Mothers and Daughters in German Literature

Mothers and Daughters in Medieval German Literature

Ann Marie Rasmussen

SYRACUSE UNIVERSITY PRESS

First Edition 1997
97 98 99 00 01   6 5 4 3 2 1

Permission by Ursula Krechel to reprint lines of poetry from "Meine Mutter," from *Nach Mainz!: Gedichte* (1977), and by Elke Erbe to reprint lines of poetry from "Das Thema startet" (1985), is gratefully acknowledged.

Permission to reprint textual material from the following sources is gratefully acknowledged: Claassen Verlag, from Elisabeth Langgässer, "Hollunderzeit," *Gedichte* (1981) and "Wolkenlandschaft im Spätjahr," *Gedichte* (1981); Indiana University Press, from "Against Women," *Satires of Juvenal* translated by Rolfe Humphries (1958) and "Mother Knows Best," *Lucian, Satirical Sketches,* translated by Paul Turner; Garland Publishing, from *Kudrun,* translated by Marion E. Gibbs and Sidney M. Johnson (1992); Kösel-Verlag, from Else Lasker-Schüler, Sämtliche Werke in drei Bänden. Bd.1 *Gedichte 1902–1943* (1990); Kümmerle Verlag, from Ingrid Bennewitz-Behr, *Die Berliner Neidhart Handschrift c (mgf 779): Transkription der Texte und Melodien,* mit Ulrich Müller (1981); Penguin UK, from *The Nibelungenlied,* translated by A. T. Hatto (1965); Philipp Reclam jun. Verlag, from Heinrich von Veldeke, *Eneasroman* (1986) and Gottfried von Strassburg, *Tristan und Isolde,* 3 vols. (1984); and Walter de Gruyter, from *Liederbuch der Clara Hatzlerin,* edited by Carl Haltaus (1966).

The paper used in this publication meets the minimum requirements of
American National Standard for
Information Sciences—Permanence of
Paper for Printed Library Materials, ANSI Z39.48-1984.

Library of Congress Cataloging-in-Publication Data
Rasmussen, Ann Marie.
Mothers and daughters in medieval German literature / Ann Marie
Rasmussen.—1st ed.
p.   cm.
Includes bibliographical references and index.
ISBN 0-8156-2709-2 (cloth : alk. paper) ISBN 0-8156-0389-4 (pbk.: alk. paper)
1. German literature—Middle High German, 1050–1500—History and
criticism.   2. Mothers and daughters in literature.   3. Women in
literature.   I. Title.
PT179.R36   1996
830.9'002—dc20   96-19775

Manufactured in the United States of America

Horcht, mich sucht meine Mutter,
Lichte sind ihre Finger und ihre Füße wandernde Träume.
—Else Lasker-Schüler

Hark, my mother seeks me,
Her fingers are lights and her feet, wandering dreams.

Ann Marie Rasmussen is associate professor of German at Duke University and author of articles on twentieth-century German women writers, German courtly love poetry, and feminist work in medieval German studies. She has taught at the University of Berne, Switzerland, and is currently working on a monograph about fifteenth-century German literature.

Contents

PART TWO

Common Mothers and Daughters
Sexual Rebellion and Constraint

Illustrations

TABLE

Preface

MEDIEVAL GERMAN SECULAR LITERATURE about mothers and daughters is without exception either male-authored or anonymous. The first text in German written by a woman dates from the early twelfth century and treats a religious topic; no secular, German language text by a woman is known to exist before the middle of the fifteenth century. Yet medieval German fiction contains many dialogues between mothers and daughters and many plots about their relationships, although this pattern has not been widely noted in existing scholarship.

I have selected prominent works—canonical texts, as it were—for my interpretive readings. The apparent exception, *Stepmother and Daughter,* owes its obscurity largely to early twentieth-century scholars' distaste for its unsophisticated style and ribald contents. Its presence in eleven fifteenth-century manuscripts shows that it must have been one of the most popular poems of its genre in late medieval Germany. Much medieval German mother-daughter material is not discussed in this book— for example, material from *Ruodlieb* (anonymous, late eleventh century), *Titurel* and *Willehalm* (Wolfram von Eschenbach, both c. 1220), *Friedrich von Schwaben* (anonymous, after 1314), *Barbali* (Niklaus Manuel, 1526), and *Denkwürdigkeiten* (Caritas Pirckheimer, 1527–28). The rhymed couplet genres, *Mären* and *Minnereden,* so popular in the late thirteenth, four-teenth, and fifteenth centuries are replete with mother-daughter stories. There is doubtless much more. I have, however, foregone a survey of mother-daughter material in order to analyze in selected fictional texts the wider implications of the mother-daughter theme as a literary and cultural paradigm. I explore each work in its historical context as a literary and cultural system deploying stereotypical representations of mothers and daughters in specific ways and for specific purposes. In the process, I chart changing usages of the stereotypes of compliant and disorderly mothers and daughters in light of a series of historical changes: the emergence of patrilineal kinship organization among the nobility, changing feudal marriage practices, and the attendant renegotiations of noble-women's exercise of power. I also discuss at length the sexualization of women that lies at the heart of the representation of femininity in medieval literature.

Each chapter in this book is devoted to a specific work, and the sequence of chapters is generally chronological. However, because it is impossible to be precise about the dates that any of these works were written, I have gently reshuffled the order of some chapters in order to highlight similarities of genre and theme. In order to keep together works indebted to the tradition of the heroic epic, the discussion of the *Nibelungenlied* (chapter 2) is followed by the discussion of *Kudrun* (chapter 3), although *Tristan und Isolde* (chapter 4) was probably written before *Kudrun*. *Die Winsbeckin* (chapter 5) may well be younger than the first Neidhart texts (chapter 6), but because it is completely impossible to date *Die Winsbeckin* with any exactness whatsoever, it is placed so as to provide a transition from the genre of epic to the genre of lyric, and from the theme of politics to the theme of sexuality. Chapter 6, on Neidhart, discusses both poems attributed to him and poems imitative of his style that were composed throughout the thirteenth and fourteenth centuries. The Neidhart texts bridge the chronological gap between chapters 1 through 5 and chapter 7, which treats a short narrative poem, *Stepmother and Daughter*, dating from the early fifteenth (or perhaps the late fourteenth?) century.

Dating medieval literature is a hazardous and complicated enterprise that at best yields vague results. At times the facts are so sparse that they can only suggest a certain century. Fixing a more limited time period based on philology, style, and intertextual references remains an informed conjecture, subject to the skeptical scrutiny of other scholars. In indicating dates, I have reproduced the parameters generally accepted in the field, relying primarily on the second edition of the *Verfasserlexikon* (Ruh 1976) and on a standard literary history, *Deutsche Literatur im Mittelalter* (Bumke, Cramer, and Kartschoke 1990). Misapprehensions are my own.

Citing medieval texts poses similar problems. Deciding what version to cite—manuscript, diplomatic reprint, edition—means adopting an opinion in a scholarly debate. Where possible, I have elected to cite widely available editions rather than diplomatic reprints or manuscripts. I do so for two reasons. First, I want to cite editions that are easily accessible to interested readers. Second, my arguments in this book address questions of theme and content, not philology and text criticism. Nevertheless, the choice to cite editions presents the reader with the illusion of a fixed and standardized text, obscuring much that is unique about the production and transmission of medieval literature. In the case of *Kudrun*, I have even, with a heavy heart, taken this erasure one step further. Stackmann's edition uses a complicated system of typefaces to reproduce different levels of editorial intervention employed in reconstructing the text. It is an excellent example of how to make the painstaking process of reconstructing a text visible to a reader. Yet I have chosen not to reproduce these typefaces, but rather to use a uniform typeface for all citations from *Kudrun*. I do so because I believe that reproducing the details of Stackmann's system would entail lengthy explanations that distract from my argument. In the case of *Stepmother and Daughter,* I rely on diplomatic reprints and manuscript transcriptions I have made. Following scholarly practice, I have made "such slight changes in orthography and punctuation as were necessary for the sake of clearness and uniformity" (Gudde 1934, iv). With the exception of *Kudrun* and the *Nibelungenlied*, English translations are my own.

While writing this book I have tried to balance the interests of specialists and nonspecialists. Where their interests conflict, I have chosen compromises that reach toward nonspecialists. For this reason the book has lengthy quotations, English translations, and plot summaries. It also includes as chapter epigraphs poems by twentieth-century German women writers that highlight thematic continuities of the mother-daughter relationship over time. All this may try the patience of scholars of Middle High German. Nevertheless, I ask these colleagues for their indulgence and, indeed, approval. It is my hope that making this book more accessible to nonspecialists will advance the visibility and the appreciation of the domain of our common endeavors, medieval German literature.

In this book I work with fictional texts. The one exception is a spiritual biography, *Leben der Gräfin Yolande von Vianden* (after 1283) by Brother Hermann, on which the first half of the introduction is focused. Including a biographical work with a religious theme points toward the wealth of material on medieval mothers and daughters in fields related to medieval literary studies. In art history, Kathleen Ashley and Pamela Sheingorn have begun the work of tracing the cultural meanings attached to St. Anne and her daughter, the Virgin Mary (Ashley and Sheingorn 1990) (Sheingorn 1993). In religious studies, Clarissa Atkinson's work on the changing ideas and practices of Christian motherhood contains a fascinating account of the uneasy relationships between St. Brigitta of Sweden (d. 1373) and her daughters, Märta, Ingeborg, Cecilia, and Katarina (Atkinson 1991, 170–84). And in religious cultural studies, the wide variety of late medieval religious material from German convents is only now becoming available in complete scholarly editions (Ringler 1980; Meyer 1995). The vast amount of material I could not bring into this work should serve as a challenging reminder of all the knowledge we have yet to produce about women in the Middle Ages.

Acknowledgments

SMALL PORTIONS of chapters 4, 5, 6, and 7 were published in different versions in the essay "Bist du begehrt, so bist du wert: Magische und höfische Mitgift für die Töchter," in *Mütter-Töchter-Frauen: Weiblichkeitsbilder in der Literatur*, edited by Helga Kraft and Elke Liebs (1993). A different version of chapter 4 appeared as "'ez ist ir g'artet von mir': Queen Isolde and Princess Isolde in Gottfried von Strassburg's *Tristan und Isolde*," in *Arthurian Women: A Casebook*, edited by Thelma Fenster (1996a). A section of the introduction appeared in German translation as "Zur wissenschaftlichen Analyse von Müttern und Töchtern im Mittelalter" (1996b). A portion of this work was supported by a summer fellowship from the University of Oregon Humanities Center and by an arts and science research council grant from Duke University.

This book has been nourished and supported by communities of colleagues, neighbors, and family. It would never have come into being, much less to an end, without their aid, advice, and encouragement. I warmly thank my colleagues and friends from Berne, Hubert Herkommer and Danielle Herkommer-Jaurent. James Rolleston and Frank Borchardt believed in me when the going was rough and saw to it that I received the research leave that made this book possible. Special thanks to Frank for answering the phone! Art Groos welcomed me into the world of medieval German studies in America. Lee Patterson's advice at difficult moments in my career has always been on the mark. Thanks to Julia Hell for reading parts of the book and to James A. Schultz for reading all of it with such great care; their astute comments improved my arguments immeasurably. Hermina Joldersma generously shared with me her collection of Low German, Dutch, and Afrikaans mother-daughter ballads. Mary Wyer's meticulous copyediting of the first draft taught me how to write, and her faith in the project gave me hope. Sally Poor's research and editing skills improved the book. Patricia Naylor tracked manuscripts and permission letters with efficiency and enthusiasm. Helene Baumann and the Staff of the Interlibrary Loan Office at Perkins Library, Duke University, were patient and resourceful. Cynthia Maude-Gembler's understanding has truly nurtured me and the project.

The writing of this book has benefited in large and small ways from the unstinting support of the North Carolina Research Group on Medieval and Early Modern Women. The intellectual commitment, the professional integrity, and the ethics of fair and generous reading practiced in our group have modeled for me what academic life can and should be. I am deeply grateful to Monica Green, Helen Solterer, and Sarah Westphal for many long conversations that helped me negotiate the perils and possibilities of academia and the intellectual life, and for sharing their struggles and successes with me.

The support and good cheer of my neighbors in North Carolina have been invaluable. I thank Barbra Roberman, Hal Sandick, Mary Kay Delaney, Fritz Mayer, Maryska Bigos, Jeff Hamilton, Beth Silberman, Ken Rose, Ricky Magnuson, and Carol Mozell—I could not have done this without you. Special thanks to Molly and Gracie Sandick; Paul, Michael, and David Delaney Mayer; and Imani Hamilton for reminding me what really matters in this world.

I owe more to the love and pride of my family than I can possibly express. I thank my parents, Sigrid and Gerry Rasmussen, for always being there to help out. Special thanks to my sister, Alis A. Rasmussen, (alias Kate Elliott) for many great talks about writing books. I thank Ingrid Bodkter, Carol Reerslev, and Karla and John Reerslev for their support and companionship during my Oregon summers. I dedicate this book to my beloved son, Arnbjorn.

Durham, North Carolina   Ann Marie Rasmussen
January 1996

Mothers and Daughters in Medieval German Literature

Studying Medieval Mothers and Daughters

> There can be no systematic and theoretical study of women in patriarchal culture, there can be no theory of women's oppression, that does not take into account woman's role as a mother of daughters and as a daughter to mothers, that does not study female identity in relation to previous and subsequent generations of women, and that does not study that relationship in the wider context in which it takes place: the emotional, political, economic, and symbolic structures of family and society. Any full study of mother-daughter relationships, in whatever field, is by definition both feminist and interdisciplinary.
>
> —Marianne Hirsch (1981, 202)

Margaret of Courtenay and Yolande of Vianden

AROUND 1240, Yolande of Vianden (c. 1231–1283), the daughter of a wealthy and influential noble family from the region of present-day Luxembourg, felt called to renounce a worldly life and become a Dominican nun. Her parents, Henry of Vianden (d. 1252) and Margaret of Courtenay (d. 1270), strongly objected. Her mother, in particular, vigorously opposed Yolande's wish. The struggle between mother and daughter raged for some eight years. Yolande's mother used every means at her disposal to dissuade her youthful daughter: pleading, berating, scolding, beating. She enlisted kin and allies, secular and religious alike, to argue with Yolande and forced her to partake in worldly festivities. Yolande's intractable resistance severed the well-connected marital engagement negotiated by her family, and the claims for compensation advanced by the fiancé threatened her parents and their vassals with economic ruin. Margaret pled and threatened; Yolande refused to budge. When the erstwhile bridegroom married an heiress and dropped his claim against Yolande's family, Margaret tried a more subtle approach. Agreeing to Yolande's choice of religious vocation, she now insisted that Yolande en-

3

ter one of the Cistercian foundations supported by her kin. Yolande refused, stubbornly clinging to her vision of the place and order to which
she felt elected. Again Margaret stormed, but a sudden change of heart finally prompted her to accede to Yolande's wishes. In 1248, with great
pomp, she gave Yolande to the Dominican convent at Marienthal, near
Mersch, where Yolande rose to the position of prioress and inaugurated a
period of prestige for the convent.

   The story of Yolande and Margaret has come down to us in a rhymed
biography of Yolande written some time after 1283 by Brother Hermann,
a monk attached to the abby of Marienthal.[1] In their story, the reader dis-
cerns a familiar, modern narrative pattern: a conflict between mother and
daughter about the shaping of female identity. From the vantage point of
the twentieth century, the story of Margaret and Yolande's struggle might
look something like this: Linked by obligations of family and status, and
dependent on each other, mother and daughter are locked in a struggle
over their conflicting visions of what a woman's place in the world should
be. The mother attempts to carry out the familial duty and responsibility
of guiding her daughter into a marriage that will reinforce valuable political and economic alliances for her family and provide wealth and
prestige for the daughter herself. The daughter revolts. She refuses identification with her mother, rejecting her mother's view of a noblewoman's place in society and her mother's right to choose for her. Instead, she
chooses for herself a way of life based on a medieval institution that often
competed with the feudal nobility for economic and political power: the
church. Freed from maternality, familial burdens, and submission to
parental or spousal rule, the daughter chooses, shapes, and occupies a different space of femininity.

   Such a reading retells the story of the protracted and bitter struggle between Margaret and Yolande according to a familiar modern paradigm: a
woman's quest for adulthood and maturity pivots on her relationship
with her mother. In the modern psychological narrative of the formation
of female identity, the mother-daughter relationship is the crucial, foundational, unavoidable, and intractable nexus of women's gendered place

---

   1. Quotations from the biography that follow in this chapter will be according to the
Meier edition (1889), *Bruder Hermann: Leben der Gräfin Iolande von Vianden,* abbreviated *Leben,*
and will be cited by line number. Translations are mine. An English translation of the *Leben*
(Lawson 1995) appeared after this book was prepared for publication.

   The author, Hermann, is probably the same Brother Hermann who in 1276 wrote a
rhymed translation of the Dominican rule at the behest of Yolande, then convent prioress. It
has not survived. Brother Herrmann died in 1307. References in the *Leben* make it clear that
the work was written after Yolande's death in 1283. On intertextual evidence, Wachinger
makes a good case for dating the *Leben* in the 1290s (1973, 243–45).

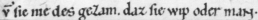

1. A girl, accompanied by a married woman and two male figures, dedicates herself to the religious life. Although this illustration is taken from a sequence of images illuminating Priester Wernher's "Driu liet von der maget" (Three Poems about the Virgin Mary), it also expresses the final resolution of the conflict between mother and daughter in the *Life of Yolande of Vianden*. The manuscript was produced around the year 1200, which is also the approximate date of birth for Margaret of Courtenay. Cracow, Biblioteka Jagiellonska, ms. germ. oct. 109, f. 21v. Courtesy of the Biblioteka Jagiellonska.

in the world, in the words of Marianne Hirsch, "the most formative relationship in the life of every woman" (1981, 200). In their relationship,
mother and daughter struggle over issues of separation and connected-
ness, of similarity and dissimilarity. Ultimately, it is a struggle for connection that can value difference, but because it takes place within the
context of a patriarchal social order that devalues and objectifies women,
this ideal is only rarely, if ever attained. Instead, the conflicts and lessons
that emerge from the mother-daughter relationship are all too often ambiguous and painful: what the mother seeks to reproduce in her daughter
may be her own subjugation; what the daughter seeks to wrest from her
mother may be a fragile and isolated independence grown from anger
and fear.

The mother-daughter relationship is often not a connection, but rather,
in Adrienne Rich's word, a "schism" (Rich 1986, 227). And so it seems for
Margaret and Yolande. Aligned with secular patriarchal interests, the
mother speaks for the father and acts as intermediary between father and
daughter. Desiring conformity and submission, she attempts to create for
her daughter a life like her own: marriage, childbearing and childrearing,
politics, diplomacy. The daughter rejects this life completely and utterly.
She insists on following a religious model that values chastity over sexuality and reproduction, humility and obedience over the self-interest of
secular politics, enclosure over diplomacy. Indeed, her chosen way of life
claims ethical and spiritual superiority over the mother's model.[2]

Between these positions there would seem to be no possibility of compromise, but Brother Hermann's story fashions a kind of happy ending
for mother and daughter. The mother capitulates without rancor, though
even in acceding to her daughter's wishes she presses upon her noble
pomp and festive clothing which mortify the daughter's sense of religious
piety and which the daughter can only bearly tolerate. The story goes no
further. However, in his introduction Meier (1889, c–ci) provides historical evidence documenting that some time after her husband's death in
1252, Margaret herself made gifts to the convent of Marienthal, entered it,
and died there in 1270. Based on these bare facts, Meier suggests another
harmonious conclusion to the mother-daughter story that is summed up
in his reimagining of Margaret's death: "her daughter, Yolande, was able
to close Margaret's tired eyes" [ihre Tochter Iolande konnte ihr noch die
müden Augen zudrücken] (1889, ci). Still different, but no longer separate, mother and daughter are connected again. Benevolently mothered
by the daughter she once treated so harshly, Margaret, in retreating to the

---

2. The daughter's refusal to marry, a standard topus in much hagiographic literature, is
discussed at length by Opitz (1988, 1990).

safety and intimacy of her daughter's care, provides Yolande's ultimate victory and vindication. For Meier, the mother-daughter struggle ends in a poignant fantasy of reconcilation and unity.

Telling the story of Margaret and Yolande in this manner adopts a modern theory of female development to understand a mother-daughter relationship from seven hundred years ago. But is such an explanation universally applicable? Although the paradigm dramatizes the story, bringing it nearer and making it more intelligible to us, the paradigm also distorts and conceals elements that are distant and alien, that do not fit in. It is often these untidy bits that pose unsettling questions to the modern interpretive paradigm, useful though a psychological framework is in highlighting the presence and the complexity of medieval mother-daughter stories. In the story of Margaret and Yolande, for example, a number of different elements challenge the explanatory force of a modern psychological model: the fact that their story is male-authored; the role played by medieval notions of nobility and lineage; and the political history of religious orders that is embedded in Yolande's insistence on becoming a Dominican.

The variegated relationship between the interpretive model offered by psychology and the historical distinctness of fictions from the distant past will concern me in the pages that follow. Reading and writing with it in mind has meant thinking through cultural assumptions about mothers and daughters and articulating the various social and cultural meanings attached to them over time. This is one way, I believe, of getting at the multiple yet specific ways in which these texts produce a plurality of discourses of mothers and daughters. In the case of Yolande and Margaret, each of the elements mentioned above—male authorship, the ideology of class and lineage, the politics of religiosity—represents a strand of discourse that brings a particular and specific pressure to bear on the shaping of the mother-daughter relationship in the *Leben*. Two of these elements, male authorship and the politics of constructing noble lineage, are crucial to this book. In explicating how such different elements converge to shape the mother-daughter story in the *Leben*, I am illustrating one of the major themes of this book: that when interpreting literature of the past we must be continually aware of the interplay between the usefulness of a modern understanding of selfhood, on the one hand, and, on the other, the social and cultural construction of categories such as motherhood and daughterhood through which we attempt to grasp a sense of self.

I begin with the issue of male authorship. Neither Yolande nor Margaret tells us her story; instead, it was composed by Brother Hermann, a member of Yolande's monastic community. In the Middle Ages, it was the rule, not the exception, that the lives of extraordinary women were chronicled by men. Although the female religious, in turning toward a spiritual life, entered a world that revered the book, the cloistered lives of chastity, obedience, humility, and contemplation they were expected to lead did not encourage the pursuit of literary achievement. Exceptions such as Mechthild of Magdeburg (c. 1210–1282), who felt obliged to mount repeated, spirited defenses of writing a spiritual autobiography, prove the point. In any case, further exploring the immediate relationship between Brother Hermann, Yolande, and Margaret—that is to say, between male chronicler and his female subjects—is impossible on the level of personal history because we possess virtually no documentation of that relationship apart from the *Leben* itself. Thus this puzzle must be recast as a question of genre and genre expectations.

What is the relationship between Yolande's story and the genre of spiritual biography through which it is fixed?[3] The medieval spiritual biography follows a set narrative pattern—a script, if you will: divine call, rejection of the secular world, testing and torment, final triumph. The third section is one of the most important, for the holy person must undergo a series of ordeals in order to prove her faith, and she is often entangled in one special relationship with an unbeliever whose torments are particularly gruesome.[4] When we view Yolande's story through the lens of the saint's life, we see that her mother, Countess Margaret, is cast in the role of the torturer-intimate, while Yolande herself represents the type of the holy person who early in life longs to cast aside all worldly ties in order to devote herself to the higher claims of a spiritual life.[5] We are not in a position to say how much, or little, of Yolande's and Margaret's experienced reality corresponded to the narrative formulas guiding the process of selection that shapes Brother Hermann's rendering of their lives. But we do see that he, like modern-day psychologists and literary scholars, creates and exploits great dramatic tension by locating the conflict of the spiritual and the secular in the mother-daughter relationship.

A further dimension of Brother Hermann's account of Margaret and Yolande's conflicting ways of being, the issue of noble lineage and nobility, is suggested by his *prooemium*, in which he praises Margaret's virtue and generosity and establishes her descent from French royalty (*Leben*, ll. 52–61). It emerges in full relief when we consult the extant historical evidence about Yolande's kin (Meier 1889, lxxxii–cxxvii). This evidence suggests that Count Henry of Vianden, Yolande's father, was a well-

3. For a detailed and nuanced discussion of this aspect of the *Leben*, see Sullivan 1994.

4. On this part of the pattern, see Cazelles 1991.

5. Yolande's father, who is deeply attached to his daughter and becomes completely morose and withdrawn when she insists on joining a convent, exemplifies a different potential trap for the spiritually inclined, the trap of familial piety and affection.

connected vassal of the count of Luxembourg belonging to the landed nobility.[6] Margaret of Courtenay, on the other hand, was descended through
her father, Peter of Courtenay II, from the Capetian dynasty and through
her mother, Yolande of Hainaut, from the most powerful and wealthy
lords of present day Belgium (our Yolande is thus named after her maternal grandmother). Margaret was closely related, both maternally and paternally, to the rulers of France, to the most powerful families of the Low
Countries, and to the crusading aristocratic adventurers who sprang from
their alliances—in some degree a cousin to the lords of Hainaut, Flanders,
Luxembourg and all the Capetian rulers of her lifetime as well as niece to
the first Latin emporer of Constantinople and sister to the second and
third.[7] Though Margaret of Courtenay and Henry of Vianden belong indisputably to the same class, Margaret's lineage is indisputably more illustrious and influential.

The knowledge that Yolande of Vianden's mother, Margaret of Courtenay, represents a more distinguished and powerful connection than
Yolande's father, Henry of Vianden, holds enormous significance for our

6. Henry of Vianden was related to Conrad of Hochstaden (d. 1270), elected archbishop
of Cologne in 1238, who plays a role in the *Leben*. One of Yolande's siblings, her brother
Henry of Vianden (d. 1267), became a prior in Conrad's household and later bishop of
Utrecht.

7. Margaret's father, Peter of Courtenay II (d. 1217), was the son of Peter of Courtenay I
(d. c. 1181), youngest brother of Louis VII (r. 1137–1180). Their father was Louis VI
(r. 1108–1137). Margaret's paternal grandfather is thus Peter of Courtenay I and her paternal
great-grandfather Louis VI. Her father's cousin, Philip Augustus, son of Louis VII and Alice
of Champagne, was king of France from 1180–1223. Margaret was thus first cousin once
removed of Philip Augustus, and first cousin twice removed from his son, Louis VIII
(r. 1226–1228).

Margaret's mother, Yolande of Hainaut (d. after 1219), was the daughter of Baldwin V of
Hainaut and VIII of Flanders (d. 1195). Her sister, Elisabeth (sometimes called Isabelle,
d. 1190), was Philip Augustus's first wife and mother of King Louis VIII. On her mother's
side, Margaret was thus first cousin to Louis VIII and first cousin once removed to his son,
Louis IX (r. 1226–1270). Yolande and Elisabeth's brother, Baldwin VI of Hainaut and IX of
Flanders, was elected first Latin emperor of the Eastern Empire (Constantinople) by the crusading Franks in 1204. Another brother, Henry, became emperor after Baldwin's death in
1205. In 1210, Henry died, and the title of Latin emperor of the Eastern Empire passed
through his sister, Yolande of Hainaut, to her husband, Peter of Courtenay II. Upon Peter's
death in 1217, the title passed first to the widowed Yolande herself and then in 1219 to Peter
and Yolande's sons (Margaret's brothers): first to Robert of Courtenay (d. 1228) and then to
Baldwin (d. 1273). Baldwin returned to the west in 1237 to raise money and wrested by force
the Margraviate of Namur from his sister, Margaret, who had inherited it in 1229 (Kienast
1975, 624–25).

For a fascinating account of the life of Margaret's maternal uncle, Baldwin I of Constantinople, VI of Hainaut, and IX of Flanders, see Wolff 1952.

understanding of the *Leben*. It draws attention to the discrepancy in Brother Hermann's portrait of Margaret, who is praised in the *prooemium* but in the narrative portrayed as a wicked figure who torments and beleaguers her daughter. But knowledge of Margaret's high birth offers a different perspective on the imperious, stubborn, and temperamental mother figure who dominates the action in Yolande's story. In the feudal world, powerful kin meant political clout. What the facts of Margaret's birth status allow us to see is that Margaret of Courtenay did not passively embody the prestige of her natal family within her marital family. Rather, she acted—dealing as an agent, brokering the influence and power that her dual kin status conferred upon her. Perhaps Margaret was a willful and domineering woman; such an interpretation of her actions, which Brother Hermann's narrative suggests, suits a modern psychological reading of Margaret and Yolande's mother-daughter relationship as one based on rivalry for paternal affection.[8] The facts we can glean about Margaret's life suggest, however, that she was also a significant political player in a world where intelligence, decisiveness, and determination were necessary to capitalize on connections that might secure and advance one's political vision of the future.

Moreover, even the meager historical information we can glean about Margaret of Courtenay allows us to recognize as narrative *choices* certain details in Brother Hermann's narrative. By virtue of her lineage, Margaret of Courtenay is better suited than Henry of Vianden to represent the power and prestige of the secular world that Yolande rejects. Overcoming the representative of such distinguished connections marks the magnitude of Yolande's victory: as Brother Hermann says, "nobility and highborn ways she crushed underfoot" [den adel und den hôen art trat sy zen vůzen under sich] (*Leben*, ll. 5948–49). And yet Brother Hermann seeks to recuperate the prestige that Margaret represents, if not for Yolande herself, then for the aura of prestige, power, and protection that it brings to the convent. The evidence of this contradiction comes at the moment when Margaret completely agrees to Yolande's wishes. Here Brother Hermann reuses an image for the mother-daughter relation that first appeared in his introduction: "I wish to bow to the tree from which we received the fruit" [ich wil dem bôime nîgen, van dem uns ist dy vruht gesant] (*Leben*, ll. 50–51). After Margaret assents, Brother Hermann inserts a series of positive, if veiled, references that stress the prestige of Margaret's lineage while subtly devaluing Margaret herself: "blessed be the family tree from which such a full bough could be guided so purely"

---

8. For this reading, see Lawson 1989, and, in particular, Lawson 1991, 113.

[gebenedîet sî der stam dâ von sô vulder ast bequam, der sich sô reine by-gen lyz] (*Leben*, ll. 5031–33) and a few lines later "for from good trees there can always be harvested good fruit" [wat y van gůden bôime wart gele-sen vruht, dy was ôich gůt] (*Leben*, ll. 5060–61). The biological metaphor of the solid (Capetian) family tree whose branch (Margaret) bears good fruit (Yolande) reduces Margaret to a passive, linking role she most surely does not play either in the *Leben* or in the historical record.

Most importantly, however, without historical information we would not know Margaret's name, for Brother Hermann never uses it. Through-out his narrative she is simply "the mother." When we remember that Brother Hermann names other members of Yolande's immediate family, including her father, and that in his first audience he may well have had people who had known both mother and daughter, the decision to render Margaret anonymous gains significance. It suggests that for Brother Hermann's story it is imperative that the unique identity of the woman who bore Yolande be suppressed and this woman become instead the rep-resentative of a generic function: a tormenter, a "bad" mother, whose only positive function is to passively link her daughter to a prestigious past. In making Margaret an exemplum of motherhood gone awry, Brother Her-mann's perspective converges with the modern psychological model, which at times sees mothers less as individuals enmeshed in a web of of-ten conflicting social and political relationships than as representatives of a monolithic, predetermined sociopsychological function.

The political history of the rise of the Dominican order is another ele-ment of the *Leben* that tells us about Brother Hermann's construction of daughterhood. Here I can provide only the briefest sketch of the ideolog-ical context within which Brother Hermann worked. Founded in 1216, the Dominican order was young and lacked the prestige and wealth of the older Benedictine and Cistercian orders. What the Dominicans lacked in tradition, they made up for in reformist zeal, taking as their particular mission teaching as well as the spiritual care of heretics and female reli-gious, both those in convents and those living as Beguines. The tension between the older, established orders and the new orders such as the Do-minicans (and the Franciscans, founded in 1210) finds expression in the *Leben*. Margaret's initial resistance to Yolande's calling is relatively easily overcome. It is not Yolande's determination to become a nun but rather her determination to become a *Dominican* nun that is a source of contin-ued conflict. Margaret repeatedly offers Yolande the choice of entering a Cistercian convent long supported by the house of Vianden, an option Yolande stubbornly rejects. But what difference can the choice of religious house possibly make?

From a Dominican point of view, the Cistercian foundation is doubtless inextricably bound up with the disreputable notions of "nobility and highborn ways" represented by Margaret herself.[9] It is easy to see how Hermann's life of Yolande participates in the greater project of writing the history of the Dominican order as the history of the triumph of virtue and reform over the corruption and privilege of the older orders. Perhaps Yolande was attracted to the learned piety of the Dominicans for this very reason. What can be only vaguely discerned are the reasons for Margaret's hostility towards her daughter's choice of religious order, a hostility all the more puzzling because we learn that she welcomes prominent Dominicans such as Walther of Meisenburg and Albertus Magnus at her court. Perhaps Margaret did indeed feel, as Hermann's narrative implies, that Yolande's choice was déclassé—under the worth of the family's station and status and of no use to Margaret in her own political plans. It is not unthinkable, however, that Yolande's parents were worried about the material security and bodily safety of a daughter living in a completely new and probably impoverished foundation (founded in 1232, Marienthal was no older than Yolande herself), enjoying little or no aristocratic protection and patronage and supported by an untried and poverty-stricken order.[10] From Brother Hermann's point of view, however, Yolande's loyalty to the Dominican order represents more than a daughter's rejection of her mother: it signals liberation from her. Whatever happened between Yolande and Margaret after Margaret's entry into the convent does not find a place in Brother Hermann's narrative. Any continuity between mother and daughter is cast off; the construction of pious daughterhood depends on the disavowal of the mother.

Brother Hermann's story of the piety and fortitude of a Dominican depends on creating and manipulating stereotypes about women and deploying them to produce stereotypes about mothers and daughters. Hermann's willful, tempestuous Margaret becomes a manipulative and unaffectionate mother. His stubborn and defiant Yolande becomes a dutiful, chaste, and pious daughter of God, who, it should be noted, advances to the position of stern yet beloved mother—that is to say, leader—of her monastic community. In Brother Hermann's view, Margaret errs as a mother because she places power over affection, control over nurture, self-interest over selflessness—all errors of mothering that Yolande as pri-

9. On the history of the Dominicans in the thirteenth century, see Bennett 1937, Hinne-busch 1966, and Freed 1977.

10. According to Grundmann (1966, 229) and Wilms (1928, 62–63), Marienthal was founded in 1232 by Dietrich of Mersch, the seneschal (*Truchseß*) of the duchess of Luxembourg, confirmed by Theodoric, archbishop of Trier, in 1235, and governed initially by a sister from the Dominican convent of Saint Mark in Strasbourg.

oress apparently corrects. Brother Hermann's political agenda and his understanding of motherhood and daughterhood reinforce each other.

The indebtedness of Yolande's biographer to a specific ideological position on religiosity and motherhood (a position that may well have coincided with Yolande's own) should remind us that the religious sphere, no less than the secular sphere, is inflected by patriarchal beliefs about women. By choosing to live her life in a religious community of women, Yolande does escape the dangers and trials of marriage, childbirth, and kin-based political strife, but she does not escape patriarchal domination. She merely moves from one patriarchally controlled sphere to another, where the norms for female conduct and virtue are different. Margaret operated from a separate set of attitudes, beliefs, and expectations about women and motherhood, however biased Brother Hermann's presentation of those norms may be. Doubtless class-based, Margaret's norms were also a function of a time, class, and clan in which male absence and death due to the Crusades created the need for noblewomen to govern.

The medieval world did not have one set of beliefs, attitudes, and expectations towards women and the roles they played as mothers and daughters. Rather, it produced different, often conflicting, models. The story of Margaret and Yolande as the story of a mother and daughter is thrice removed from us: by the passage of time, by male authorship, by the loss of evidence. It cannot satisfy any wish for an authentic woman's voice from the Middle Ages. Yet I believe, and I hope this book will show, that male-authored stories about medieval women, such as Brother Hermann's *Leben der Gräfin Iolande*, can contribute to women's history because they can reveal to us a great deal about the contradictions of medieval models for mothers and daughters, contradictions that I attribute to the real, historical circumstances of medieval women's lives. At this level, Brother Hermann's story is indeed authentic. It produces a discourse about medieval mothers and daughters that is fraught with contradiction. In so doing, it frames some of the conflicting attitudes and beliefs within and through which medieval women lived their mother-daughter relationships.

In the case of Brother Hermann's *Leben*, the tension between the discourses of literature and history magnify these contradictions; the *Leben* is, after all, a biography, a genre that straddles the fence between literature and history. Yet fictional stories of mothers and daughters also produce their own, internal oppositions, for they participate in and contribute to historically specific social and cultural discourses about women that are also fraught with contradiction: theological positions of the medieval church that proclaimed the equality of souls before God while inscribing women's inferiority on earth, organization of kinship in the medieval aristocracy that both relied on and sought to diminish the role of women, aristocratic structures for allocating economic and political resources that both depended on and sought to radically limit women's access to power, notions of femininity that in the sacred sphere idealized virginity and in the secular sphere required motherhood.

Such contradictions point out that mother-daughter stories, whether fiction or biography, are in the largest sense about the patriarchal social order in which they arose, an order in which men commanded most of society's economic and political resources. Mother-daughter stories are thus about power, about the social construction of relationships of domination and subordination as they inflect relationships between men and women and between women themselves. Mother-daughter stories can tell us about the complex power relations that install and maintain patriarchy and about the contradictions and ambiguities of patriarchy's operation. They can reveal the assumptions about women's power, women's sexuality, and women's relationships to one another upon which patriarchal order rests. Mother-daughter stories are about the schism between women that the power relations of patriarchy create. But because the patriarchal order is a diffuse, contradictory, and flexible set of institutionalized power relations (attributes that probably account in part for its longevity), the mother-daughter story can also stake out positions that amend or subvert the dominant social order.[11] Mothers and daughters—sometimes together, sometimes apart—can object, hesitate, resist, speaking and acting different versions of femininity. The crux is the extent to which mothers and daughters manage to share their knowledge. In some medieval fictions we can see medieval mothers and daughters divided by patriarchy. In others we can see the solidarity of medieval mothers and daughters operating within the limited agency they can claim in a patriarchal social order. The stories of medieval mothers and daughters amplify a fundamental and perplexing issue underlying any literary or historical investigation of women: the conditions under which women in a patriarchal social order succeed or fail in transferring their knowledge and power to other women.

Interpretive Models and Assumptions

The Psychology of Mothers and Daughters

At its most basic, the mother-daughter relationship is a genealogy, grounded as a metaphor in biological and physiological process, made meaningful through individual, social, and cultural investment. The

---

11. For a group of extraordinary essays about writing the history of medieval women from sources that are at best indifferent to women and often hostile to them, see Rosenthal 1990. On medieval patriarchy, see Judith M. Bennett 1989 and 1996.

mother-daughter relationship is about the production and transmission of knowledge about women between women: about bodily pleasure and pain, about the dangers of oneness and the anguish of isolation, about self-love and self-loathing mirrored in and experienced through an intimate other of the same sex. These are issues that Adrienne Rich explores in her chapter devoted to mothers and daughters in *Of Woman Born: Motherhood as Experience and Institution* (1986, 218–55). Rich's pioneering reflections on the fierce ambiguities of identity, knowledge, and power that energize the mother-daughter relationship remain, to my mind, among the most instructive and moving available to us.

Much feminist theory joins Rich in viewing the mother-daughter relationship as being a key to explaining how women acquire gender identity in a patriarchal society.[12] One of the most influential studies has been Nancy Chodorow's *The Reproduction of Mothering: Psychoanalysis and the Sociology of Gender* (1978). In her quest to answer the question of why women mother, Chodorow turns to a psychoanalytic analysis of mother-daughter relationships that employs both Freudian and object-relations theory. Chodorow begins with an account of the primary identification between mother and infant and traces how this primary, preoedipal relationship between mother and child develops differently for boy children and girl children. Boys come to perceive themselves early as being bodily different from their mothers, which makes their switching to their fathers for gender identity both more clear and more difficult: the bodily distinction of having or lacking a penis strongly demarcates difference, yet the child's profound, primary emotional bond with the mother makes the intimate, emotional oneness with this powerful but differently gendered figure threatening. According to this theory, the boy child is thus likely to develop a clearly separate sense of self but to fear intimacy. In contrast, girls identify both emotionally and bodily with their mothers. Since there is no pressing psychic need for the girl child to distinguish herself from her mother, she develops a sense of self that is more connected to others, but she fears the loss of this connection, that is to say, she fears separation.

> Women's mothering, then, produces asymmetries in the relational experiences of girls and boys as they grow up, which account for crucial differences in feminine and masculine personality, and the relational capacities

12. Examples of significant research on the role of the mother-daughter relationship in contemporary female identity formation include Benjamin 1988; Chodorow 1985; Flax 1978 and 1985; Hirsch 1981; Irigaray 1981; Kristeva 1985; Mens-Verhulst, Schreurs, and Woertman 1993; and O'Barr, Pope, and Wyer 1990.

and modes which these entail. Women and men grow up with personalities affected by different boundary experiences and differently constructed and experienced inner object-worlds, and are preoccupied with different relational issues. . . . From the retention of preodipal attachments to their mother, growing girls come to define and experience themselves as continuous with others; their experience of self contains more flexible or permeable ego boundaries. (Chodorow 1978, 169)

For women, this early drama of personal identity formation has a deep and abiding social consequence. Women learn to establish personal, emotional connection and avoid emotional disconnection, to seek oneness in intimate relations and avoid the pain of separateness even at the cost of maladjustment and neurosis. From this process daughters learn to be mothers.

In our society, a girl's mother is present in a way that a boy's father, and other adult men, are not. A girl, then, can develop a personal identification with her mother, because she has a real relationship with her that grows out of their early primary tie. She learns what it is to be womanlike in the context of this personal identification with her mother and often with their female models (kin, teachers, mother's friends, mothers of friends). (Chodorow 1978, 175)

A final dimension of this process is that it includes learning to choose a love object, usually of the opposite sex. In learning to be heterosexual, the boy has an easier path, for when he learns to identify himself as a male, he can maintain the force of the preoedipal, emotional bond with his mother by loving a woman. A girl, on the other hand, undergoes a far more difficult process, for learning gender identity through similarity complicates the transfer of the preoedipal attachment to the opposite sex.

The paradigms of psychoanalysis and its explanatory categories of connection and disconnection, separateness and oneness inform much of feminist literary criticism on mothers and daughters from the past twenty years.[13] From the vast number of recent publications, I mention here only

13. The number of titles is so vast that it far exceeds the scope of this note; almost all examine the mother-daughter relationship in modern culture or in the work of women writers. Some important recent bibliographies and studies by scholars in fields such as English, French, Slavic literature, and art history include Carter 1993, Donovan 1989, Farrell 1991, Forsyth 1981, Haigh 1994, Homans 1986, Kloepfer 1989, Payne 1983, Pearlman 1989, Spitz 1990, Walters 1992, and Weeks 1990.

In addition, a number of important works have appeared on the subject of the mother-daughter relationship in modern German literature, such as Kraft and Kosta 1983; Kraft and Liebs 1993; Müller 1991, whose research examines both male- and female-authored texts; Shafi 1991; and Valtink 1987.

Marianne Hirsch's *The Mother/Daughter Plot: Narrative, Psychoanalysis, Feminism* (1989). Hirsch uses psychoanalytic criticism to analyze how fiction represents the formation of individual female subjects within familial structures. Of particular interest to Hirsch is the "maternal" plot, the ways by which the maternal becomes inscribed as objectified, repressed, or unspeakable; the ways daughters try to "disidentify" with silencing notions of the maternal or, alternatively, to find a connection to the maternal that allows them some measure of autonomy; the ways, finally, in which the maternal seeks a voice, a subject position of its own.

What *Of Woman Born, The Reproduction of Mothering, The Mother/Daughter Plot,* and this work share is a recognition that it is useful to think in terms of similarity and dissimiliarity between women and in terms of continuity and discontinuity between women when analyzing the mother-daughter relationship as a key moment in the social and cultural reproduction of femininity. As I wrote, however, I discovered that the psychoanalytic approach, which tells about gender, sexuality, and language in the context of *individual* identity formation and works so well for the analysis of nineteenth- and twentieth-century *women* writers, who must continually struggle to create discursive, intellectual, and social space for themselves, does not work well for anonymous or male-authored medieval fictions about women. I believe that medieval people enjoyed, as we do, a sense of self, but where is the individual to be found in my medieval texts? The approach that looks at how women writers maneuver to create or reject women-centered plots can locate a critical consciousness— the woman writer—who reflects, critiques, and creates and thus to some degree stands outside the fictional structures she makes and the social structures in which she lives. Because she is a woman writer, her work offers a unique perspective on the urgencies, the pressures, the demands, the rewards and penalties of the mother-daughter plot. However, the mother-daughter stories analyzed in this book offer no such distance, no such critical locus allowing such a step away from the cultural and social scripts for mothers and daughters. Rather, the medieval mother-daughter stories tend to exemplify conflicting assumptions and norms about women. They are not so much representations of inner, psychic drives as they are representations of the historical forces, material conditions, and social and cultural discourses through which medieval women shaped their lives and through which their lives were shaped.

This book, then, it turned out, could not be about the transindividual emotional and bodily processes by which a patriarchal social order is originated and maintained, however, fragmentarily or critically, *in individual psyches,* whether fictional or real. What it could be about were the cultural and literary conventions by which medieval mothers and daughters are represented, and the assumptions and contradictions upon which those conventions rest. In taking this approach, my book differs as well from the little scholarly work that has been done on medieval mothers and daughters. Niki Stiller's pioneering studies, for example, use a psychoanalytic approach but pay less attention to the historical circumstances and conditions of medieval texts (1980a, b). Works in German studies, such as Lydia Miklautsch's (1991), mainly recount the attitudes laid out within the texts. My own short essay in a recently published volume rehearses some of the arguments expanded in this book (Rasmussen 1993). Above all, I see in medieval mother-daughter stories no implicit alignment between the maternal and silence, or sacrifice, or submissive compliance, nor between the filial and rebellion or disruption. What remains is the mother-daughter relationship as a source of profound connection or disconnection for women, a place where fears and anxieties about women's similarities and dissimilarities are acted out, an arena where women's strategies for learning to survive in a patriarchal social order find elemental representation.

The Politics of Nobility

Mother-daughter stories are culturally conditioned narratives, stories about the choices mothers and daughters have in a patriarchal social order and about the culturally conditioned ways—the scripts, the stereotypes, the roles—through which their stories can be told. Finding the traces of such cultural processes in literary texts means delving into the evidence and arguments of women's history in order to explore how historical and literary evidence about medieval women intersect. An early example of this approach is Penny Schine Gold's *The Lady and the Virgin* (1985). The book's subtitle, *Image, Attitude, and Experience in Twelfth-Century France*, points to the distinct realms of literature and history: from literature and religious culture we learn something about images of and attitudes toward women; from history we learn something of their lived experience and material circumstances. Gold explores not just the continuities between image, attitude, and experience, but also the discontinuities and contradictions between them.

A slowly growing body of German scholarship explores similar themes. In "Vom Familienzwist zum sozialen Konflikt" (1988), Claudia Opitz examines hagiographic texts in light of noble marriage practices in the twelfth, thirteenth and fourteenth centuries with a view to working out what this evidence might tell us about the ideological and practical constraints guiding medieval women's life choices. Petra Kellermann-Haaf's *Frau und Politik im Mittelalter* (1986) discusses both historical evidence regarding noblewomen's activities in post-Carolingian Germany and a wealth of epic texts. Unlike Gold, Kellermann-Haaf relies for her historical discussion primarily on secondary literature. However, Kellermann-Haaf's study is energized by the dynamic manner in which it stakes out and claims as a productive field of inquiry the tension between literary and historical evidence. Thus, Kellermann-Haaf not only brings together documentation from disparate sources on medieval German noblewomen but also generates a method of analysis that seeks to establish contradiction and suspend synthesis. This critical practice proves very productive for a field such as medieval women's history because it yields a new set of interpretive problems that can form the basis for future research.[14]

The fresh approaches needed for thinking about medieval women are being generated in the work of scholars such as Monica Green (1993), Helen Solterer (1991, 1995), and Sarah Westphal (1996), to name only a few. On the subject of mothers and daughters, a recent article by the historian John Carmi Parsons (1993) sheds new light on this poorly understood relationship within royal and aristocratic families. Arguing against the thesis that noble daughters were automatically marginalized and devalued in agnatic (i.e., paternal) lineages, Parsons claims instead that "marriage and matrimonial endeavors were a common ground that closely touched upon the self-perceptions of medieval noblewomen. . . . These women so utilized the incidents of international marriage to vindicate for themselves an active role in that arena, and thereby won a not insignificant modicum of power" (1993, 77). He goes on to argue that in the aristocracy this power and the value of consent to marriage could energize the mother-daughter relationship because it emphasized the daughters' choice to "conform to their families' desires and to the behavior of royal women as a group" (78).

At a fundamental level, Parsons is seeking as a historian to reexamine and charge with new meaning women's place in the agnatic kinship structures of the medieval aristocracy, a place defined by "multiple family allegiances" (1993, 77). Miriam Teresa Shadis (1994) follows a similar strategy in reevaluating the lives and careers of two royal sisters, Berenguela de León (1180–1246) and Blanche de Castille (1188–1252), who became queen of León and queen of France, respectively. I take a similar approach in the first half of this book, linking the mother-daughter configurations in epic texts with the organization of kin and and the allocation of power in the medieval aristocracy of twelfth- and thirteenth-century Europe. Taking up this strategy has meant drawing on the history

14. See, for example, Morrison 1994 on fifteenth-century German texts produced in the households of royal women.

of the medieval aristocratic family, in particular, the patrilineal organization of noble families, a mode of kinship organization that arose during
the tenth and eleventh centuries in France (Duby 1980) and in Germany
in the mid-eleventh century (Leyser 1968, 32–36) (Freed 1995). This agnatic line of descent (from the Latin term *agnatio,* meaning "paternal kin")
is what David Herlihy terms "a kind of fellowship of males, stretching
backwards and forwards over time" (1985, 82).[15] The appearance of these
dynastic lineages is connected to the new ways of allocating economic
and political resources that evolved in medieval Europe, the "rise of feudal principalities and the implantation of feudal institutions—fiefs and offices—widely across Europe" (Herlihy 1985, 92).

This introduction is not the place to provide a lengthy explanation of
the evolution of the feudal system. I wish only to remind the reader that
it changed over time, in large measure because of the opposing principles
of division and consolidation embedded within it: partible versus inpart-
ible inheritance, conditional versus hereditary title to fiefs and offices, ter-
ritorial versus imperial bases of power. What such tensions indicate is that
the agnatic lineage cultivated the appearance of permanent ownership of
office, territory, wealth, and power, a stability such lineages often did not,
in fact, possess. As Karl Leyser suggests:

> Stem-seats could thus permutate with bewildering frequency within fami-
> lies or change hands so that the traditions of one kin were thrown into the
> keeping of another and then passed on again to a third. It was not only the
> failure of direct male heirs . . . which brought about these situations. The
> proliferation of castles by which individuals and later whole families came
> to be named thus did not necessarily stand for a more stable and unequiv-
> ocally patrilineal family structure. (Leyser 1968, 50)

Just as it is important not to overestimate the permanence of agnati-
cally defined aristocratic families, so it is equally important not to overex-
aggerate the predominance of patrilineal kin organization in the medieval
nobility. Patrilineal descent is what Jack Goody terms a "unilineal mode
of reckoning" (1983, 223), which traces kin only through the male sex. Its
complement is matrilineal descent, which is traced through the female
sex. However, there are also *bilateral* modes of reckoning descent, often
traced through the *cognatio,* which "sometimes meant . . . maternal kin
but more usually . . . referred to the bilateral range of kin on both sides,

---

15. A useful appendix defining kinship is included in Goody 1983, 222–39. See also the
introduction in Jones's study of German kinship terms (1990, 1–14).

one's ego-oriented or personal kindred, that is, the range of kin traced through father and mother" (Goody 1983, 222–23). Societies can and usually do contain several types of kindred organization. Often, different kindred structures are organized to achieve different specific functions: the agnatic lineage may be designed primarily to protect the kindred's patrimony against ruinous division, thus giving rise in medieval Europe to the notion of primogeniture; the *cognatio* may have defined "a domain of affective ties" (Herlihy 1985, 83). The agnatic line's need for written transactions about the transfer of wealth, title, and power has lent it great visibility in the surviving records. Yet Goody, Herlihy, and Leyser all stress that in the European nobility of the twelfth and thirteenth centuries, bilineal descent networks continued to exist side by side with patrilineal ones. In the case of Scandinavia, for example, Birgit and Peter Sawyer argue that "throughout the Middle Ages kinship systems continued to be bilateral at all social levels, and normally the families of both partners in a marriage helped to endow the new family" (Sawyer and Sawyer 1993, 213). In thinking about the kinship systems of the medieval aristocracy, then, it is imperative to keep Herlihy's conclusion in mind: "Nowhere did the [agnatic] lineage truly replace the old, bilateral kindred; rather, it was superimposed upon it" (1985, 83).

For the medieval aristocracy of the twelfth and thirteenth centuries, maternal kindred mattered enormously, both for the claims that could be advanced through them and as political players in their own right (Leyser 1968, 1970).[16] In this book, I have paid attention to the mother-daughter relationship in twelfth- and thirteenth-century epic texts as an indicator of the importance of maternal kin. Such an enterprise, of course, could also be carried out through an examination of mother-son relationships. Focusing on the mother-daughter relationship, however, shifts the emphasis to a less visible and more fragile site for creating or denying kinship and its privileges and authority. It might also be possible to ask if medieval texts attempt to create matrilines, descent networks traced exclusively through female kin. This is something that the *Eneasroman,* for example, seems to do in a negative way, in the sense that it actively works *against*

---

16. A thesis regarding the *Iwein* frescoes in the castle at Rodenegg provides a fascinating argument for how a noblewoman's high status might find pictorial glorification: the emphasis on the widow Laudine in this representation of the Arthurian romance may well be connected to the marriage between Arnold III of Rodank and the widow Mathilda of Hohenburg, who as a free noblewoman was her husband's social superior (Freed 1995, 224–49). Freed's study analyzes the marriage strategies of the nobility in the archdiocese of Salzburg, 1100–1343. On Austrian noblewomen in general see also Schwob 1982. A recent study both sums up the German literature on the Rodenegg mural cycle and provides a lucid account of its iconography and *pictorial* narrativity (Rushing 1995, 30–90).

the possibility of an enduring, political mother-daughter connection. However, truly matrilineal kin structures over generations are, to my knowledge, virtually unknown in the medieval European nobility of the High Middle Ages, although Shadis's work does point toward noble-women's active construction of matrilines in contexts of royal patronage (1994, 252–302; 1996). Nevertheless, remaining within unilineal systems of kin reckoning and attempting to see if the patriline suppresses the matri-line runs afoul of the lack of historical evidence. It has proven more pro-ductive to focus instead on how the mother-daughter relationship stands in for the *cognatio,* the bilateral kindred descent systems whose continued importance is documented for the European nobility. In the case of the *Eneasroman,* it is indeed impossible to distinguish the matrilineal from the bilineal because only two female generations, mother and daughter, are represented.

Focusing on the mother-daughter relationship does more than make visible in fictional texts the bilineal, or cognatic, descent group. More sig-nificantly, it makes visible the relationship between the agnatic and bilat-eral systems of kin organization as a site of social and political struggle and contest. For the two systems stand in a power relation to each other, with competing claims on rights, privileges, wealth, and power. It is here that the multiple family allegiances of European noblewomen enter into the picture. Women pass between families. At times they appear as objects whose exchange between patrilineal families on the marriage market se-cures political alliances while keeping wealth, influence, and power within the noble class (Fisher and Halley 1989, 1–17). Yet at other times they can be seen as active agents in constructing and maintaining both agnatic and cognatic kin networks. This is the argument I advance in chapter 3 about the anonymous, thirteenth-century epic *Kudrun.* Far from seeing the medieval aristocracy as a world where the ascendancy of ag-natic kin relations and the passive role of women were taken for granted, a close look at the mother-daughter relationship shows us a world in which competing and contradictory social codes and descent structures offered a field for women's agency and action.

Mother-Daughter Conversations about Love

Mothers and daughters talk about sex. Such dialogue, a literary con-vention reaching back to classical literature, characterizes the mother-daughter relationship as a sexual alliance between women. It takes as its bodily and social point of departure the daughter's sexual maturation, for the daughter's sexual maturation marks her transition to female adulthood. The mother teaches her daughter love lore. In so doing she reproduces a female sphere of activity, initiates her daughter into the patriarchal social order, and prepares her daughter for the role that awaited virtually all sexually active medieval women: motherhood. Modern daughters are said to learn female gender identity from their mothers as very small children, before and during their coming to consciousness in language; medieval adolescent daughters in these texts are taught the rules and protocols of female gender identity from their mothers in an overtly didactic, pedagogical manner.[17] Still, modern and medieval accounts agree that in order to understand the reproduction of femininity one must investigate the social and cultural representation of sexual desire and explore the mechanisms by which such discourses are transferred between women.

The literary motif of the mother-daughter conversation about love and the model for learning female gender identity it advances were first discussed by Trude Ehlert in her groundbreaking article, "Die Frau als Arznei" (1986). In a reading of *Die Winsbeckin,* Ehlert argues that the image of women in male-authored medieval German poetry is constructed from a male perspective in which women function exclusively as mediators of men's pursuit of happiness. As her title suggests, women become men's "medicine," and women's reward for fulfilling this role is social prestige: "In dieser ganz aus der Perspektive des Mannes definierten Minnebeziehung wird die Frau zum passiven Medium männlicher Selbstvervollkommnung und Selbstwertsteigerung abstahiert" (Ehlert 1986, 61) (In this love relation, which is completely defined from a male perspective, woman is abstracted into a passive medium for a man's pursuit of self perfection and for the heightening of his self esteem).

The female identity that is created in this way is synonymous with sexual identity. Such a sociosexual female identity is passive and reactive, for it depends on the woman's becoming an attractive and compliant object of male desire. Ehlert dubs this role women's "instrumental function" (1986, 44), a notion that is central to this book.

Women's instrumental function and the sexualization of women, the reduction of women to their function as sexual objects, go hand in hand, pervading medieval representations of mothers and daughters. The ancient literary motif of mothers and daughters talking about sex, passion, and marriage spans both halves of the book and appears in many genres. The epic *Eneasroman* features a lengthy conversation between mother and daughter on the subject of the nature and causes of love. The *Nibelungen-*

17. An important study of medieval and early modern advice for girls in German literature (Barth 1994) situates the readings precisely in a pedagogical context and therefore discusses the Latin tradition as well as conduct literature such as the *Der Ritter vom Turn* that is addressed to daughters by fathers.

lied contains a similar, though highly abbreviated, exchange. *Die Wins-beckin*, the Neidhart poems, and *Stepmother and Daughter* all take as their starting point the motif of the mother and daughter conversing and debating about sexual desire and the choice of a male partner. Only two texts in this book do not contain a mother-daughter conversation about love: *Tristan und Isolde* and *Kudrun*. In the case of the former, the love potion given to the daughter by the mother embodies, to a certain extent, the love lore so intimately connected with mothers and daughters. The epic *Kudrun* alone contains not so much as a hint of this motif.

Nevertheless, the literary convention of mothers and daughters conversing about sex and love takes on different meanings, which fall out along the lines of genre and class. In epic texts such as the *Eneasroman* and the *Nibelungenlied*, the motif of the mother-daughter conversation about love converges in salient ways with political issues, since for medieval noblewomen the choice of a marriage partner was usually a matter of state. In the lyric texts, however, the emphasis shifts from politics to sexuality. *Die Winsbeckin* is a kind of transitional piece, for it features a mother and daughter of the nobility but lacks a political context for the choice of a partner. The Neidhart poems and *Stepmother and Daughter*, feature women of the lower classes: rural women, peasant women, poor urban working women. In these texts, the conversations between mothers and daughters are about choices for sexual activity: a knight or a rich peasant boy, a lover or a husband, a poor suitor or a rich one, an inexperienced suitor or a married one, illicit or licit sex, sex for pleasure or sex for money. Often they choose both alternatives.

Through the mother-daughter relationship we can see how the sexualization of medieval women is arrayed along class lines. When aristocratic mothers and daughters discuss erotic passion, their conversations draw on Ovidian love lore; both in the *Eneasroman* and in *Die Winsbeckin*, the symptoms described show clear affinities to lovesickness, an ailment of mind and body caused by sexual desire that was recognized by medieval physicians as a melancholia-like illness unique to the wealthy (Wack 1990). Mothers and daughters of the lower classes, in contrast, do not experience lovesickness; they experience—and act on—a strong desire to have sex. Thus the aristocratic mothers and daughters seem to illustrate the notion that the monogamy upon which noblewomen's honor rested might be secured if a daughter could be led to understand and act on her desire in class-specific terms. The lower-class mothers and daughters, on the other hand, seem to illustrate the tenet that any program for the social control of sexuality placed in the hands of women is bound to fail.

Mother-daughter stories, then, are not timeless fables about female maturation. Neither do they possess a single, unifying principle that explains the production of femininity in patriarchy. Their meanings are not fixed. Rather, the mother-daughter stories of medieval German fiction are socially, historically, and economically conditioned; versions differ, depending on genre, time, and class. Mother-daughter stories tell us something about competing modes of constructing kinship in the medieval aristocracy. They show us differing modes of sexualizing women. They embody the tensions between what is innate and what is learned, between compliance and disorderliness, between conformity and rebellion, between collaboration and resistance. Whether arguing or agreeing, mothers and daughters in medieval German literature show us women in the process of performing cultural work that interrogates the vexed and contradictory, yet historically specific, scripts through which patriarchal ideals of womanhood take shape.

PART ONE

Noble Mothers and Daughters

Conflicts of Sentiment and Power

❧ I ❧

Unruly Mother, Exemplary Daughter

*The Construction of Female Power and Passion
in Heinrich von Veldeke's* Eneasroman

Ich sehnte mich nach Mutterlieb
Und Vaterwort und Frühlingsspielen,
Den Fluch, der mich durchs Leben trieb,
Begann ich, da er bei mir blieb,
Wie einen treuen Feind zu lieben.
—Else Lasker-Schüler, "Frühling" (1986, 79)[1]

THE MOTHER-DAUGHTER STORY in Heinrich von Veldeke's *Eneasroman* (c. 1170–c. 1185), a German adaption of the anonymous Old French antique romance, the *Roman d'Eneas* (c. 1160), in turn based on Virgil's *Aeneid*, is probably the first sustained mother-daughter interaction in German literature.[2] The queen and her daughter, Lavinia, appear in one of the first works to introduce the new discourse of sexual passion, which originated in the Old French cultural sphere, to German-speaking territories. *Romantic love*, the name I will use for this new paradigm of sensibility, links sexual desire and passionate suffering with an intense erotic attachment to a single individual. In the Middle Ages, notions of romantic love were closely linked to the disease of lovesickness, which was considered a class-specific ailment of the nobility, who alone possessed enough leisure

1. "Spring": I longed for mother love / and father word and spring games; / the curse that drove me through life, / because it stayed with me, I began / to love it like a loyal enemy.
2. I quote from the Kartschoke edition (1986) of Heinrich von Veldeke's *Eneasroman;* citing line number. Kartschoke's edition, derived from Ettmüller's, gives both numbering systems that have evolved for Heinrich's work: Ettmüller's page and line numbering system and the continuous line numbering used by Behaghel (1882) and by Schieb and Frings (1964–1970). I follow the continuous line numbering system.
   The standard edition of the Old French *Roman d'Eneas* is by de Grave (1925–1929). All translations of the Old French are from Yunck (1974) and are cited by page number. The most detailed comparison of these three related texts remains Dittrich (1966). See also Minis 1959 and Ruh 1977.

to experience it (Wack 1990, xi–xii). Unlike courtly love, which seems to have depended on the impossibility of any sanctioned social union between the lovers, romantic love in its fictionalized forms often led to marriage.

It is no accident that lengthy and subtle characterizations of noblewomen and the conventions of a new discourse of erotic longing should enter German literature hand-in-hand, as it were. Whether fantasized, fetishized, chastised or idealized, woman, the "opposite sex," is constructed as the indispensable "other" in a new discourse on erotic attraction and suffering that contributes to the advance of such vernacular genres as courtly love poetry and Arthurian romance and leaves its mark on such diverse areas of knowledge as the lore of medicine, religious thought, and the practice and writing of piety.[3]

It is well known that the medieval *Eneas* stories rewrite their antique source in order to celebrate the erotic anguish of its heroine and hero, Lavinia and Aeneas, according to a model of romantic love that resolves the pain and pleasure of sexual desire in marital bliss. What has less often been noted is that the medieval tales of *Eneas* complicate the story of romantic love between man and woman by grounding it—indeed, founding it—in a story of the conflicted emotional and political attachment between mother and daughter. This theme, already well developed in the *Roman d'Eneas,* is expanded and intensified in the *Eneasroman.*

In the *Eneasroman* father and daughter never once speak; it is the mother who informs her daughter about love and politics and teaches her about a woman's place in society. Yet the dynamic of the mother-daughter relationship in Heinrich's *Eneasroman* anticipates in salient ways the traditional Freudian psychoanalytic model describing the origins of female heterosexuality and the development of a socially acceptable female gender identity: the daughter must break with her primary love object, her mother, in order to engage in heterosexual love.[4] Furthermore, the mother-daughter relationship in the *Eneasroman* reveals that what appears to be a timeless, apolitical fable about a young woman's emotional maturation is, in fact, part of a larger, socially conditioned narrative about the cultural struggle over medieval noblewomen's contested right to exercise political power.

---

3. Wack (1990) explores the confluence of love lore and medicine, Cazelles (1991) the influence of the new discourse of love on saint's lives, and Bloch (1991) the connection between the invention of the concept of romantic love and misogyny.

4. The standard essays by Sigmund Freud on female identity formation are "Einige psychische Folgen des anatomischen Geschlechtsunterschieds (1925); "Über die weibliche Sexualität (1931); and "Die Weiblichkeit" (1933).

Summary of the *Eneasroman*

In both the *Eneasroman* and the *Roman d'Eneas,* the mother-daughter relationship is staged through lengthy conversations between the queen and Lavinia.[5] These conversations have no precedent in Virgil's work, where mother and daughter never speak to each other.[6] *The Roman d'Eneas* invents two mother-daughter dialogues, to which Heinrich's *Eneasroman* adds a third (ll. 9748–990; ll. 10497–721; ll. 13012–92). The first and second mother-daughter conversations in both the Old French and the Middle High German suspend the forward movement of the plot at a significant moment. Aeneas flees Troy and lands in Carthage, where the ruler, Queen Dido, falls in love with him. The two become lovers, but Aeneas abandons Dido to continue his journey. Dido commits suicide. While underway, Aeneas descends into the underworld, where his father, Anchises, shows him the illustrious royal dynasty that will issue from him. Aeneas and his Trojan followers arrive in Italy, which is ruled from the stronghold of Laurentum by King Latinus and the queen. The royal couple's only child, Lavinia, is betrothed to Turnus, a local prince and the queen's champion, a betrothal signaling Turnus is Latinus's successor. However, King Latinus immediately recognizes in the hero Aeneas the man whose succession to his throne has been prophetically foretold. Understanding that Aeneas's sudden but divinely sanctioned appearance renders moot the betrothal of Lavinia and Turnus, Latinus attempts to negotiate a peaceful termination of the engagement so that Lavinia will be free to marry Aeneas. Instead, war breaks out between the Trojan interlopers led by Aeneas and the native Italians led by Turnus, who is spurred on by the queen. The enemies engage in a series of battles concluding with the deaths and splendid burials of two opposing champions: first the Trojan ally, Prince Pallas, slain by Turnus; and then the Italian ally, the Amazon queen, Camilla, slain by Aeneas. A stalemate is reached. The two sides arrange a truce; Turnus and Aeneas agree to meet in single combat. In the interim between the truce and the duel, the first and second mother-daughter dialogues take place.

The first and lengthiest of the dialogues is set up as a conversation about love between an innocent daughter and her knowledgeable mother,

---

5. In Virgil's epic the queen is named Amata, but in both the *Roman d'Eneas* and Heinrich's *Eneasroman* she is anonymous. Heinrich refers to her as *diu kuniginne* (the queen), a practice I will follow here.

6. In Virgil, mother and daughter appear together in the journey to sacrifice (book 11, ll. 477 ff.). In addition, Lavinia reacts to Amata's vow to die (book 12, ll. 64 ff.) and to her death (book 12, ll. 605 ff.).

who explicates the question "What is erotic love?" in terms derived from Ovid. The queen uses her superior knowledge to prod Lavinia towards a display of affection for Turnus. Lavinia speaks for the first time, questioning her mother's pronouncements and evading her directions. After this mother-daughter conversation, Lavinia begins the first of her famous monologues on love that connect her awakening sensibilities with Dido's tragic passion. Then Venus herself intervenes, causing Lavinia to fall passionately in love with Aeneas in spite of the queen's equally passionate disapproval. The second mother-daughter conversation, which ensues, dramatizes the breach between Lavinia and the queen that frees Lavinia to reveal her passion to Aeneas.

In the Old French version, this second conversation also marks the queen's final appearance in the story. Battle breaks out again between the Italians and the Trojans, but Aeneas, now knowing of Lavinia's passion and himself inflamed with love through Venus's devices, slays Turnus. Lavinia and Aeneas finally meet in person, declare their mutual love, and Aeneas offers sumptuous gifts. At this point Heinrich inserts a final conversation between the queen and Lavinia, in which the queen violently berates Lavinia before withdrawing to die. With the marriage of Aeneas and Lavinia, the epic is done. Both versions conclude with a dynastic tableau recounting again the success of the royal patrilineage Aeneas has founded.

Power and Love

What might have been the Old French poet's source for his amplification of the mother-daughter relationship? As mentioned above, it is not developed in Virgil, and the Old French literature that predates the *Roman d'Eneas* offers no models of mother-daughter conversations. No scholar of Old French appears to have pursued the question of the poet's source for this invention; rather, scholars point to Ovid in general as the inspiration for the love discourse which the Old French poet fashioned in the *Roman d'Eneas* (Yunck 1974, 209–11, nn. 132 and 133). Insofar as they partake of the Ovidian love motifs, the mother-daughter conversations are thus thematically central to what Lee Patterson has called "the *Eneas* poet's boldest act of revision" (1987, 177), the introduction and elaboration of Ovidian eroticism in a tale of conquest and empire building.

Patterson argues persuasively that, far from being merely an ornamental or entertaining digression, Ovidian eroticism is inextricably linked to the epic's discourse of war and power. The medieval *Eneas* epic establishes a "profound bond between the inner world of erotic experience and the historical world of martial deeds" (1987, 178). According to Patterson, this linkage serves a political purpose, for it "establishes an analogy between the creation of a mutual love and the founding of an empire based upon that love" (1987, 177). These thematic connections can also be analyzed in generic terms, for the Old French romance *Roman d'Eneas* represents a kind of hybrid between the older genre of the heroic epic or *chanson de geste*, such as the *Chanson de Roland*, and the fledgling genre of romance. Simon Gaunt argues that the *Roman d'Eneas* "provides a bridge between epic and romance, between two ideologies, enacting a conscious movement towards an ideology in which love and sexuality regulate the bellicose tendencies of the medieval aristocratic male rather than male bonding within a male brotherhood" (1992, 9).[7] This is not to say that in enacting the end of the heroic epic the medieval *Eneas* tales overthrow patriarchal authority. Rather, they reinscribe patriarchal authority by means of a new ideology of power that is founded on a hierarchy of gender and sexuality—in short, by means of romantic love.

The genre of romance creates new notions of masculinity; it also creates new notions of femininity. In the *Eneas* story of conquest and dynasty building, the mother-daughter dialogues provide a female foundation for the new order of gender relations. They adjust the apparent elevation of women in romance ideology to the continuing subordination of women in the areas of political and military activity. Romantic love, then, is critically implicated in the way the *Eneasroman* constructs sexual love and political power as categories that are mutually exclusive for women. To put it another way, the representation of mother and daughter in the *Eneasroman* reveals how the discourse of romantic love depends on a hierarchy of gender relations that reserves the exercise of political power for men. The mother-daughter presence in the *Eneasroman* thus tells two stories: that powerful women are dangerous and that in the ideology preferring male rule and the father-son lineage, the mother-daughter connection ultimately does not matter.

In a general sense, all the female characters in the *Eneasroman* provide compelling examples of the notion—prevalent not just in the Middle Ages—that love and political rule are fundamentally incompatible for women. Most scholarship on this issue focuses on the parallels and contrasts between the Aeneas/Dido and Aeneas/Lavinia relationships.[8]

---

7. Gaunt argues that the deaths of the warrior companions Eurialus and Nisus in the *Roman d'Eneas* represent a *mise en abyme* of the end of the "male bonding" ideology of the *chanson de geste* (1922, 24–25).

8. Patterson 1987 and Gaunt 1992 have already been mentioned. See also Groos 1976, Kartschoke 1983, Rusinek 1986, and Kasten 1988.

Dido's incapacity to reconcile passion and power is both obvious and calamitous; Lavinia's complete subordination to both the "law" of love and to Aeneas is linked to her utter disinterest in political matters. The political and martial prowess of the woman warrior, Camilla, is predicated on her sexual disdain for men.[9] Finally, the queen illustrates a further position on the continuum of this apparent incompatibility of love and power for women. Heinrich portrays her as an entirely political creature, a woman whose pursuit of political domination deprives her of love— both the capacity to give it and the capacity to be its object. This understanding of the queen's role and function is supported by the medieval texts' suppression of the name given the queen by Virgil: Amata, beloved. Indeed, because the *Aeneid* was well known in the Middle Ages, the queen's anonymity in the medieval adaptations may well have been understood as an interpretive cue by many members of the medieval audience.

Heinrich's adaptation imagines the mother-daughter story as the absolute clash between two incompatible principles: the mother symbolizes power; the daughter, love. To develop this clash, the *Eneasroman* amplifies its source's representation of the queen as an unruly woman who endangers the social order—in effect, demonizing her. At the same time, the *Eneasroman*, following its source, presents Lavinia as a desirable woman who inverts the stereotype of the disorderly woman. In submitting to paternal rule in the guise of romantic passion (for, in her choice of husband, she follows her father's wishes), the compliant and desirable Lavinia stabilizes the social order.

What makes this connection by inversion particularly compelling in the *Eneasroman* is that the unruly woman and the compliant woman are *genealogically* linked by the fact that they are used to portray a mother and a daughter. Power-crazed noblewomen and submissive noblewomen are nothing new in medieval literature; what is intriguing in this tale about the *re*foundation, through Aeneas, of patriarchal inheritance and lineage, is that this pair of female stereotypes is projected into the mother-daughter relationship, that is to say, into the story of maternal inheritance and lineage. In a time and class when genealogy meant history and was a sought-after guarantee of authority and power, the parent-child relationship was an important political link that was exalted for fathers and sons but negated for mothers and daughters. Far from being static, the dominant medieval notion of genealogy as a succession of fathers and sons had to suppress or vitiate competing notions of kinship, among them that of mothers and daughters.

9. On the Amazon queen Camilla in Veldeke's work, see Westphal 1996.

The mother-daughter story in the *Eneasroman* allows us to see traces of this social process. According to Simon Gaunt, the mother-daughter "episode is . . . subject to analysis in terms of a dispute between paternal and maternal authority" (1992, 14), a dispute in which maternal authority is constructed as "pseudo-authority," and linked, through the mother-daughter relationship, to the project of discrediting maternal genealogy and women's right to power. Both the Old French version and Heinrich's reject a notion of mother-daughter relationship as the site of the transfer of power between women. This repudiation of maternal-filial power must be taken into account in any interpretation of the second set of feminine stereotypes invoked by the text, the erotically experienced mother and erotically innocent daughter of the mother-daughter dialogue, stereotypes that propose an apolitical mother-daughter relationship based in the realm of sentiment. The way these stereotypes are deployed and the way they clash against each other reveal deeply rooted cultural ambivalence about powerful noblewomen and the place of the mother-daughter lineage in a patriarchally structured social order, an ambivalence that resonates with our historical knowledge about the lives of aristocratic women in the Middle Ages.

The Queen in the *Eneasroman* and the *Roman d'Eneas*

In tracing the *Eneasroman's* agenda of legitimating paternal authority and discrediting maternal authority, we must first examine how the German adaption changes its source's representation of the queen into a disorderly woman. To explore the implications of this characterization means returning to the beginning of the story, for the queen is established as a significant actor long before the first mother-daughter dialogue takes place. Even before she makes her first appearance, her political actions are presented as meddling in the affairs of state. Welcoming Aeneas's envoys, Latinus offers Aeneas Lavinia's hand in marriage, together with the lands and authority that follow with her: "Whether I desired it or not, the gods have given her to him" [ich wolde oder enwolde, / die gote hânt si ime gegeben] (ll. 3966–67).[10] However, Latinus goes on to explain that this magnificant gift comes with a bothersome political encumbrance: Lavinia is already engaged to Turnus. Latinus goes on to explain how this engagement, which he claims to have opposed, came about: "my wife the

10. All translations are my own, but I have consulted the English translation by Thomas (1984).

Queen gave me no peace, so finally I had to act on this matter in a way I wish I had avoided" [mîn wîb diu kuniginne / diu ne liez mich nie gerûn, / ê ich der mite mûste tûn, / des ich gerne hete enboren] (ll. *3970–73*). In a word, the queen has nagged him into it.

The scenes immediately following the king's public reception of Aeneas's envoys—the quarrel between Latinus and the queen over which husband Lavinia is to have, the queen's warning message to Turnus, and Turnus's reply—set up the king and queen as political enemies in the matter of their daughter's marriage. Like the mother-daughter conversations, this sequence of scenes is one of the Old French poet's innovations. Heinrich's version not only adopts this plot line but it also intensifies the portrayal of the queen as an angry and ungovernable woman. The Old French version places the decisive quarrel between Latinus and the queen in public. The queen enters the reception hall, where the king has been receiving messengers, and sits down beside him. Expressing her "wish and desire" (Yunck 1974, 121) that Latinus uphold the engagement to Turnus, she acquaints Latinus with Aeneas's past history of seducing and abandoning women (i.e., Dido), expresses her fear that he will do the same with Lavinia, and points out that Turnus will not fail to put up a fight. Although the narrator has told us that the queen is "sorrowful and angry" (121), her speech seems quite calm, touched even with a hint of sophisticated, courtly wit: "This man [Aeneas] is in great need of repose, for he has labored many a day rowing on the sea" (121). Latinus's reply is also short, clear, and devoid of emotion: Aeneas is the divinely sanctioned husband. Only after the queen sees that she cannot sway her husband does she retire to her chamber, where, weeping, she gives vent to her anger, sorrow, and frustration.

In the Old French version we see the queen adapt her demeanor to the space she occupies: in public she shows the calm self-possession of a sovereign; in private she weeps. In contrast, the queen in the German adaption is shown only in private and only in one mood: anger. Heinrich removes the royal couple's dispute (ll. *4144–4344*, nearly three times longer than the Old French version!) from a public setting. The queen goes to the king's chamber; at the end of the scene, he walks out on her, leaving her to rage on alone in the *kemenât* (chamber), the private room where the entire quarrel has taken place. The queen's gestures speak before she does; we are told that she enters the private room so out of control and ill-bred that she violates protocol by sitting down without bowing in greeting (ll. *4153–55*). The argument between the queen and Latinus then begins, with the enraged queen accusing the king of being out of his mind ("dû bist ûzer sinne," l. *4170*). She violently berates him for breaking Lavinia's engagement to Turnus in favor of the cowardly, wastrel vagabond Aeneas, going on to express the fear that Aeneas will use Lavinia and abandon her as he has Dido. Replying with great detachment, the king does not assert his authority but rather invokes an outside agent: he calmly describes for the queen the divine causation of his action.

It is at approximately this point that the scene in the *Roman d'Eneas* ends. In the *Eneasroman,* however, Latinus continues his speech and shifts the terms of the discussion. The issue for him is not Aeneas, or even Dido, but rather the queen's anger and loss of self-control. What does she expect to gain, the king asks, by this show of anger (ll. 4260–62)? A list of the words the king employs as he describes, to her face, his wife's conduct makes a truly impressive compendium of Middle High German expressions for "being enraged" and "disorderly conduct": *bedwingen mit ubellîchen dingen* (to compel with evil behavior, l. 4264); *ir zornet zunmâzen* (you rage excessively, immoderately, l. 4276); *ungefûge zorn* (unseemly anger, l. 4277); *ungemach* (aggravation, l. 4286); *unzuhte* (lack of discipline, unruliness, l. 4317); *grôze undolt* (intense impatience, extreme lack of self-control l. 4321); *fravelheit* (arrogance, l. 4332); *freissam* (frenzied, fierce, l. 4333). Following this speech, Latinus rejoins his male councilors, leaving the queen to rage on alone.

Heinrich goes beyond his source to polarize the conflict between the king and the queen, amplifying the characterization of each, the queen negatively and the king positively. Throughout the *Eneasroman,* Heinrich strengthens Latinus's kingly bearing and his alignment with Aeneas's cause.[11] Nevertheless, the king does not succeed in curbing the queen's disruptive force. She remains a tenacious power broker behind closed doors. Wringing her hands and weeping in fury after the king's exit, the queen writes Turnus a letter—in her own hand, Heinrich tells us—giving Turnus her account of the dishonor that has befallen him, reminding him of her affection, and promising him advice and material support should he elect to drive the interloper out of Laurentum. This treasonous letter produces the predictable results: Turnus assembles his army.

---

11. As Dittrich points out, "Nur in Veldekes Eneide bekennt sich König Latinus gegenüber Turnus mit Entschiedenheit zu Eneas, verteidigt ihn, bewährt den *fride* schützend durch Gesinnung und Wort, ja kündigt demjenigen den Entzug der königlichen Huld an, der etwas gegen den Troer zu unternehmen wagen sollte" [Only in Veldeke's Eneide does King Latinus declare himself forcefully against Turnus and for Aeneas, does he defend Aeneas, does he protect and keep *fride* (peace) through his intentions and his words. Yes, he even threatens anyone who might venture against the Trojan with the loss of royal favor] (1966, 228).

In the *Roman d'Eneas*, the queen gives a speech during the hand-wringing scene, immediately before she sends a messenger to Turnus.[12] In this speech, she articulates again the reasons for rejecting Aeneas, and she couches her concerns specifically in terms of Lavinia's honor and safety: "He [Aeneas] shall have none of my daughter unless he pays very dearly for her. Neither daughter nor mother will ever fall under his protection" (Yunck 1974, 123). By having the queen repeat, while alone, the fear she has already expressed to the king, the Old French offers a more charitable view of the queen, whose motivations are founded partially in her concern for the welfare of her child. This concern can be read as a signal of loving maternal attachment, intended to complicate the characterization of the queen. We also see that the queen is concerned for her own welfare. The phrase "fall under his protection" suggests that she expects to outlive her husband and as a widow become dependent on the goodwill of her son-in-law. Perhaps a sense of medieval reality intrudes here, for widowhood may have brought greater opportunities to medieval women, but it also put them at great risk. In any case, we see that the queen is anxious about her own future and this existential, rather than political, dread humanizes her. In the *Eneasroman*, however, a parallel speech does not exist; in one descriptive sentence, the text goes from the queen's gestures of grief and rage to the business of the letter. The hints of the queen's sentimental attachment to her child and of her anxieties about her own well-being have been struck from Heinrich's version. Such a deletion is particularly noteworthy in an adaptation that almost always lengthens rather than abbreviates its source. In removing all implications that the queen is motivated by anything other than anger and thwarted political ambition, Heinrich removes from the German queen any sign of human attachment.

The Politics of the German Queen

After the outbreak of open hostility between the Trojans and Turnus and after Latinus's unsuccessful attempt to mediate between them, Heinrich inserts a scene that has no parallel in the Old French version, one that

---

12. This scene is one of the two in which Heinrich "modernizes" by moving the action from the sphere of the spoken word to that of the written word. The other instance is the scene in which Lavinia hesitantly reveals to her mother the name of the man she loves (Eneas) : in the Old French she explodes—or, as Gaunt argues, assembles—the name by speaking the syllables one by one (ll. 8551–61); in Heinrich's version she writes the syllables on a wax tablet, using a golden stylus (ll. 10618–27) (Gaunt 1992, 17–18). Heinrich introduces the motif of the "exploded" name in the conversation about love between Dido and her sister Anna as Dido stammers out the name of her beloved (ll. 1521–34).

even further demonizes the queen (ll. 4947–5000): a short dialogue between Turnus and the queen that takes place in the queen's chamber. Received in courteous friendship by the queen, Turnus apprises her of his intention to "drive Aeneas back over the sea" (ll. 4973–75). The queen again pledges Turnus her assistance:

> Turnus, my dear son, I believe you. Follow up your words with deeds, and I will help you, with advice and council, early and late, day and night, however I may and can, with skill and with cunning. I will give you much wealth, which you can readily accept, because you've got the right point of view.

> Turnûs, lieber sun mîn,
> des wil ich gewis sîn,
> alsô dû spriches alsô tû
> dâ wil ich dir helfen zû
> mit sinne und mit râte
> beidiu frû und spâte
> unde naht unde tach,
> als ich kan unde mach,
> mit listen und mit fûgen.
> ich gibe dir schaz genûgen,
> den dû gerne nemen maht,
> wande dû bist wol bedaht. (ll. 4979–90)

By addressing Turnus as "son," the queen makes clear that in her mind his engagement to Lavinia is as good as a marriage. Indirectly she reminds Turnus that he can add to his social status as her vassal and to his political status as her champion the familial rank of "dear son." In other words, the queen expresses a way of comprehending the world in which these three categories—the social, the political, and the familial—are inseparable from one another. By granting Turnus familial status as her son, the queen increases his social and political investment in continuing the war with Aeneas. Further, the queen's offers of wealth, influence, and power mimic seigneurial power. She attempts to rule by establishing hierarchies and authority through these gifts. The queen thus attempts to operate within the political system we know as feudalism, the system of administrative and military bonds between nobility that secured governance in the Middle Ages. What is significant about the *Eneasroman* is that it aligns feudalism, the dominant medieval mode of rule, with the unwholesome figure of the queen, setting her, and by implication, the version of feudalism she acts out, in opposition to a political system in which rule is based instead on conquest and divine authority.

The queen's success in inciting Turnus to intractable hatred by appealing to his wounded pride and by promising him material and political support is largely responsible for the strife that overtakes Laurentum. That is to say, in the *Eneasroman* the power struggle between Aeneas and Turnus results from the weakness of an ineffectual king who has been unable to control his ambitious and treasonous wife. Certainly the *Eneasroman* suggests that the lack of love between the two fuels this catastrophic state of affairs. Its portrayal of the queen further implies that her behavior is to blame for the breach. The queen is disobedient as well as unlovable, refusing to follow her husband's example and orders in conforming to a preordained plan. Because she is an ambitious queen who meddles in affairs of state, the queen endangers not only the harmony of the family, but also the welfare of the entire country. In short, the German queen is presented both as a ruthless woman who will stop at nothing to consolidate her influence and power and as an agent of social destruction. Domestic strife, symbolized by this disorderly woman, is thus to blame for the civil strife that will rend the kingdom of Laurentum. Such a representation of the queen suggests a fear among the medieval German aristocracy that "uppity" women will break down a patriarchally controlled social order and unleash the forces of chaos.

The *Eneas* stories are silent on the issue of whether the kingdom and fortresses of Italy belong to the king or to the queen. The rights of land and kin by which king and queen might assert their claim to control the fate of Lavinia and the kingdom are left obscure, yet there are important historical dimensions to their dispute over Lavinia's marriage. Gaunt points out that this dispute reflects the struggle over exogamous and endogamous marriage practices, that is, choosing marriage partners from outside (*exo-*) or inside (*endo-*) one's extended kin. This issue was debated between the Catholic church and feudal nobility from the late eleventh century onwards (Gaunt 1992, 14–15). The divine plan, which favors Aeneas and which King Latinus immediately accepts, coincides with the sustained campaign of the Catholic church to impose strict exogamy on the nobility. Turnus is a "local likely lad" (Gaunt 1992, 14), and the queen's selection of him is consistent with the endogamous marriage practices of the feudal nobility. Further, the queen's participation in the choice of a son-in-law, rendered in the text as meddling, suggests a marriage system in which mothers and maternal kin play formidable roles in the alliance politics of feudal marriage making. The medieval *Eneas* texts make Lavinia an object of exchange between Latinus and Aeneas in an exogamous marriage that asserts the dominance of a patrilineal genealogy. At the same time, however, the texts set up Turnus as an object of exchange between the queen and Lavinia in a proposed endogamous marriage that would uphold the influence of a maternal lineage. The *Eneas* epics both depict and discredit a notion of matrilineality, illustrious descent that a mother would pass to her children. The genealogy with which the epic concludes deemphasizes Lavinia's status; it is a list of Aeneas's royal offspring, whose renown comes from their father, not their mother. But the battle over the status of the mother's influence is fought long before, and the site of that struggle is the relationship between the queen and Lavinia.

The unlovable and all-too-powerful woman thus becomes at once an argument against matrilineality and an argument for female complacency, secured through notions of romantic love, within the patriarchal social order. The queen embodies the maternal authority that is disclaimed in the *Roman d'Eneas* and roundly repudiated in the *Eneasroman*. She is portrayed as an unruly and emotionally profligate woman whose insubordination against her husband's rule is in large part responsible for the war that breaks out in the kingdom of Laurentum. She provides a negative example against which the ideal embodied in Lavinia's exemplary subordination to paternal authority can triumph. Rather than inherit from and connect with her mother, Lavinia renounces her matrilineal heritage and chooses instead to be an exemplary daughter within the patriarchal family. The story of the queen and Lavinia can thus be seen as the struggle between an unruly royal mother and an exemplary daughter. In the ensuing scenes between mother and daughter, Heinrich sharpens his portrayal of the queen as a destructive force of nature that is beyond any rational control.

The First Mother-Daughter Conversation about Love

After it has been established that the queen is too powerful and willful politically, she disappears from the action. For some five thousand lines, the narrative is dominated by bitter fighting between the forces of Aeneas and Turnus, each losing a champion (Pallas and Camilla, respectively). At last Aeneas and Turnus agree to meet in single combat; the future of the Italian kingdom rests upon the outcome of this duel. At this politically charged moment, the queen reappears. She reenters the narrative by initiating a lengthy conversation with her daughter.[13] The queen's talent for persuasion has already been amply demonstrated, both indirectly in Lat-

13. The causal connection between the impending duel and the queen's action is made in the *Eneasroman* through a *dô/dô* (when/then) clause: "When single combat between Turnus and Eneas had been consented to, then late one night the queen summoned her daughter to her in her chamber" [Dô der kamph gelobet was, / des Turnûs und Enêas . . . dô was diu kuniginne / eines âbendes spâte / in ir kemenâten. / ir tohter sie vor sich nam] (ll. 9735–36; ll. 9740–43).

inus's claim that the queen has nagged him into agreeing to the first betrothal, and directly, in the letter to Turnus and the conversation with him
invented by Heinrich. She now sets out to exploit her knowledge and
rhetorical abilities, as well as her maternal intimacy with her daughter, in
order to enlist Lavinia in Turnus's cause.

In the Old French, the first conversation between mother and daughter (ll. 7857–8024) consists of short exchanges between the two women
alternating with longer explanations from the queen. In the Middle
High German, this first conversation, nearly half again as long (ll.
9745–9990), is clearly structured into four long monologues by the
queen, each followed by a question-and-answer session in which
Lavinia, in voicing her doubts and objections, raises a topic to which
the queen's next monologue responds. The final coda, only twenty lines
long, which shows us the queen's anger and Lavinia's fear, provides a
transition to the ensuing action. The entire conversation may be sum-
marized as follows:

1. The queen: Hatred for Aeneas and love for Turnus (ll. 9749–88)
   Q/A: Identification of Love (ll. 9789–820)
2. The queen: Nature and symptoms of Love (ll. 9821–51)
   Q/A: Pain of Love (ll. 9852–68)
3. The queen: Remedies of Love (ll. 9869–87)
   Q/A: Fear of Love (ll. 9888–96)
4. The queen: Love and Fortune: Cupid (ll. 9897–9965)
   Q/A: Fear of Love (ll. 9966–69)
5. Coda. The queen: Threats (ll. 9970–83)
   Q/A: Lavinia's insistence on her innocence, departure of the queen
   (ll. 9984–90)

This first and longest of the mother-daughter conversations seeks to
define mother and daughter in accordance with the notions of power and
love discussed above. Although the queen's purpose as a mother is ostensibly to instruct her daughter in the lore of love, she first confronts
Lavinia not with talk of love, but rather with the cold, hard facts of marriage politics. According to the queen, Lavinia's father has robbed Lavinia
of honor and wealth ("daz dir dîn vater hât genommen / michel gût und
êre," ll. 9752–53) by contracting a marriage to the landless Aeneas rather
than the well-situated Turnus; Aeneas intends to kill Turnus, who loves
her; and Aeneas intends to use force to take Lavinia, whom he desires
only for her inheritance. While in the *Roman d'Eneas* the queen also emphasizes the desirability of Lavinia's loving Turnus, the *Eneasroman*
heightens the hostility of the speech, adding the notion of Latinus's mis-
deed and stressing the dishonor and violence of Aeneas's intentions.

Therefore you have just cause to be hostile towards him [Aeneas] and not to show him the slightest honor of any kind; from this you must desist, and you should justly hate him, for he wants to take you violently here and now, in order to inherit your father's realm. If you wish to bring happiness and act well, daughter, then love Turnus.

> dar zû hâstû rehte scholt,
> daz dû im ungenâdich sîs
> unde im neheine wîs
> niemer êre getûst,
> want duz wole lâzen mûst
> und in von rehte hazzen salt,
> wander dich mit gewalt
> hie wil erwerben
> unde wil erben
> dînes vater rîche.
> ob dû sâllîche
> unde wole welles tûn,
> tohter sô minne Turnûm.[14] (ll. 9772–88)

The conversation is further characterized by the introduction of new stereotypes: the experienced and the innocent woman. The queen's persuasiveness and knowledge is juxtaposed to Lavinia's innocence, which at times borders on obtuseness. This distinction is obvious in Lavinia's replies to her mother's speech. Indeed, Lavinia's first words, the first she speaks in the entire epic, verge on slapstick, at once introducing and making fun of her youthful innocence. (For ease in reading I have designated the speakers in my translation throughout.)

L: "With what should I love?"
Q: "With your heart and mind."
L: "So I'm supposed to give him my heart!?"
Q: "Yes, do that."
L: "But then how can I go on living?"
Q: "You aren't supposed to give it to him like *that*."

14. Here there is again an echo of the Anna-Dido conversation about Eneas: Anna advises Dido to give in to her passion for Eneas, a passion that brings about Dido's death; the queen advises Lavinia to avoid loving Eneas, a love that will in fact bring about a fortuitous marriage and the foundation of a successful dynasty. In both cases, because the advice of the female confidant regarding Eneas is wrong, there is a hint that women in general are ignorant (in the case of the queen willfully and selfishly so) when it comes to comprehending the place, rights, and duties of "divine heroes".

"wâ mite sal ich in minnen?"
'mit dem herzen und mit den sinnen.'
"sal ich im mîn herze geben?"
'jâ dû.' "wie soldich danne geleben?"
'dune salt ez im sô geben niht.' (ll. 9789–93)

It is Lavinia's persistent questioning that provokes the mother to explain. The experience/innocence motif is bound up with the teacher/novice motif as well. The queen is instructing Lavinia, who proves a skeptical and difficult pupil. Yet this exchange between mother and daughter, also cast as one between master and apprentice, both colludes and collides with the overt content of the teachings, the topic of love. For the conversation includes not only what the queen has to say overtly about love—which is a compendium of medieval love lore derived from Ovid—but also, in light of the queen's political agenda, what the two say to one another covertly. In particular, the queen introduces the notion that Lavinia is not who she seems: "But you are not as simple and as inexperienced in this matter as you act" [dune bist ouch sô tumb niht, / sô dû dar zû gebâres] (ll. 9952–53). Here we see the first indication that in this text the stereotypes of experience and innocence are not only being enacted but also being manipulated.[15]

Lavinia's questions begin with the comic exchange cited above, in which she apparently mistakes her mother's suggestion of a metaphorical exchange of hearts for a surgical operation.[16] This confusion of symbolic and literal levels of meaning sets the tone for the entire exchange: Lavinia's persistent display of ignorance that prods her mother into explanations. After all, she cannot comply with her mother's command to love Turnus (it is hardly a request) if she does not know what her mother is talking about. Who, she asks her mother, is Love (diu Minne)?[17] After her mother's short explanation, Lavinia says that she has never met Love and wishes to wait a while before she does. When the queen as-

15. Miklautsch summarizes the content of the three mother-daughter conversations, but without drawing conclusions that go beyond the stereotypes (1991, 246–53).

16. The "heart-taking" motif was probably recognized by Heinrich's audience as being imbued in the comedy of high literary discourse. In Hartmann von Aue's Iwein, for example, the narrator takes up the motif to characterize the love bond between the wedded couple, Iwein and Laudine, at their first parting, and then adopts a skeptical attitude in the ensuing exchange with Lady Love (Vrou Minne) (Iwein, ll. 2995–3028). The narrator says: "That woman and man could ever live without a heart is a miracle I have never witnessed; and yet in this case it came to pass as she predicted" [wan swâ wîp unde man / âne herze leben kan, / daz wunder daz gesach ich nie: / doch ergienc ez nâch ir rede hie] (ll. 3021–24).

17. Two manuscripts read wat is minne (what is love). I follow Kartschoke's edition and Dittrich in using the reading "who."

serts that Love will make Lavinia happy, she expresses doubt. The following exchange precipitates the queen's speech on the nature and
symptoms of love. Having been told who love is, Lavinia inquires about
its composition.

Q: "As soon as you begin loving, much joy will come to you."
L: "I am not sure, Lady, if that is so."
Q: "You can be certain of it."
L: "Then tell me what love is."
Q: "I can't describe it to you."
L: "Well then, don't try."

> 'swenne dus beginnest,
> dir wirt vil liebe dar zû.'
> "ichn weiz, frouwe, weder ez tû."
> 'dû maht es wesen gewis.'
> "sô saget mir denne waz minne is."
> 'ichn mach dirs niht gescrîben.'
> "sô solt irz lâzen blîben." (ll. 9814–20)

Lavinia's doubts and questions almost lead to the breakdown of the
conversation only some seventy lines from its beginning. When the queen
admits her inadequacy ("I can't describe it to you"), Lavinia responds
with a spoken shrug of the shoulders—"don't try." This indifference
goads the queen into her second speech (ll. 9821–51), which provides a
neat if conventional summary of the symptoms of lovesickness—love
turns you hot and cold, interferes with sleeping and eating, induces
melancholy—and a description of love's irresistible force (Wack 1990). At
the end of it, the queen herself comments on the length of her speech:
"Well, I have never before talked so much about this" [nû is des vil
manech tach, / deich nie sô vil dar abe gesprach] (ll. 9850–51). This time,
when her mother signals that she may be reaching the limits of her knowledge, Lavinia initiates another question-and-answer exchange, pressing
her mother on the basis of the symptoms described. Lavinia again focuses
on the literal level of what she has heard, on the actual symptom (fever,
moodiness), rather than on the symbolic discourse of love invoked by her
mother's words.

L: "Lady, is love a disease?"
Q: "No, but close."

> "frowe, is denn minne ungemach?"
> 'nien si, niwan nâhen bî.' (ll. 9852–53)

Although the queen asserts that love's pain is sweet, Lavinia expresses the wish to renounce love altogether. The queen responds to this pronouncement with her third speech (ll. 9869–87), in which she recites the remedies of love: the joy and happiness of love itself. But Lavinia proves a stubborn pupil, obstinately asserting her objections, and the queen's irritation at her daughter's obtuseness colors her answers.

L: "But at first love is very bitter, before the sweetness begins to work?"
Q: "You don't grasp how it works: love itself reconciles the bitterness."
L: "The torment before that is too great."
Q: "Love always works in such a way that it heals without salves and potions."
L: "The preceding torment persists too long."

> "sis aber von êrist vil unsûze,
> ê diu senfticheit kome?"
> 'dû erkennest ir niht ze frome:
> si sûnet selbe den zorn.'
> "diu quâle is zû grôz dâ bevorn."
> 'si tût daz dicke under stunden,
> daz si heilet die wunden
> âne salben und âne trank.'
> "diu arbeit is ab ê vil lank." (ll. 9888–96)

This short altercation is followed by the mother's fourth monologue (ll. 9897–965) on the role of fate and fortune in love, a speech that includes the famous allegory of Cupid and the two arrows of love to which I will return below. The mother concludes this important speech as follows:

Love gives and apportions joy after sorrow. You should remember well that both of these come from love. But you are not as simple and as inexperienced in this matter as you act. Even if you were two years younger than you are, you can be certain that you would not be learning love too early. Besides, you are physically mature enough, and you are beautiful, too. Keep in mind that I will always reward you, with affection and with gifts, for someday you must love. Therefore, love the bold warrior and noble prince Turnus.

> si gibet unde teilet
> daz lieb nach dem leide.
> daz saltû merken beide,
> daz des von minnen vil geschiht.
> dune bist ouch sô tumb niht,
> sô dû dar zû gebâres.

ob dû junger wâres
zweier jâre dan dû sîs,
dû mohtest wole sîn gewis,
dun gelernst ez nimmer ze frû.
dû hâst ouch lîb genûch dar zû
gewahsen unde scône.
daz ich dirs immer lône
mit minnen und mit gûte,
diz behabe in dînem mûte,
want dû mûst doch minnen phlegen.
von diu minne den kûnen degen
Turnûm den edelen vorsten. (ll. 9948–65)

After delivering this axiomatic instruction that both joy and sorrow come from love, the queen returns to the urgent political business at hand. Lavinia's failure to comprehend her lessons is a severe impediment to the queen's plans, and it provokes the queen to comment on Lavinia herself. Lavinia is being willfully stupid, the queen says; she is both intellectually and physically mature enough to understand what she is being told. In effect, the queen claims not to believe Lavinia's expressions of ignorance and fear, and she offers Lavinia a new bargain. Love is inevitable, but if Lavinia will agree to accept Turnus, her mother promises to sweeten the deal with her continued love and with wealth.

Most striking here is the parallel to the scene in which the queen promises her "son," Turnus, goodwill and riches in exchange for his continued resolve to combat Aeneas (ll. 4979–90). In the present scene, too, the queen is attempting to negotiate a political alliance, in this case with her daughter. As she did with Turnus and as any wealthy and powerful aristocrat of Heinrich's time might have done, the queen uses the traditional tokens of a feudal power alliance, favor and gifts, to meld familial ties with the alliance politics of the nobility. With Turnus the primary political alliance could be strengthened by a familial bond; with Lavinia the primary familial bond is a springboard for a political alliance. For the queen, the familial tie between herself and Lavinia is not outside or above the framework of other relational categories such as the social (teacher/novice) and the political (ruler/subject); rather, all three are intertwined.

The queen clearly hopes to secure lasting power by negotiating political alliances with both Turnus and Lavinia. From her perspective, the proposed marriage between Turnus and Lavinia represents an alliance that is, in the final analysis, a familial *and* political bond between mother and daughter. Implicit in this arrangement is that loyalty between mother and daughter could be the foundational nexus of connection and power. The fact that the queen is so obviously fashioned as a disreputable figure obscures the expression of political authority that her proposals of alliance entail. Through her tactics the queen advocates a power-oriented notion of marriage that contradicts the love lore she teaches, subordinating sexual passion to political and social expediency. The queen thus offers Lavinia a marriage that stakes a claim to women's exercise of political power. The queen's negotiations concerning this marriage provide Lavinia with an example of the rights and authority she might someday claim for herself.

At this point in the story Lavinia has no articulated understanding of love or power, and she remains unpersuaded that her interests lie in maintaining an alliance with her mother.

L: "I cannot do it, and I dare not do it."

Q: "Why?"

L: "Because of the torment."

Q: "But it is a great happiness."

L: "How can it be happiness?"

Q: "God knows, my dear daughter, I am certain that you must love, no matter how unwillingly you do so. If I ever discover that you wish to love Aeneas, disgracing us by giving your heart to the Trojan, I will have you slain. I will torture you to death before you become his wife. He will do without a wife such as you, and he will never enjoy your love."

L: "You can certainly forbid me this, because I have no intention of doing it." Then the lady fell silent. In anger she left, looking at her daughter most malevolently, the mighty queen.

> "ich ne mohte noch getorsten."
> 'war umbe?' "dorch die arbeit."
> 'jâ is ez michel senfticheit.'
> "wie moht daz senfticheit sîn?"
> 'got weiz, liebe tohter mîn,
> ich weiz wol daz dû minnen mûst,
> swie ungerne dû ez tûst.
> wirde ich des innen,
> daz dû Ênêam wilt minnen
> und uns sô entêres,
> daz dû dîn herze kêres
> an den bôsen Troiân,
> ich heize dich ze dôde slân
> unde martere dînen lîb,
> ê dû iemer werdest sîn wîb.
> her enbirt wol solhes wîbes,
> hern sal dînes lîbes
> niemer sich genieten.'
> "ir moget mirz lîht verbieten,

ichn gewans nie willen."
dô sweich diu frouwe stille,
in zorne gienk si hin dane
unde sach die tohter ane
vile ungûtlîche
diu kuneginne rîche. (ll. 9966–90)

The crescendo of malevolence articulated by the German queen stands in sharp contrast to the neutrality of the *Roman d'Eneas* on the subject of the queen's political and emotional investment in the conversation with Lavinia. In the Old French version, when Lavinia insists that she wishes to avoid Love's acquaintance, the queen simply leaves: "she did not wish to force her [i.e., Lavinia] any further, since she saw that it was of no avail" (Yunck 1974, 214). In contrast, all the inventions of the German text— which include the queen's suspicions that Lavinia is dissembling, the queen's murderous threats, and her wicked glare—are shocking and run counter to the many expressions of parental love found elsewhere in the story (for example, Aeneas's father, Anchises, and the parents of Pallas). The threats make it clear that the queen has failed in both her political strategy and her maternal role. The hostility directed at her only child completes the demonization of the queen enacted in the *Eneasroman;* the enraged queen, frustrated in her political ambitions, is represented as an unnatural mother, devoid of human affection.

Innocence, Experience, and Romantic Love

Lavinia's stubborn resistance to her mother's teachings is not only a manifestation of Lavinia's sexual inexperience, but also, as the queen says, a strategy. Lavinia *is* sexually inexperienced, as the ensuing plot makes clear. However, her persistent misunderstandings and her obstinance hint that her innocence is also a ploy to steer the conversation away from the direction the queen wishes to give it, away from saying either yes *or* no to the issue of loving Turnus. Lavinia's cleverness, which is demonstrated a few episodes later when she devises the arrow-and-letter scheme to tell Aeneas she loves him, is already suggested by her responses to her mother. Protocol dictates that she cannot end the conversation—the difference in rank between mother and daughter is retained throughout the dialogue in differing pronouns of address, with Lavinia addressing the queen as *îr* and the queen addressing Lavinia as *du*. However, nothing can prevent Lavinia from exhausting and exasperating her mother with objections, questions, and artful confusion. This behavior contrasts with that of the Old French poet's Lavinia, whose

2. The queen standing at the doorway of Lavinia's chambers (above) and forbidding her daughter on pain of death to love Aeneas (below). Her words are a rhymed paraphrase of Heinrich's text rather than a direct quotation: "If you ever love the Trojan, it will cost you your life" [Minnest du iemer den troian so mustu du din leben werden an]. Both the queen ("diu chuniginne") and Lavinia ("ir tohter Lavine") are identified by name in the picture frames. From Heinrich von Veldeke, *Eneasroman*, Berlin, Staatsbibliothek zu Berlin Preußischer Kulturbesitz, ms. germ. fol. 282, f. 64v (1220–1230). Courtesy of the Staatsbibliothek zu Berlin Preußischer Kulturbesitz, Handschriftenabteilung.

responses have no overtones of willful misunderstanding. The Lavinia of the *Eneasroman*, however, is not only resisting love; she is also resisting her mother.

Heinrich's "naïve" Lavinia is not entirely naïve. She both embodies and deploys the stereotype of the innocent maiden in order to elude her mother's control. The queen's nasty threats and malevolent glare are not totally unprovoked. In the mother-daughter conversation about love the words of the two characters call the stereotype of innocence itself into question, revealing the more conventionally misogynist notion of womanhood lurking behind it: the craftiness of women, women's perceived ability to *be* innocent and *play at* being innocent at the same time. There is, in this scheme of things, no such thing as female innocence.

Refocusing attention on the queen, we see that the *Eneasroman* invokes and dismantles the stereotype of the experienced mother. The fact that the character who teaches about love is fashioned as a monstrous figure standing outside any category of affection shows the extent to which the *Eneasroman* seeks to separate the ideal of love, as presented in love lore, from the experience of romantic love. For all the queen's detailed knowledge, for all her preaching about love, she behaves as if love were solely of instrumental value. What then does she know about the discourse of passionate sexual desire and the notion of romantic love? A great deal, the text seems to tell us, and nothing. The queen is well informed about love lore, but she never hints, nor are we shown, that she has any personal experience of love; indeed, her constant anger is presented as the polar opposite of romantic passion. Such an angry woman, the *Eneasroman* implies, cannot partake of the joys of romantic love. Lavinia, in contrast, though ignorant of love lore, becomes the *Eneasroman*'s expert on the emotional practice of erotic passion. The master/apprentice structure underlying the stereotypes of experienced mother and innocent daughter has been inverted: the true "master" of romantic love is Lavinia, whose monologues on loving undercut her mother's theoretical superiority. A generational duality is set up in the intellectually knowing mother, who is angry, and the emotionally knowing daughter, who is—in the end— happy. Such an opposition suggests that, for women, the new discourse of romantic love in the *Eneasroman* seeks to privilege the experience of love over lore about love. It further suggests that intellectual knowledge is devalued when it is held by women.

That in privileging the experience of love the *Eneasroman* participates in the creation of a new love lore—the discourse of romantic love—is one of the ironies of the situation. The dominant position of the new ideology of romantic love, as well as the differing positioning of mother and daughter in relation to it, is in fact suggested by the queen herself. In her fourth monologue, before exhorting her daughter to marry Turnus, the queen relates to Lavinia the story of Lord Amor's (Cupid's) two arrows or darts. This story can be read as an allegory of how Lavinia's passion and the queen's rage are *both* responses to the inescapable ideology of the new discourse of romantic love.

> He [Amor] carries in one hand a box, and in the other two darts, with which he shoots mightily, as I wish to tell you. One dart is made of gold, and Amor uses it all the time. Whoever is wounded by it loves passionately and lives with torment. Never can he be accused of inconstancy. The other dart is made of lead. Whoever is wounded deep in his heart by it will always resist true love, hating and reviling it. He will never desire anything that comes about out of love.

> ein buhsen hât her an der hant,
> in der ander zwêne gêre:
> dâ mite schûzet er vil sêre,
> als ich dir sagen wolde.
> ein gêr is von golde,
> des phleget her alle stunde.
> swer sô eine wunde
> dâ mite gewinnet,
> vil starklîch er minnet
> und lebet mit arbeite.
> neheiner unstâticheite
> ne darf man in zîen.
> der ander gêr is blîen,
> von deme tûn ich dir kunt:
> swer dâ mite wirdet wunt
> in sîn herze enbinnen,
> der is der rehten minnen
> iemer ungehôrsam,
> her hazet unde is ir gram.
> swaz sô von minnen geschiht,
> des ne lustet in niht. (ll. 9916–36)

The allegory of the two darts shows that the ideology of romantic love can furnish an explanatory model for the behavior of both women, for it articulates the belief that passionate devotion to love and abhorrence of it alike spring from the same source. Wounded by the golden dart, Lavinia embodies the desirable female object of romantic love and will furnish a submissive female body for erotic passion. Wounded by the lead dart, the queen is enraged, yet her anger is explained (away) as a toxic reaction to all-powerful love. Her wisdom cannot overcome the fact that she is the adversary of true love, not its advocate. The many other reasons for her actions we read from the text—perhaps the queen knows the futility of "love" as a binding concept in patriarchy, perhaps she has reason to be angry about her lack of power, perhaps reason to be angry at her daughter for rejecting the proffered political alliance—are thus conjured away.

The allegory of the two darts also implies that the queen does not stand completely outside the experiential framework of romantic love embodied by Lavinia. The queen's anger, when explained as a function of love's power, further undermines her claim to expertise. To put it another way, the notion that her anger is but a poisoned reaction to love's rule denies her agency and mastery. It weakens her contention that, because love is coercive, Lavinia should also consider tangible rewards. From this perspective, her pupil, Lavinia, not only surpasses her but unmasks the anger that undercuts the queen's claim to authority. In contrast, Lavinia's prestige derives from her ability to submit to the new "law" of passion. Her reward for rejecting her mother and for enduring the trials and suffering of romantic love is her marriage to Aeneas, a union that legitimizes paternal authority. The ideology of romantic love secures the patriarchal social order, an alignment that has the effect of recasting that order in apparently benign terms of sentiment.

Despite her feigned ignorance, Lavinia has learned enough about love to understand it when it hits. Indeed, Lavinia openly acknowledges the validity of her mother's teachings in a later monologue, remarking that "even if she [the queen] had not spoken to me about it [love], it still would have come about like this. Perhaps knowing so much about it now can be of use to me, for I am both hot and cold inside" [al hete sie mirs niht gewagen, / ez wâre doch alsus komen. / eteswaz mach mir daz gefromen, / daz ich nû sô vil drumbe weiz, / wandich bin kalt unde heiz / an mîme lîbe enbinnen] (ll. 10088–93). Still later, she notes: "My mother told me the truth, the wise queen" [mîn mûter sagete mir wâr / diu wîse kuneginne] (ll. 10234–35). The queen is thus an unwitting instrument of the patriarchal order, an order to which she nevertheless stubbornly refuses to submit.

The Second Conversation between Mother and Daughter

Lavinia's refusal to be controlled by her mother is underscored by a series of episodes leading to the fated union with Aeneas. Espying Aeneas from a fortress window, Lavinia is stung by Cupid's arrow. In the long monologue that follows (ll. 10061–496), Lavinia diagnoses her lovesickness on the basis of her mother's teachings, reproaches her mother (!) for telling her about love, and then retracts the blame because "I do not love as she advised me [loving Aeneas rather than Turnus], I cannot reproach her" [ichn minne niht daz sie mir riet, / ich ne darf niht von ir klagen] (ll. 10086–87). Brooding about the now inevitable confrontation with her mother, for she can neither conceal nor confess the cause of her lovesickness from this "clever woman" [*listich wîb*] (l. 10136), Lavinia reviews and affirms all the love lore she has heard, swears she will never love Turnus (ll. 10336–37), and suffers the torments of true love. She spends a sleepless night and then attempts to lie to her mother about the cause of her suffering:

> "Lady, I am bewildered. I don't know what's wrong with me, whether it is a sickness or a fever. That I am in the throes of something I have noticed myself." "God knows," said she, "my daughter, however good you are at lying, you can't fool me. Tell me the truth."

> 'frowe, ich bin verirret,
> ichn weiz waz mir wirret,
> weder diu suht oder der rite,
> dâ ich bin bevangen mite,
> daz is mir wol worden schîn.'
> "got weiz" sprach si "tohter mîn,
> swie wol dû kunnest liegen,
> dune maht mich niht betriegen,
> dû mûst der wârheit jehen." (ll. 10515–23)

This exchange introduces the second dialogue between mother and daughter (ll. 10515–724). At first, Lavinia tries to avoid telling her mother what is wrong, while the queen presses her for an admission of whom she loves. After the famous confession scene, in which Lavinia, unable to speak Aeneas's name, writes it on a wax tablet (ll. 10621–27), the queen launches into a tirade, cursing her daughter as dishonorable, accusing Aeneas of homosexuality, and reminding Lavinia of Dido's terrible fate.[18] This attempt to dissuade Lavinia is in vain because love has made her a staunch defender for Aeneas; he is, she says, a noble lord, a decent man, a child of the gods. Emboldened by love, Lavinia even talks back to her mother:

> He is descended from the gods, no matter how much you in your anger berate him and impeach his honor. You should have stopped doing that.

---

18. In this matter the Old French version is considerably more forthright than the German adaptation. In the *Roman d'Eneas*, the queen details her charge of sodomy against Aeneas; for example, "he prefers the opposite trade: he will not eat hens, but rather loves very much the flesh of the cock" (Yunck 1974, 226). In the *Eneasroman* she merely says: "he never loved a woman. It is improper to speak of what he does with men, so that he doesn't desire women" (ll. 10646–49).

3. Lovesick Lavinia (above) in conversation with her angry and suspicious mother (below). In the top frame, Lavinia beseeches "Lady Love" for mercy: "Have mercy, Lady Love. Alas, what has become of my previous feelings, for now I suffer torment" [Gnade frowe minne owi war sint min sinne chomen dz ih het e daz mir nu ist so unsanfte we]. In the bottom frame, the queen scolds Lavinia, "Tell me quickly and loudly what has happened to you, you nasty piece of work" [Sag mir drat uber lut waz ist dir geschehen du ubel hut], while Lavinia answers evasively, "Lady, I am confused, I don't know what is wrong with me" [Frowe ih bin verirret ih ne waiz waz mir wirret]. As in fig. 2, the words are a rhymed paraphase of Heinrich's text. From Heinrich von Veldeke, *Eneasroman*, Berlin, Staatsbibliothek zu Berlin Preußischer Kulturbesitz, ms. germ. fol. 282, f. 69r. Courtesy of the Staatsbibliothek zu Berlin Preußischer Kulturbesitz, Handschriftenabteilung.

> her is von den goten geborn,
> swie ir in dorch ûwern zorn
> scheldet alsus sêre
> und sprechet im an sîn êre:
> daz mohtet ir wol lâzen. (ll. 10683–87)

The queen again responds with rage. Apparently forgetting that she had earlier believed Lavinia mature enough for love, she now mocks her for chasing men at such a young age (ll. 10690–92). If she must have some man, why not Turnus? (ll. 10694–96) Fearfully, Lavinia pleads dementia—love has robbed her of heart and reason—but the queen scolds and threatens until, we are told, the weeping Lavinia faints. The queen again threatens her daughter, now unconscious, and leaves the room in anger (ll. 10699–721).

In the first conversation, miscommunication between mother and daughter carried the interaction forward and made it possible for them to talk to each other. The disclosures of the second conversation, however, demonstrate that their positions are completely irreconcilable. When Lavinia's loyalty to romantic love becomes clear, mother and daughter have nothing more to say to each other.

In the context of these irreconcilable differences, Lavinia's fainting is not only an escape from an intolerable situation but also a kind of death. Having openly defied her mother, Lavinia faints—dies—as her mother's daughter in order to awaken—be reborn—as her father's. Lavinia's fainting scene marks the point where she relinquishes her always tenuous alliance with maternal authority and fully transfers her allegiance to paternal authority. Further, the economy of emotions governing the mother-daughter relationship is recapitulated in this scene: to the mother is allocated rage, to the daughter is allocated not only sexual passion but also fearfulness, expressed as fear of her mother.

Lavinia's transfer of allegiance to paternal authority is rewarded by the loss of this fear, although she remains fearful that Aeneas may not love her. Indeed, the fear of unrequited love now spurs her on to defy her mother. Awaking, Lavinia considers and rejects her mother's slurs on Aeneas, commenting "May God curse wicked counsel!" [got verwâze bôsen rât] (l. 10784). Taking action in her own behalf, she writes a love letter to Aeneas and winds it around the shaft of an arrow, and tricks a paternal relative through a series of persuasive lies. When she tells him that she fears the Trojans are planning an assault on her father's honor ("ich vorhte sie verrâten / mînem vater al sîn êre," ll. 10866–67), he is convinced to shoot the letter-arrow from the castle into a group of Trojan warriors milling about below (ll. 10785–912). Lavinia's persistent resistance to her mother's claim on her loyalty—furtive in the first dialogue, open in the above scene—is condoned by the text as an indication of Lavinia's loyalties to the distinctly patriarchal authorities of the gods, her father, and the conquering spirit of her destined spouse. In so doing, she attains the romantic ideal—marriage to her true love.

The Third Conversation between Mother and Daughter

In the *Roman d'Eneas*, the queen leaves the room after Lavinia faints—there is no comment on her state of mind—and is never mentioned again. She is consigned to narrative oblivion, as it were.[19] In contrast, Heinrich recounts the queen's death and links it to a third, completely new mother-daughter dialogue. This last exchange between Lavinia and the queen follows Lavinia and Aeneas's first meeting and immediately precedes their wedding. On learning of Aeneas's extravagant gifts, the queen screams abuse at Lavinia for her refusal of her mother's legacy:

> How happy you are now, you nasty piece of work, about the pain in my heart! Believe me, I regret that I ever bore you, and that I didn't kill you the moment of your birth!

> wie frô dû nû bist, ubel hût,
> mînes herzen rouwen!
> dû maht mir des getrouwen,
> mir is leit daz ich dich ie getrûch
> daz ich dich niht ze tôde slûch,
> als schiere sô ich dich gewan. . . . (ll. 13022–29)

She expresses bitter regret that she ever married Latinus, who now intends to pass the rulership of his kingdom to Aeneas. The legal point that Aeneas will be *king,* and not prince consort, is clarified only in Heinrich's version (Dittrich 1966, 427).[20] The queen insists that she cannot survive seeing Aeneas and Lavinia "going crowned before me" [vor mir gekrônet

19. Some scholars have suggested that the Old French poet, in his haste to complete his story, simply forgot to tie up this loose end of the plot. However, it is also possible that suppressing this plot line was linked with the court for which the Old French poet probably composed the *Roman d'Eneas,* the Anglo-Norman court of Henry II and Eleanor of Aquitaine. By conveniently omitting the scandalous demise of the king's wife, the poet might have been avoiding a scandalous—or, at the very least, unchivalrous—comment on the all too real, powerful, and imperious Queen Eleanor, whose political quarrels with her husband were later to escalate into open strife. Once the poem was removed in time and place from a court in which the fictional figures resonated with flesh-and-blood monarchs and patrons, such delicacy would no longer be necessary.

20. Dittrich goes on to point out that "erst mit der ausdrücklichen Betrauung des Eneas als männlichen Erben an Sohnes Statt ist die Möglichkeit weiblicher Erb- und Thronfolge grundsätzlich ausgeschaltet" [only when Aeneas has expressly been designated male heir in place of a son can the possibility of female inheritance and succession be excluded on principle] (1966, 427).

soldet gân] (ll. 13048), surpassing her political position. The detached tone of Lavinia's response indicates how completely she has overcome her previous fear of her mother. Lavinia praises Aeneas and reminds her mother that it is romantic love and not any political considerations that have guided her choices: "Even if I could win ten kingdoms with another man, I would not be able to love him, and would rather choose death" [moht ich zehen kunichrîche / mit anderm man gewinnen, / ich mohte in niht geminnen, / ich wolde kiesen ê den tôt] (l. 13072–75). Calmly, Lavinia counsels her mother against an angry response:

> "I advise you loyally not to do something out of anger that no one will condone," she said, "my dear mother." "Curse you for that," replied the queen and threw herself on her bed. In great torment she lay I know not how many days, until death entered her heart and took her person (body) violently."

> "ich râte û trouwelîche daz,
> daz ir dorch zoren niene tût
> daz nieman ne dunke gût
> (sprach si), liebiu mûder mîn."
> 'des mûzest dû unsâlich sîn'
> sprach diu kunegin dâ wider
> und viel an ir bette nider.
> mit grôzen rouwen si lach
> ich ne weiz wie manegen tach,
> unz ir der tôt inz herze quam,
> der ir den lîb unsanfte nam. (ll. 10382–92)[21]

The queen's words are her last. Her rage has become symptomatic of powerlessness, not power. The mother-daughter relationship and the legacy that it might have ensured are now dead. With her violent curses the queen has negated the mother-daughter relationship, and Lavinia has renounced her legacy by being everything her mother is not—kind, loving, submissive to her husband, unconcerned with political power. The story suggests that the daughter can attain the position of mother-of-a-new-dynasty, given Lavinia in the twice-repeated genealogical table of Aeneas's descendants, only when her unruly mother is purged from the story. Indeed, the mother-daughter relationship literally disappears from the story. The queen's death is not mourned, and in a text that relishes the solemnities of funereal pomp, there is no mention of her

---

21. The ambiguity of the lexeme *lîb*, denoting "person" but carrying the secondary meaning "body," is particularly apparent here.

burial. Instead, the sentence following the queen's death describes the joy and heightened sense of prestige Aeneas now feels and the physical pleasure he can now take, as often as he pleases, in Lavinia's body. The wedding follows.

Only after the mother dies can Lavinia marry—that is to say, fulfill the promise of romantic love in the experience of erotic bliss. The queen's death is thus a transition to the wedding. In a kind of hideous anticipation and inversion of Lavinia's marriage bed, the death scene is recounted in the language of sexual intercourse: "the queen . . . threw herself on her bed. In great torment she lay I know not how many days, until death entered her heart and took her person (body) violently." What for Lavinia, within the ideal of romantic love, is coded as urgency and passion, for the queen becomes violence and death. We are led to believe that Lavinia, bedded by the man she loves, Aeneas, will consent and submit passionately; but bedded by death, the queen is taken violently, that is to say, raped. This explicit death-as-rape, a horrible end for a wicked character, contrasts with the decorous silence the *Eneasroman* maintains around the subject of Lavinia and Aeneas's first sexual union.

The sexual violence of the queen's death harks back to the allegory of Cupid and the two darts. For all her political clout, the queen cannot escape the ideology of romantic love, which is organized to include special, sexual punishment for women who refuse to submit to its rule.[22] For her there is none of the erotic pleasure with which romantic love promises to reward its disciples, but only a prolongation of torment. It is her female body that renders the queen vulnerable to this violation. As we have seen, the queen's body is alluded to throughout the story, with her dramatic entrances and exits and malevolent glances betraying her immoderation, anger, and loss of control. Even when the queen does not speak, her body language talks for her, expressing her rage. Not only must her voice be silenced, her body must be disciplined as well. The queen's death-as-rape in the *Eneasroman* is emblematic—an image of a female body that is resistant, undisciplined, and yet vulnerable to sexual violence.

The Daughter and Gender Identity

The mother-daughter bond represents a challenge to the discourse of romantic love that must be suppressed. When Lavinia, in the very first question-and-answer exchange of the first conversation, asks her mother, "How can I turn my affections to a man?", she suggests that her affections

22. On rape and romance, see Gravdal 1991 and 1992.

currently rest with her mother, and that one must be lost in order to gain the other. That such a question could also be a part of Lavinia's strategy to avoid the subject of Turnus only reinforces the reading that the "other" must be the mother. In this sense, the rewards the queen promises Lavinia have a compensatory quality; you will not have to lose my love, says the mother. Love and happiness could come from the mother, or at least not be lost, though the *Eneasroman* insists that with *such* a mother these promises are illusory at best.

A further challenge is implicit in the way gender is assigned in the mother's first teachings about love. Describing the interactions of the feminine noun *love* (in German, *diu minne*) and the person love has smitten, the queen always uses masculine pronouns to describe the lover to Lavinia. There is a certain gender dissonance in the fact that the love actor is male, because he represents the role Lavinia will find herself in. The queen is offering Lavinia the role of love actor. Through her use of masculine pronouns to describe the state her daughter will embody, the queen claims not only that Lavinia will eventually be happy but that she will also be empowered to act, to become an agent of her own happiness. And indeed, we have seen that Lavinia is empowered to rebel against her mother and disclose her passion. However, she refuses the step her mother wishes, the step in which she would seize her empowerment instrumentally in order to make an alliance with her mother through Turnus. This refusal leads, as we have seen, to the breakdown of the mother-daughter relationship.

The dynamic of the mother-daughter relationship in the *Eneasroman* resembles in salient ways the traditional Freudian psychoanalytic dynamic describing the origins of sexuality and the learning of a socially acceptable gender identity: the daughter must break with her mother in order to learn heterosexual love. For a girl, this process is more mysterious, complex, and dangerous than the analogous process for boys. Boys are said to maintain the opposite sex, represented first by their mother and later by their lovers, as their primary love objects. They learn masculinity, through their identification with their fathers, as a new power relation to that other. Girls, however, must switch the gender allegiance of their primary love object, a switch that can be accomplished only at the cost of attempting to suppress the mother (Chodorow 1978). Indeed, in the *Eneasroman* Lavinia's fear of (hetero) sexuality and her fear of her mother are entwined; when Lavinia conquers the first, she conquers the second as well. From this perspective, the queen is both suppressed and replaced, for although Aeneas represents the victory of patriarchal and paternal rule in the story, he does not replace the king in Lavinia's life, he replaces her mother.

The story's ending of marital bliss casts the queen as the foil against which love emerges, a temporary association on the road to an allegiance that will discard the mother altogether. Yet the queen makes her position into an offer of affiliation—in the familial, social, and political senses—in order to establish an enduring bond between mother and daughter that might resist the erosion of noblewomen's political power. The medieval *Eneas* stories offer us no compromise between these positions; the mother is struck down, while in the guise of romantic love the father prevails. The nuanced difference between the medieval French and German versions in this regard is striking. Though both stories suggest that some check on the mother figure is a necessary precondition of Lavinia's conformity, in the *Roman d'Eneas* she lives on in oblivion, a shadow in the wings. Her power, though diminished, survives. In the *Eneasroman*, however, the queen is evicted from the story. First demonized and then dispatched, the queen is set up to discredit her own exercise of power altogether. Her death is a necessary precondition both to Lavinia's long and happy marriage and to Aeneas's long and happy rule. Still, for the modern reader the German queen becomes an outraged shade, bearing the intensity of the anxieties that made her and haunting the story's production of romantic discourse, female identities, and happy endings.

The continuity in medieval and modern notions of the processes by which sexuality is socially encoded is striking. The *Eneasroman* is particularly compelling because it tells the story of the creation of a normative female sexual and gender identity as the story of a power relation of inequality, in which women must submit to male rule. The fixing of gender hierarchies is thus an integral part of the establishment and perpetuation of patriarchal rule. Yet at the same time that the *Eneasroman* anchors the story of patriarchal rule in a notion of desirable femininity in which women submit to men and voluntarily forgo political influence for love, its portrayal of the queen suggests a conflicting account of women's power. If we set aside for a moment the ideology of romantic love that frames the queen as an unlovable and power-mad woman, we note that the queen is fearless, assertive, and anything but submissive, and that she apparently commands a great deal of wealth and support in her own right. The fact that in the *Eneasroman* the portrait of the queen is drawn in such villainous terms—monstrous, cruel, ruthless, self-serving—leads us to investigate the range of power that noblewomen might have wielded in the intricate networks of kin, land, wealth, and rule of the medieval aristocracy. For it could be that the monstrousness of this imaginary queen reflected a very real anxiety about the considerable authority, influence, and wealth of aristrocratic women.

Historical Noblewomen, Patrilineality, and the *Eneasroman*

There are well-known examples of politically assertive noblewomen from the last decades of the twelfth century, the time during which Heinrich von Veldeke was composing his book. Eleanor of Aquitaine (c. 1125–1204) comes to mind. So does Constance of Sicily (1154–1198, r. Sicily 1189–1198), who in 1186 married the son and successor of Frederick Barbarossa, Henry VI (1165–1197; r. 1191–1197). Royal families used the rights of noblewomen to defend and secure regional or dynastic interests (Schulze 1983, 24–27). In 1188 another son of Barbarossa, Conrad (d. 1196) became engaged to the presumed successor to King Alfonso VIII of Castile, Berenguela (1180–1246), then eight years old. The Castilean party wished to ensure that Conrad be prince consort, *not* king, if Berenguela should succeed her father. This was agreed to and made legally binding in a contract dated April 23, 1188.[23] From the point of view of the Staufer dynasty, Frederick Barbarossa was, through his sons, trying to expand the dynasty's influence and power (Dittrich 1966, 427). However, for the royal families of Sicily and Castile, Constance's and Berenguela's political and legal rights were grounds upon which to resist the imperialist politics of the German dynasty.

Imperial politics was not the only realm in which noblewomen could wield influence and power. Although poorly researched, there appear to have been formidable kin alliances forged through women as well as influential women figures within the aristocratic circles where Heinrich von Veldeke found his patrons. According to the epilogue to the *Eneasroman*, Heinrich's chief patrons were the sons of the landgrave of Thuringia, Ludwig II: Ludwig III (d. 1190); Henry Raspe (III) (d. 1180); Friedrich, count of Zeigenhain; and, above all, Hermann I (c. 1160–1217), who was landgrave from 1190 until his death.[24] Their mother, Jutta of Swabia (d. 1191), the daughter of Duke Frederick II of Swabia, was Frederick Barbarossa's half-sister. Their father's marriage to Jutta, which allied his family to the rising Staufer dynasty, was a political step up for the rising Ludovingian family.

23. See Rassow 1950. The contract is also discussed by Dittrich (1966, 427) and by Kellermann-Haaf (1986, 282–83). Shadis (1994) gives a lengthy explication of the treaty that illuminates the gender politics of the marital alliances sought by royal families and the role—at once powerful and vulnerable—played in those politics by marriagable daughters. The marriage between Berenguela and Conrad was dissolved some two years later. Berenguela married her cousin, Alfonso IX of León, in 1198, with whom she had five children, and was repudiated by him in 1204. She survived two younger brothers and in 1217 claimed the throne of Castile for her eldest son, Fernando III (Castile 1217–1252; León 1230–1252) based on the rights of succession set out in the contract of 1188 (1994, 55–73).

24. On Hermann's numerous activities as a literary patron, see Bumke 1979, Lemmer 1981, and Peters 1981.

Landgrave Hermann I was thus cousin, through his mother, to the Staufer emperor Henry VI mentioned above and to Henry's brother, Philip of Swabia (ruled as German king 1197–1208). During his long and tumultuous reign, Herman I relied often on a strong alliance with his neighbor to the east, Ottokar I, king of Bohemia, another cousin, this time through the marriage of his father's sister, Jutta, to Vladislav II, king of Bohemia.[25] In other words, a man such as Hermann I owed no small measure of his standing to the wealth and the connections of kin that women secured for him, for these could fortify common strategic and political aims.

In imperial politics, where the legal and social systems of different groups and regions often clashed, aristocratic women's legal and economic rights could become a kind of testing ground. In regional politics, it might be argued that kinship networks were based not so much on the *exchange* of women between noble families in marriage as on the way in which married women always represented one family while living with another. And in imperial and regional German politics alike, the fragility at the heart of the system of patrilineality—the death of male heirs—opened up a space in which women could assert inheritance rights on behalf of their sons. Here, too, we can find examples in the house of the Ludovingians. The widow of Dietrich, margrave of Meissen, was Jutta of Thuringia (d. 1235), Hermann I's daughter. She defended her son Henry's inheritance rights against the encroachments of her stepbrother, Landgrave Ludwig VI, through a strategic remarriage (Patze 1974, 33). When Hermann I's last son, Henry Raspe (IV), died in 1247 without issue, a number of competing claimants sought to enlarge their territories. Raspe's niece, Sophia of Hesse (d. 1282; daughter of Hermann I's son, Ludwig IV, and Saint Elisabeth of Hungary) fought long and hard with her cousin, Henry of Meissen (d. 1288; son of Hermann I's daughter, Jutta, and Dietrich of Meissen) for territories in the landgraviates of Hesse and Thuringia. Though Sophia's party did not succeed in overturning Henry's claim to Thuringia, it did secure succession for her son, Henry I (d. 1308), in Hesse (Patze 1974, 42–48; Kellermann-Haaf 1986, 295).

We are still left with powerful mothers and powerful sons; given the kinds of evidence that survive from the Middle Ages, this connection has left the clearest traces.[26] Even in this context it seems a striking irony that

25. Hermann I's alliances to the family of his second wife, Sophia of Wittelsbach, daughter of the Count-Palatine Otto I of Bavaria, also played a role in his politics.

26. Shadis (1994, chap. 5) begins the project of tracing the mother-daughter connections of feudal noblewomen through their practices of patronage, particularly as patrons of the Church and in the establishment of burial places for themselves and their families. She argues that the royal women she studies "follow generally matrilineal preferences, influencing generations of daughters and granddaughters" (1994, 253–54).

in the *Eneasroman* it is the queen, so clearly coded as evil, who attempts to uphold a legal marriage contract and tries to bring about a marriage in a manner consistent with the norms and conventions of the aristocratic audience of this tale, noblemen and noblewomen who presumably would have thought more than twice about marrying their daughters to impoverished upstart foreigners of dubious lineage with nothing but their ambition to recommend them. Tracking historically what the connection between mothers and daughters might have meant in families such as these is a task that remains to be done. For the time being we are left to interpret stories like the *Eneasroman*, which also talk in broad terms about the organization of kinship itself. As Lee Patterson argues regarding the *Roman d'Eneas:*

> the *Eneas* contributes both to the myth of continuity that the Anglo-Norman ruling class promoted and to the privileging of lineage, and of primogeniture, that was so crucial to the Norman social and economic structure. . . .
> It is just this ideology of continuous lineage—of genealogy—that the *Eneas* presents in an especially unproblematic form. It is the unproblematic nature of its representation that is most worthy of note; clearly the text functions as a propagandistic resolution of social and political oppositions that were historically far less tractable. Henry II's own inheritance of the throne, after all—if, in fact, "inheritance" is the right word for so aggressive an act of appropriation—was hardly as rectilinear as the model of Roman foundation prescribed; . . . With the *Eneas* Henry was thus possessed of a celebratory epic that relentlessly suppressed, as he was himself literally suppressing, the very real disruptions that marked the reality of Anglo-Norman politics and society. (1987, 179–80)

What Patterson says here about the uneasy fit between the propagandistic intent of a work and the "less tractable" realities surrounding it is illuminating. More important, however, is how far the *Eneasroman* departs from the *Roman d'Eneas*'s model of presenting the idea of continuous lineage, of genealogy—by which Patterson means the relation of father and son—unproblematically. Indeed, perhaps Patterson overstates the case for the *Roman d'Eneas*. Both works show us that the idea of continuous male lineage must engage in a struggle with the *mother* over the daughter, a struggle that is intensified in the *Eneasroman*. By demonizing the mother and sentimentalizing the daughter, the *Eneasroman* seeks to render their connection to one another immaterial. Legitimizing paternal genealogy, then, means discrediting maternal authority and denying a sense of lineage based on the mother-daughter filiation. Telling the story of the founding of a dynasty based on patrilineality is also the story of disrupting matrilineal descent. This matrilineal descent surely represents not just itself but also other pressures standing in the way of consolidating and transferring power—such as local rights, competing claims, regional politics—in a line of fathers and sons. For patrilineal descent to be made unproblematic, the mother-daughter relation must be made problematic. The possibility of a *political* mother-daughter relationship must be undercut, and women who win out, like Lavinia, must be seen to remove themselves voluntarily to a familial sphere where their willing subordination will be rewarded with love. Underlying the *Eneasroman*'s commitment to the privileging of continuous father-son lineage is the construction of the mother-daughter relationship as repudiation, a repudiation that legislates against the ability of the mother-daughter relationship to function as the site of the transfer of knowledge and power over time between women. That is the secret that lies revealed—not all concealed—at the heart of this story.

✥ 2 ✥

Exemplary Mother, Unruly Daughter

The Mother-Daughter Dialogue and the Nibelungenlied

Als mit dem Wind sie
Persephone rief
und an dem Ufer der
Lethe entschlief:
Über sich Plutons
berauschtes Gesicht,
Unterwelt über sich,
Oberwelt nicht.
—Elisabeth Langgässer, "Wolkenlandschaft im
Spätjahr" (1981, 137)[1]

THE WOMAN WHO TRANSGRESSES the boundaries of normative femininity in the *Nibelungenlied* is not the mother, as in the *Eneasroman,* but the daughter, Kriemhild. The *Eneasroman* represents the mother as an aberrant female who usurps power and so must be displaced by a daughter who conforms to patriarchal expectations. The *Nibelungenlied* represents the mother, Uote, as a minor character whose short, stereotypical lessons about love in no way address Kriemhild's relentless pursuit of power. The topos of the disorderly mother that underwrites the mother-daughter dynamic in the *Eneasroman* differs sharply from the topos of the disorderly daughter in the *Nibelungenlied,* and this generational shift parallels far-reaching differences in the plots. In the *Eneasroman,* the disruptive mother is overcome, a new dynasty founded by means of the daughter's body, and the story progresses from the chaos of warfare to peace and civil order. In the *Nibelungenlied,* the miscommunication between mother and daughter foreshadows the unchecked and uncheckable disorder

1. "Autumn Landscape with Clouds": When with the wind she / shouted for Persephone / and on the bank of the / Lethe fell asleep: / over her Pluto's / drunken face, / netherworld above her, / not the upper world.

Kriemhild unleashes in the unfolding story; two old dynasties meet cataclysmic ends as the story progresses from tenuous civic peace to warfare, from a fragile order based on chivalry to a heroic order celebrating the robust bonds between fighting men.[2]

Moreover, the differences between the disorderly female protagonists point to the epics' contrasting attitudes towards the passage of time. Affirming the Virgilian project of patriarchal conquest by discrediting the queen, the *Eneasroman* seeks to promise justice in the present and hope for the future; it sets out to be understood as fundamentally a work that is optimistic about history. In contrast, the *Nibelungenlied* projects a far darker view of history. In it, the present is dominated by insult, injustice, and treachery, burdened by the grievances of the past. This present moves inexorably toward an apocalyptic ending. Mobilizing rather than dispersing past injuries, it violently amputates from the work the dimension of futurity. The *Eneasroman* and the *Nibelungenlied* represent history in alternate modes: in the former, it is the story of progress; in the latter, the story of decline. Each work, however, enacts its version of the principle of historical change by representing women as the source of the terrors and turmoil that threaten the social order.

Summary of the *Nibelungenlied*

When the sixteenth-century compiler of the voluminous manuscript known to scholars as the *Ambraser Heldenbuch* gave the anonymous *Nibelungenlied* the heading "Ditz Puech Heyſſet Chrimhilt" [This Book is Called Kriemhild], he merely articulated a tendency that dominates the poem: Kriemhild is the poem's pivotal character, whose presence unites the two halves of this epic.[3] In the first half, the hero Siegfried leaves his kingdom on the lower Rhine in order to win the hand of the beautiful Burgundian princess Kriemhild, whom he has never seen. The arrival of the pugnacious Siegfried at the Burgundian court in Worms precipitates a crisis among its rulers, Kriemhild's brothers, Gunther, Gernot, and Giselher, and their relative and adviser, Hagen, for Siegfried is too strong to be driven away, too unreliable to be offered a binding political alliance, and too dangerous to be ignored. The Burgundian rulers therefore at-

2. Jaeger comments on the use of both the chivalric order and the heroic code. "In the *Nibelungenlied* the two codes, courtesy and warrior valor, are not harmonized; they stand one next to the other in ethical parataxis" (Jaeger 1985, 192–93).

3. On this question see, for example, Anderson 1985, which includes a bibliography of significant scholarship on Kriemhild.

tempt to use Siegfried for their own ends: he leads a crushing military defeat of the invading Saxon armies, and he uses his knowledge and superhuman strength to dupe the Icelandic princess Brunhild (a maiden warrior figure) into marrying Gunther. Siegfried's reward for these labors is the hand of Kriemhild in marriage. The deception of Brunhild culminates after Gunther and Brunhild's wedding night, when Gunther is unable to consummate the marriage because he does not possess the strength to subdue his bride. In despair, Gunther allows a disguised Siegfried to take his place in the marriage bed. Siegfried and Kriemhild then depart for Siegfried's kingdom.

Some ten years later, Brunhild is still pondering the puzzle of Siegfried and Kriemhild's marriage. If Siegfried is Gunther's vassal, as she has been lead to believe, why has Gunther dishonored his sister by marrying her beneath her station? And why has Gunther never called upon Siegfried to discharge the political services of a vassal? Siegfried and Kriemhild are invited to attend a grand festival in Worms, during which Kriemhild and Brunhild quarrel violently over issues of status and rank. Brunhild demands a demonstration of fealty from Kriemhild; Kriemhild vehemently asserts first her equality with Brunhild and then, fatefully, her superiority. To uphold this claim, Kriemhild displays to Brunhild, before a crowd of people, a belt and a ring that the disguised Siegfried stole from Brunhild during the night her marriage was consummated. She follows up this revelation by openly calling Brunhild Siegfried's concubine. (Although we are never told, we may presume that at this moment Brunhild finally understands what truly transpired that night.) Publicly humiliated, Brunhild demands that Hagen avenge her disgrace: Siegfried must die. Gunther attempts to smooth things over, but in vain. Hagen becomes the agent of Siegfried's death, first tricking Kriemhild into betraying the secret flaw in Siegfried's invincibility, then engineering the hunt that takes the Burgundians and Siegfried away from court, and finally wielding the spear that stabs Siegfried to the heart. Hagen is also the agent of Kriemhild's humiliation, dumping Siegfried's body before her chamber, stealing the immense treasure she has inherited from Siegfried, and then sinking it in the Rhine. Nevertheless, Kriemhild, who has been a dutiful daughter and loving wife, decides against a return to Siegfried's kingdom. She makes peace with her brothers (but not Hagen) and stays in Worms.

The second half of the story begins thirteen years later with a new courtship: the mighty king of the Huns, Etzel, seeks the hand of the widow Kriemhild in marriage. Kriemhild is loath to remarry; her brothers are eager to see her gone, but Hagen counsels heatedly against this remarriage, which would furnish her with unlimited wealth and power. Finally, however, Kriemhild accepts and leaves Worms for Etzel's court in Hungary. Seven years pass. Messengers from Etzel arrive in Worms inviting the Burgundians to festivities. Again Hagen urges caution, for he does not believe that Kriemhild has forgotten Siegfried's unavenged death, but his words go unheeded and the Burgundians depart. Upon their arrival at the Hunnish court, they learn that Kriemhild still grieves for Siegfried. Kriemhild quickly reveals her true intentions: she seeks Hagen's death. She promises a Hunnish vassal riches, castles, and a high-born wife in return for massacring the unarmed Burgundian pages. Hagen retaliates by murdering Ortlieb, the son of Kriemhild and Etzel. This unleashes open battle between the Burgundians and the Huns. Kriemhild turns the formidable might of the Hunnish kingdom against her brothers, who take refuge within a palace hall. Refusing Kriemhild's offer of safe passage if they will turn Hagen over to her, the Burgundian warriors battle to the death while defeating thousands of Hunnish opponents. In the end, only Gunther and Hagen survive as the captives of Dietrich, one of the German allies of the Hunnish court. An enraged Kriemhild has Gunther murdered and then confronts the bound Hagen, who is still carrying Siegfried's sword. When Hagen mocks her, she takes Siegfried's sword and decapitates Hagen. At this, Hildebrant, another German ally of the Huns, hews Kriemhild to pieces. The epic closes with the cries and laments of the survivors resounding on the battle site.[4]

The Mother-Daughter Conversation about Love

The *Nibelungenlied*'s first chapter (*âventiure*) is devoted to Kriemhild. She is introduced in the second stanza of the epic as the first of many protagonists, one stanza before her brothers, Gunther, Gernot, and Giselher, who make their entry into the epic as her guardians. The mother-daughter exchange is also contained in the first chapter. After naming more Burgundian kin and vassals and establishing the splendor of the court that surrounds Kriemhild, the poet switches to a short, intimate scene between Kriemhild and her widowed mother, Uote. This scene contains the first of Kriemhild's three prophetic dreams predicting the tragedies that will permeate her life, the so-called falcon dream. It is followed by a brief mother-daughter dialogue, which, I quote here in full:[5]

---

4. For general introductions to the *Nibelungenlied*, see Haymes 1986, Andersson 1987, and Ehrismann 1987.

5. Hereinafter, the original, cited by stanza number, is from *Das Nibelungenlied*, edited by Bartsch and de Boor and revised by Wisniewski (1979). The translation, cited by page number, is from Hatto 1965.

4. Kriemhild's dream. Kriemhild lies sleeping. Above the foot of the bed, the struggle of three birds represents the content of her dream. Another woman, probably Uote, her mother, stands in the doorway. Her hand gesture represents speech; perhaps she is waking Kriemhild, perhaps interpreting the dream. From an illuminated manuscript of the *Nibelungenlied* dated 1414, known as the Hundeshagen Codex, Berlin Staatsbibliothek zu Berlin Preußischer Kulturbesitz, ms. germ. fol. 855, f. 3r. Courtesy of the Staatsbibliothek zu Berlin Preußischer Kulturbesitz, Handschriftenabteilung.

Living in such magnificence, Kriemhild dreamt she reared a falcon, strong, handsome and wild, but that two eagles rent it while she perforce looked on, the most grievous thing that could ever befall her.

She told her dream to her mother Uote, who could give the good maiden no better reading than this: "The falcon you are rearing is a noble man who, unless God preserves him, will soon be taken from you."

"Why do you talk to me of a man, dear Mother? I intend to stay free of a warrior's love all my life. I mean to keep my beauty till I die, and never be made wretched by the love of any man."

"Do not forswear it too firmly," rejoined her mother. "If you are ever to know heartfelt happiness it can come only from a man's love. If God should assign to you a truly worthy knight you will grow to be a beautiful woman."

"Let us speak of other things, my lady. There are many examples of women who have paid for happiness with sorrow in the end. I shall avoid both, and so I shall come to no harm." (Hatto 1965, 18)

> "In disen hôhen êren troumte Kriemhilde,
> wie si züge einen valken, starc, sœn und wilde,
> den ir zwêne arn erkrummen. daz si daz muoste sehen,
> ir enkunde in dirre werlde leider nimmer gescehen.
>
> Den troum si dô sagete ir muoter Uoten.
> sine kundes niht besceiden baz der guoten:
> "der valke, den du ziuhest, daz ist ein edel man.
> in welle got behüeten, du muost in sciere vloren hân."
>
> "Waz saget ir mir von manne, vil liebiu muoter mîn?
> âne recken minne sô wil ich immer sîn.
> sus sœn' ich wil belîben unz an mînen tôt,
> daz ich von mannes minne sol gewinnen nimmer nôt."
>
> "Nu versprich ez niht ze sêre," sprach aber ir muoter dô.
> "soltu immer herzenlîche zer werlde werden vrô,
> daz gesciht von mannes minne. du wirst ein sœne wîp,
> ob dir noch got gefüeget eines rehte guoten riters lîp."
>
> "Die rede lât belîben", sprach si, "frouwe mîn.
> ez ist an manegen wîben vil dicke worden scîn,
> wie liebe mit leide ze jungest lônen kan.
> ich sol si mîden beide, sone kan mir nimmer missegân." (st. 13–17)

Kriemhild's falcon dream, foreshadowing the love and loss of Siegfried that will be the catalyst for the destruction of Kriemhild's entire birth family and their vassals, is the subject of much scholarship, most of it oriented toward establishing the origins and histories of the falcon motif (*Stoffgeschichte*).[6] In this chapter, however, I am interested not in antecedents but in a different set of conventions, those of the mother-daughter dialogue. These conventions help explain two sets of dissonances generated in the episode: first, the dissonance between the somber dream and Uote's correct but terribly understated interpretation of it; second, the dissonance between what I call the pragmatic conclusions Uote and Kriemhild draw from the dream—that is to say, Uote's assumption that Kriemhild will marry—and Kriemhild's desire to repudiate love and marriage. These dissonances are made manifest through the *Nibelungenlied* poet's skillful linkage of the falcon dream with the stereotypical figures of the knowledgeable, experienced mother and the naïve daughter.

The first of these motifs appears in stanza 15. It is the stereotype of the innocent maiden who desires to forswear erotic love both to maintain her beauty and (the more common motif) to avoid sorrow. The representation of Kriemhild as an innocent maiden is similar to that of Lavinia in the *Eneasroman*, although Lavinia's fear of erotic love can also be read, in part, as a conscious exploitation of the convention to shield herself from her mother's scrutiny. Both characterizations of the fearful virgin daughter are touched by a hint of comedy—Lavinia's exaggerations ("How will I live without my heart?") are intended to indicate a naïveté about the world that is also implied in Kriemhild's statement that she can avoid aging ("keep her beauty") if she avoids men.[7] Like Lavinia, Kriemhild is expressing a fear of sexual experience.

Uote's response draws on the stereotype of the knowledgeable and experienced mother whose duty is to teach her daughter about the social and personal benefits of erotic passion, insist on love's inevitability, and safeguard her for marriage. Like the queen in the *Eneasroman*, Uote is portrayed as an experienced woman who introduces her daughter to the ways of the world. Uote succinctly defines heterosexual love (*mannes minne*) as a woman's path to worldly happiness: in the German this phrase means "being loved by a man" ("it will happen from a man's love"), not "loving a man." In other words, the promised happiness will

6. For a structuralist analysis of all three dreams dreamt by Kriemhild in the *Nibelungenlied*, see Frakes 1984, which cites much earlier literature.

7. The characterization of the unnamed daughter in *Die Winsbeckin*, which I discuss in chapter 5, follows similar conventions. Her naïveté is created from equal parts of bewilderment and indignation that produce unintentionally comic effects.

come about for the daughter when she becomes the favored object of a man's desire. Uote then counters Kriemhild's wish to preserve her attractiveness; it is not the rejection of sexual experience, she says, but the embrace of it that guarantees female beauty. She also suggests that sexual experience and the happiness issuing from it are in line not just with the order of the world but also with the transcendental order, for God will have a hand in assigning, even blessing (*segnen* carries both meanings) Kriemhild with a suitably chivalrous warrior-husband. In sum, these teachings represent, in much condensed form, a version of the romantic love discourse I discussed in chapter 1.

One aspect of the convention of the naïve daughter is that she resists her mother's teaching. Kriemhild, too, wishes to avoid passion and even, like Lavinia, to change the subject (st. 17). Kriemhild advances an alternate paradigm of love that contests her mother's confirmation of love and implicitly labels it unrealistic; Kriemhild is not so sheltered that she does not have some knowledge of the mixed and unpredictable effects of love's dominion. It is this suspicion about men and their ability to bring happiness to her that leads her to repudiate love. Her skepticism suggests a will *character* to seek her own path, a will toward self-definition, a resistance to the patriarchal order. The mother is aligned with conformity, the daughter with defiance. But because this skepticism, this resistance, is spoken by a woman who is defined as naïve by the conventions within which she is speaking, Kriemhild's notion of self-determination is undercut. The conventions of the mother-daughter motif suggest that Kriemhild's resistance and her strategy of avoiding pain by avoiding love are equally unrealistic. The convention signals that her self-determination is naïve, even comic, her renunciation of the world impossible. Kriemhild's opposition to her mother's social conformity thus also becomes an embellishment of the stereotype of the naïve daughter. At this point in the story, then, Kriemhild's statement of nascent independence appears to fulfill the characterization of her as a naïve daughter.

Kriemhild's rejection of erotic passion is, in fact, quietly set aside as the story unfolds. Yet her repudiation of erotic love is not comic, as Lavinia's was, but ironically tragic. Kriemhild's determination to shape her own future develops within the somber context of the falcon dream. The dream transforms her pious and girl-like wish into a grimly inverted foreshadowing: Kriemhild will experience both deep passion for Siegfried and unstaunchable grief at his death, and she will both suffer and inflict irremediable harm. And if the falcon dream anticipates symbolically Siegfried's violent death and Kriemhild's violent grief, then the rhyme pair *tôt/nôt* (death/anguish) of Kriemhild's first speech, (st. 15), spoken to her mother, quite literally anticipates the last stanza of the *Nibelungenlied*:

"I mean to keep my beauty till I die, and never be made wretched by the love of any man." (Hatto 1965, 18)

> sus scœn' ich wil belîben unz an mînen tôt,
> daz ich von mannes minne sol gewinnen nimmer nôt. (st. 15)

At the end of the epic, this rhyme pair sounds the story's last chord and titles the work *Nibelunge nôt* [The Nibelungs' Last Stand]:[8]

I cannot tell you what happened after this, except that knights and ladies, yes, and noble squires, too, were seen weeping there for the death of dear friends.

This story ends here:
such was
The Nibelungs'
Last Stand. (Hatto 1965, 291)

> Ine kan iu niht bescheiden, waz sider dâ geschach:
> wan ritter unde vrouwen weinen man dâ sach,
> dar zuo die edeln knehte ir lieben friunde tôt.
> hie hât daz mære ein ende: daz ist der Nibelunge nôt. (st. 2379)

It is fitting that Kriemhild speak this first echo of the ending, for it configures her own end and the destiny she inflicts on others. Bookended by this rhyme repetition, the epic of betrayal, anguish, and death unfolds. The maiden Kriemhild knows examples of women who have paid for love with unhappiness, but she herself is destined to become the epitome of them all.

The Foreshadowing of Tragedy and the Breakdown of Stereotypes

Knowledge of the *Nibelungenlied*'s tragic ending marks the poem from its very first stanzas. The first chapter is one long foreshadowing. Besides Kriemhild's falcon dream, the poet leaves no doubt that all these splendid and powerful Burgundian knights are destined to meet a "sad end":

They held sway at Worms beside the Rhine, and were served in high honour by many proud knights from their territories till their dying day, when the enmity of two noble ladies was to bring them to a sad end. (Hatto 1965, 17)

---

8. The rhyme pair *tôt/nôt* (death/anguish) reoccurs throughout the epic, for example, in stanzas 1020, 1056, 1284, 1541, 1700, and 2014.

Ze Wormez bî dem Rîne si wonten mit ir kraft.
in diente von ir landen vil stolziu ritterscaft
mit lobelîchen êren unz an ir endes zît.
si sturben sît jæmerlîche von zweier edelen frouwen nît. (st. 6)

He also gives away that their misfortune will be brought on them by Kriemhild for the murder of her husband:

What terrible vengeance she took on her nearest kinsmen for slaying him in days to come! For his one life there died many a mother's child. (Hatto 1965, 19)

. . . wie sêre si daz rach
an ir næhsten mâgen, die in sluogen sint!
durch sîn eines sterben starp vil maneger muoter kint. (st. 19)

This explicit foreshadowing of the epic's outcome in the first chapter often irritates students reading the book for the first time. Not knowing the story beforehand, they feel robbed of a curiosity about the outcome that for them constitutes a part of the pleasure of reading. The foreshadowing clearly disturbs their sense that a plot must work with surprise and suspense to unfold successfully. Medieval readers might have had a different response. Because it seems likely that the *Nibelungenlied* draws on legendary material that was widely circulated orally, the foreshadowings could have affirmed what listeners and readers already knew. In so doing, such foreshadowings would have promised continuity between past and present, between oral and written literature, and established a sense of a community between the poet and his audience. For both modern and medieval reader or listener, however, foreshadowing shifts the emphasis of the story from events and outcome to the artistry of the telling.

This is an important point for the mother-daughter conversation and the falcon dream, because they appear to be embellishments of the legendary material introduced by the anonymous author of the *Nibelungenlied*, in partial imitation, perhaps, of the mother-daughter scenes in the *Eneasroman*. The *Nibelungenlied* employs the representations of experienced mother and naïve daughter that suggest the courtly discourse of romantic love. In connecting these conventions with the forecasts of certain tragedy that structure the first chapter, however, the *Nibelungenlied* also unsettles them. The stereotypes of experienced mother and naïve daughter, so carefully deployed in this scene, are just as carefully disturbed by the context into which they are placed. In light of the bleak destiny awaiting all the characters, a new question asserts itself: Who is, in fact, unworldly and unwise here, the mother or the daughter? A mother who ignores the enormous anguish and despair implicit in the text of her daughter's dream ("the most grievous thing that could ever befall her") betrays her inexperience, her own naïveté. Conversely, the practical conclusions this daughter draws from her dream suggest wisdom beyond her years. The dissonances are cast as a miscommunication between mother and daughter, but they carry implications exceeding that frame.

On the level of simple decoding there is no disagreement between Kriemhild and Uote: the falcon dream bodes ill. Uote's interpretation acknowledges this portent—saving divine intervention, Kriemhild's lover will quickly come to no good end—but it fails to pay proper heed to the intensity of the suffering the dreaming Kriemhild feels, an intensity that is the key to the dream's prophetic urgency. Uote's advice that erotic love will lead to happiness seems to ignore Kriemhild's pain and the urgency of the dream's message altogether, as though the loss of a husband were a solemn, but not disastrous, matter. In any case, Uote interprets the dream properly, but she nevertheless does not understand its significance. In light of Kriemhild's destiny, Uote's teaching that erotic love is the path to a woman's happiness is not untrue—Kriemhild does indeed experience "the joys of love" with Siegfried—but it is trite, and, in the manner of many fictional dream interpretations, fatally incomplete. Uote comprehends neither the dream's true import nor the significance of the fact that her beautiful but otherwise as yet unremarkable daughter has dreamed it: Kriemhild has been singled out for an unenviably singular fate.

Kriemhild does not refashion the dream's meaning at all. Her response focuses instead entirely on what her mother ignores, the anguish she felt in the dream. She disputes her mother's conventional praise of erotic love by citing the authority of other women's experience to back up her claim that in time anguish will override pleasure (st. 17). This move into the realm of experience implicitly contests the experiential basis of Uote's teaching. Together with the chapter's foreshadowings it implies that Uote, and by extension the discourse of romantic love she mouths, is naïve.

Kriemhild then moves to forestall the dream's terrible predictions by repudiating erotic love, which in the context of her gender and estate is, in effect, a renunciation of marriage. Casting off such worldly concerns suggests the option of a religious way of life, of joining a convent. As Yolande's story teaches us, for young, unmarried noblewomen in the twelfth and thirteenth centuries such choices were probably neither common nor easy. Among the German aristocracy of this period, daughters do not appear to have been perceived as burdens, whose dowries depleted the family coffers, but rather as significant political assets, whose marriages built feudal alliances. They were expected to marry, and it would appear that most of them did. This context supports the stereotype of the young and inexperienced woman when it suggests that the notion of repudiating erotic love and marriage is idealistic and naïve. Nevertheless, the actions such a repudiation implies have in Kriemhild's case self-protective and self-directed implications. In the terrible context of the falcon dream, Kriemhild's limited experience of the world, which differs from her mother's, and her naïveté produce a deep and dark ambivalence about the notion of romantic love. The interplay of foreshadowing and stereotype let us see that in her naïveté, which is not yet imbued with the rules of the patriarchal order, Kriemhild is wiser than her experienced mother.

In any case, the dream and Kriemhild's disavowal of erotic love are not brought up again. Kriemhild forgets both when she encounters Siegfried, and so mother Uote's conventional wisdom is, for a time, proved right. Yet Kriemhild's grief will also come to pass. The multilayered discordancy between experience, conventionality, and idealism in Uote's and Kriemhild's pragmatic responses to the dream reveals that the almost complete miscommunication between mother and daughter is itself a part of the unfolding tragedy.

The Hero as Subject and Object

The connection between the symbolism of the falcon dream and the mother-daughter dialogue is linked to the gendering of narrative positioning in the *Nibelungenlied*. One of the most fascinating interpretive dilemmas of the *Nibelungenlied* is that it offers both a plethora of heros and a dearth of them. Who is the hero: Siegfried, Hagen, or Kriemhild? Each seems qualified and disqualified in equal measure; the larger-than-life Siegfried by his unheroic death, the warrior Hagen by his villainy, the faithful Kriemhild by her bloodlust. In any case, from the perspective of the male protagonists' stories, Kriemhild is an obstacle in plots centered first on Siegfried in part 1 and then on Hagen in part 2. She is a resisting force that these male heroes must either assimilate or overcome.[9] Siegfried's story is tragic: he never fully attains the position of authority that corresponds to his status as (super)hero because of his love for Kriemhild and the betrayal of Brunhild entangled with it. Kriemhild is twice the unwitting instrument of Siegfried's tragedy. First, in the argument with Brunhild (chap. 14), Kriemhild attempts to defend Siegfried's status as a freeborn prince who is socially and politically the equal of the

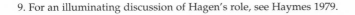

9. For an illuminating discussion of Hagen's role, see Haymes 1979.

Burgundians by publicly flaunting evidence that supports her case but also proves that Siegfried betrayed Brunhild. Although Kriemhild makes her point, the public humiliation of Brunhild and the disgrace of the Burgundian court make the assassination of Siegfried inevitable. Second, Kriemhild is directly responsible for disclosing knowledge that leads to Siegfried's death when she reveals to Hagen that there is one vulnerable spot on Siegfried's body (chap. 15). Though Kriemhild is Siegfried's loving wife, in his story she represents an obstacle that cannot be integrated into his story and is, in the end, responsible for his unheroic death.

In Hagen's case, the goal is not worldly authority as ruler or king, but rather the authority of fulfilling the role of loyal vassal, and above all, of attaining the fame and honor that the ideology of the heroic code offers. Where Siegfried fails, Hagen succeeds—in the sense that the ending of the epic is simultaneously a catastrophe for the Burgundian and Hunnish dynasties and a triumph for the warrior ethic that Hagen embodies. In the first part of the epic, Hagen's primary opponent is Siegfried, but in the second part this position is assumed by Kriemhild, who, in her quest for revenge, becomes Siegfried's representative. Indeed, Kriemhild finally attains the goal she seeks by murdering Hagen herself. Yet Hagen resists Kriemhild's purpose to the end, driving her to ever greater acts of violence and even manipulating the order of the final deaths so that by dying last he can be certain that the knowledge she craves will be forever withheld from her. By dying, Hagen wins. In Hagen's story Kriemhild becomes a symbol for an obstacle he successfully overcomes.

These observations can be systematized according to a structuralist logic. It can be argued that the "deep structure" of medieval narratives is determined by a single compressed formula: "A knight seeks and finds adventure." In this formula content is not merely form; it becomes a narrative principle, one that can generate new stories. Challenge, departure, battle, return: these stations are combined and recombined into new episodes, plots, and texts. Such a formula resembles the plot typologies of folktale and myth (Haymes 1979, 150). This model often also tells the story of transformation, of growth. The youthful hero undergoes various tests, proves his worth, integrates new wisdom into his self-understanding, and at the end of the story assumes his rightful claim to social authority. Though the father/son relationship is not necessarily treated specifically in the formula, it is nonetheless a narrative of maturation; the son becomes, perhaps not biologically but certainly socially and structurally, a father.

Such a model informs, for example, the Arthurian romances *Erec, Iwein,* and *Parzival,* and the harmony with which these works close is a function of this structure. When Erec takes over his inheritance from his father, when Iwein assumes the rule of a kingdom that parallels the

Arthurian one, when Parzival unites the realm of the Grail with the
realm of Arthur, the order of the world is both renewed and confirmed.
The model even holds a certain explanatory power for the tragedies of
Tristan in Gottfried's *Tristan und Isolde* and for Siegfried, because it suggests that tragedy occurs when a son, for whatever reason, is unable to secure the position of patriarch (father) that, by right of inheritance, might
be his. Tristan relinquishes his right to the authority of the position as father no less than four times: he turns over the kingdom he has inherited
from his biological father to his foster father and the foster father's sons;
he succeeds in the bridal quest of obtaining Isolde for his uncle Mark in
marriage, thereby doing himself out of the position as Mark's heir; he relinquishes his beloved Isolde to Mark instead of marrying her himself,
thereby foregoing the possibility of founding a new realm; finally, he refuses to consummate the marriage with Isolde-White-Hand, thereby
again refusing to found a new dynasty. Siegfried does become king in the
"Netherlands," but the events in Burgundy and his love for Kriemhild
prevent him from assuming the mythical-fantastic inheritance represented by Brunhild. In this sense, in the *Nibelungenlied* the fates of
Kriemhild and Siegfried contrast: Siegfried's tragedy stems from his willful rejection of the woman who embodies this aspect of his destiny (i.e.,
Brunhild), while Kriemhild's tragedy *is* her destiny.

In sum, the protagonists in these stories act; they exist as agents in a dynamic give-and-take with the world around them. Significant for our understanding the *Nibelungenlied* is the fact that this narrative model frames
the positions of subject and object in terms of gender. The subject position,
for example, is devised as male, a point powerfully argued from the point
of view of myth criticism by Teresa de Lauretis.

> In the mythical text, then, the hero must be male regardless of the gender of
> the character, because the obstacle, whatever its personification (sphinx or
> dragon, sorceress or villain), is morphologically female—and indeed, sim-
> ply, the womb, the earth, the space of his movement. As he crosses the
> boundary and "penetrates" the other space, the mythical subject is con-
> structed as human being and male; he is the active principle of culture, the
> establisher of distinction, the creator of differences. Female is what is not
> susceptible to transformation, to life or death; she (it) is an element of plot-
> space, a topos, a resistance, matrix and matter. (1987, 43–44)

De Lauretis's suggestions for reading myths can be applied to medieval literature as well. Women in medieval epics, for example, are
usually defined in relation to the hero. As mother, princess, beloved,
helper, or opponent of the hero, women play important roles, but they often remain, narratively speaking, places, obstacles, tests through which
the hero must pass in order to fulfill his destiny. Thus, in the narrative the

female character's story merits greater attention, or less attention, according to the value that it has for the hero's story.[10] In the structure of these stories, female characters are objects that the subject, the hero, must either obtain and possess or defeat and make disappear. The social construction of femininity in this cultural text assumes the construction of "woman" as the Other, the object against which the *male* hero's status as subject, the "I," is defined—against which, indeed, the concept of masculinity is constructed.

As de Lauretis points out, the alignment of gender with the structural positions of subject and object does not mean that all heroes must be portrayed as men. Sought-after marriageable noble maidens occupy such an object position, but through marriage or inheritance they can possess aspects of the active subject position, as I shall show in the next chapter. Under certain circumstances, medieval women, both in history and in fiction, were heroes; that is to say, they came to occupy the subject position for shorter or longer periods of time. When they did so, it was often *in place of* men. The scope of their power was often "a function of male absence" (Erler 1992, 30): the absence of a brother, which could make a woman an heiress; the absence of a husband, which could make her the lord of the manor, guardian, regent, or well-to-do widow. While women may occupy and represent the subject position temporarily, their *sex* precludes them from embodying it. In fictional texts, this issue translates into one of narrative positioning: powerful women slip between the object and subject positions, never fully contained in the first, never fully owning the second.

Kriemhild as the Falcon

Viewed from the perspective of Siegfried's and Hagen's stories, Kriemhild is an opponent, an object. In her own story, however, she slowly assumes the role of a self-determining subject. The tension between these two positions is integral to the portrayal of Kriemhild. Further, as we shall see, the mother Uote becomes in this regard Kriemhild's foil, remaining solidly within the bounds of the conventional object position out of which Kriemhild so flamboyantly breaks.

At first, Kriemhild's station confines her to a largely passive role. This passivity is illustrated by the manner in which her marriage to Siegfried comes about. Kriemhild falls for Siegfried the minute she sets eyes on

10. This is, of course, true for minor male characters as well, but a male character such as Gawain in *Parzival*, who is set up as a kind of "shadow" protagonist, both represents a test for the hero and is also an agent in his own right.

him, but she plays no part in arranging the marriage; it is instead a result of political bartering between her brothers and Siegfried. Kriemhild's brothers cynically display her in order to keep the formidable Siegfried at bay and give her to Siegfried as a part of a duplicitous exchange for Brunhild. That Kriemhild loves Siegfried is immaterial to their tactics, but it does make the intrigue easier to manipulate. The conventionality of Kriemhild's passivity is strengthened by the portrayal of Uote in part 1. With three adult sons who govern, the widowed Uote is uninvolved in political affairs. Her role is largely ceremonial: she escorts Kriemhild to court (chap. 5); supplies rich clothing to her children (chap. 4 and 6); is taken leave of by departing guests (chap. 5); and leads the procession that meets Brunhild on her arrival in Worms (chap. 10). A related aspect of Uote's ceremonial role is that it is largely accessorial; Uote's displays of wealth and gifts of riches function to bolster her sons' rule. Yet Uote plays no role in the many scenes in which political matters are decided. She is absent from the discussions that negotiate the unions of Kriemhild with Siegfried and Gunther with Brunhild, and she is neither consulted nor advised about the marriages.

Before her marriage, then, Kriemhild is much like her mother, a passive figure whose functions and activities are largely ceremonial, and she is a valuable political asset, too. As a marriageable maiden of royal birth, Kriemhild can be strategically deployed by her brothers according to their self-interests. Kriemhild's marriage to a powerful man, however, launches her into the political scene and gives her scope to act in her own right. She emerges in the subject position at pivotal moments in part 1, most notably in chapter 14, when she and Brunhild rail at each other publicly, with disastrous results.

Siegfried's murder is a crushing blow that moves Kriemhild to a new point of potential independence: widowhood. The widowed Uote's model provides a conventional foil against which to measure Kriemhild's behavior. After Siegfried's death, Kriemhild appears to follow her mother's example of withdrawing from politics. Kriemhild rejects her father-in-law's offer for her to return to the Netherlands in the role of regent for her and Siegfried's infant son (st. 1073–83). Instead, following the advice of her brothers and other relatives, who urge her to stay with her mother (st. 1077), she remains behind in Worms. Although the *Nibelungen* poet attributes Kriemhild's withdrawal to grief, we notice that in deciding to remain a daughter, Kriemhild relinquishes the role of mother, appearing to choose continued dependence over the authority and independence that being regent would bring her.

But this is not the whole story, for widowhood also grants Kriemhild opportunities to extend her claim to the status of self-governing subject.

As genuine as Kriemhild's grief appears to be, she also appears at times to be exploiting the social conventions of widowhood in order to pursue the course of action she has determined for herself: avenging Siegfried's slaying. She refuses to make peace with Hagen. She gives away her vast marital dower so freely and generously that we can believe Hagen's claims that she is using it to build alliances. This wealth also proves that as a widow Kriemhild is vulnerable; Hagen's theft of it goes unpunished. It is during the knight Rüdiger's proxy courtship of Kriemhild in the name of King Etzel, however, that we see Kriemhild carefully and consciously maneuver to get what she wants. Although her brothers consider the offer before they allow it to be brought to her, they can no longer dispose of Kriemhild as freely as before. It takes strong urging by her brothers and her mother for Kriemhild to consider the match. Exploiting the tension between her brothers' interest in this new political alliance (as well as their wish to be rid of her) and her own reluctance to remarry, she demands from Rüdiger, in return for her consent, the promise that he will "avenge her wrongs." This crafty oath—Rüdiger is ignorant of the circumstances of Siegfried's murder—will prove Rüdiger's undoing, for Kriemhild will hold him to it.

Kriemhild's astute negotiations with Rüdiger demonstrate how far she has moved from the passive role of exemplary widowhood embodied by her mother. Uote continues to speak with the same voice as her sons, although her assertions of affection, which are uncolored by political exigencies, ring truer than those of Kriemhild's brothers. Yet the image of the experienced mother summoned in the mother-daughter dialogue of the first chapter has faded indeed. Uote is apparently ignorant of her sons' role in Siegfried's death, and this ignorance gives her counsel to Kriemhild a decidedly ironic ring:

> "Dear child," said Queen Uote to her beloved daughter, "do as your brothers counsel you. Take your kinsmen's advice, then things will turn out well for you. I have seen you grieving and lamenting for such a long time now." (Hatto 1965, 160)

> Dô sprach diu vrouwe Uote ir lieben tohter zuo:
> "swaz dîne bruoder râten, liebez kint, daz tuo.
> volge dînen friunden, sô mac dir wol geschehen.
> ich hân dich doch sô lange mit grôzem jamer gesehen." (st. 1246)

In choosing remarriage, Kriemhild leaves her mother's example behind forever, and Uote becomes a negligible character. However, she is not forgotten. As Kriemhild gives secret orders to the messengers who will carry the fateful invitation from Hungary to Worms, she reminds them to "tell my mother of the exalted life I lead" (Hatto 1965, 180). Uote is to be reassured that her daughter has done well. We see the messengers carrying out this command with courtly flourish. As they do so, they make the mother-daughter relationship a site of nostalgic longing.

"My lady sends you her duty and loyal affection," began Swemmel. "And if it were possible for her to see you often, rely on it, there is nothing on earth could make her happier."

"That is not possible," answered the Queen. "However pleased I should be to see my darling daughter, she, as noble Etzel's consort, alas, lives too far away. May she and Etzel always be blessed with happiness!" (Hatto 1965, 184)

> "Ja enbiutet iu mîn vrouwe," sô sprach Swemmelîn,
> "dienest und triuwe. möhte daz gesîn,
> daz si iuch dicke sæhe, ir sult gelouben daz,
> sô wær' ir in der werlde mit deheinen vreuden baz."

> Dô sprach diu küneginne: "des enmac niht gesîn.
> swie gerne ich dicke sæhe die lieben tohter mîn,
> so ist leider mir ze verre des edeln küneges wîp.
> nu sî immer sælic ir und Etzelen lîp." (st. 1454–55)

Uote's reply embellishes the notion of an affectionate, apolitical mother-daughter connection. At the same time, the very sentiment Uote expresses—"May she and Etzel always be blessed with happiness"—demonstrates how far removed she is from the political realities of her court and her family.

Kriemhild moves far beyond her mother's example. In widowhood Kriemhild staked a claim to the status of a self-determining subject. Her marriage to Etzel completes it. During the climactic scenes at Etzel's court, Kriemhild issues as many commands as any male ruler. She dispenses wealth, promises political favors, negotiates with the enemy herself, sends warriors into battle, calls in her political debts. Throughout the epic, Uote's role remains ceremonial and passive but Kriemhild moves from being a pawn in the action, to having an effect on events, to being a decisive influence in the final scenes. Though linked perhaps still by ties of affection, mother and daughter become so dissimilar as to be complete opposites.

But Kriemhild's development from object to subject, which I have sketched out as a progressive development, is articulated in the *Nibelungenlied* as a dynamic of increasing contradiction. As Kriemhild slips between the object and subject positions, she is never fully contained by the object position but can never fully embody the subject position. When exemplified through Kriemhild, these two narrative positions contradict each other; it is, in part, this contradiction that fuels the story's cataclysmic ending. When Kriemhild is fully realized as a self-determining subject in part 2, she has completely transgressed her role as object, and that transgression endangers the stability of the social order. When she wields real power from a position of authority (when she, as ruler, treats men as objects), death results for vassal and kin, friend and foe alike. Her actions as a subject are perceived as evil, uncontrolled and uncontrollable. In sum, when Kriemhild is not contained by the status of object, she knows no political, social, or moral boundaries. As a subject she embodies excess. Such a portrayal of Kriemhild suggests a fear that when a woman is not confined by the limits of her object status, she will recognize no boundaries at all. Kriemhild's subject status, then, is not only a transgression of male perogative but also a threat to the gender ideology that underwrites the narrative structure itself.

Kriemhild's slippage between the positions of subject and object—this dynamic of increasing contradiction—is also prefigured in the falcon dream. In the dream Kriemhild takes an active role in rearing the falcon that is killed before her eyes; as the dreamer she is a passive vessel, a medium through which fate is revealed. The romantic discourse Uote mouths must overlook Kriemhild's foreboding that for her an ordinary life as a woman will lead to an extraordinary destiny. Kriemhild will not be like her mother, a minor character who fills a necessary function in the family but is otherwise socially conventional and politically insignificant. For Kriemhild's falcon dream also speaks of the dreamer. The falcon symbolizes Kriemhild, her construction of herself as an actor on the political playing field in the second half of the epic and the violent death she suffers as a result. The falcon is an image of herself in the role of subject, a symbol of those aspects of herself that are culturally encoded as masculine, that are accessible to her only when she acts "like a man." Kriemhild's falcon dream foretells that she will shatter the boundaries of her object status, usurp the role of subject normally reserved for men, and pay for it with her life. Therein lies her greatness and her tragedy.

⇜ 3 ⇝

Mother, Daughter, Foster Mother

The Politics of Lineage and the
Socialization of Women in Kudrun

Einfaches Liedchen. Die Sternbilder ziehen,
Rosenblatt, Hollerbaum duften verwandt.
Schlafe du, träume du! Beide Marien
binden und lösen dir Windel und Band.
—Elisabeth Langgässer, "Hollunderzeit", (1986, 106)[1]

THE ANONYMOUS EPIC *Kudrun* (c. 1230–1240) is preserved in a single, early modern compilation manuscript, the *Ambraser Heldenbuch* (c. 1504–1516).[2] Internal evidence suggests that the author of *Kudrun* possessed a wide-ranging knowledge of medieval German literature, including but by no means limited to the *Nibelungenlied,* but there is no evidence to suggest that *Kudrun* was known or even read beyond the narrowest circle of its authorship. There are no allusions to it in other works, no listings in library catalogues or book collections, no manuscript fragments with

---

1. This poem was written in 1947 and dedicated to Langgässer's daughter, Cordelia. "Elderberry Time": A simple little song. The constellations pass by, / rose leaf and elder tree are scented alike. / Sleep and dream, little one! Both Madonnas / bind and loosen your swaddling and bands.

2. For a complete description of the manuscript, see Bäuml 1969, 2–6.

Our only clue to the text's premodern reception comes from its place in the carefully thought-out sequence of texts in the *Ambraser Heldenbuch*, in which *Kudrun* follows the *Nibelungenlied.* The titles given to these epics in the manuscript make it clear that women are the main protagonists. To designate the *Nibelungenlied* the manuscript says, "Ditz Puech Heÿſſet Chrimhilt" [This Book is called Kriemhild], while for *Kudrun* it says, "Ditz puech ist von Chautroun" [This Book is about Kudrun]. The placement of the *Nibelungenlied* and *Kudrun* in this manuscript interrupts a series of texts about the hero Dietrich and his offspring that are compiled in "biographical order" (Wild 1979, 44) following the father/son principle. Clearly, this grouping of epics indicates thoughts on the complex interrelationship of gender and power. On the relationship of the *Nibelungenlied* and *Kudrun* to the text groupings in the *Ambraser Heldenbuch*, see Wild 1979, 28–44).

which to compare the surviving copy. Taken all together, these factors so complicate questions of dating, authorship, sources, influences, and provenance—already complex enough for most works making use in some way, as *Kudrun* does, of the traditions of *Heldendichtung*—as to render these issues less dilemmas than enigmas.[3]

Yet the obscurity of *Kudrun* in its own time cannot detract from the fact that it offers one of most unusual, sustained treatments of the mother-daughter theme in medieval German literature. Like Gottfried's *Tristan, Kudrun* does not contain a mother-daughter conversation about love, but *Kudrun* also ignores notions of erotic love such as those symbolized in *Tristan* by the love potion. *Kudrun* is concerned instead with the complex interrelationships of kinship, marriage, and rank, and it uses the mother-daughter plot both thematically and structurally to organize the telling of such a tale. Unique in its transmission, its lack of interest in notions of romantic love, and its doubled mother-daughter plot line, *Kudrun* provides a compelling account of medieval noblewomen in which love and power do not necessarily contradict each other. Further, *Kudrun* shows its female protagonists continuously and actively creating for the daughter, Kudrun, a bilineal pedigree from the paternal line of her mother, Hilde, as the primary kin-based source of their mutual claims to high social and political status. Although this pedigree clearly draws on notions of patrilineality, patrilineality is the subordinate part, put to use in the service of defending a bilineal kin system and noblewomen's ability to wield power and determine their own kinship alliances. Finally, the *Kudrun*-poet differentiates his or her meditation on noblewomen's use and abuse of power through the figure of Gerlint, Kudrun's ambitious would-be mother-in-law, who functions as a foster mother to Kudrun. In imagining Gerlint according to the stereotype of a disorderly woman, the poet expands the mother-daughter relationship into a system of oppositions that elaborates in unexpected ways on the role of birthright and fostering in the formation of socially acceptable notions of womanhood.

3. On issues such as the legendary background of the work, collatteral ballad texts, the internal strophic evidence of earlier versions, the clues and riddles presented by the source manuscript, and the vexed problems of dialect, place, and date of authorship, see Stackmann's excellent introduction to the Bartsch edition (1965) and Gibbs and Johnson's fine introduction to their translation (1992).

Scholars have been unable to agree even on the genre to which *Kudrun* should be assigned. In an interesting article Wailes (1983) makes a case for reading it as a romance rather than a heroic epic.

Summary of *Kudrun*

The *Kudrun* story is composed in four-line stanzas whose meter closely resembles the stanza of the *Nibelungenlied;* the entire poem numbers 1,705 stanzas. The epic is divided into thirty chapter-like sections that the manuscript calls "events" or "adventures" (*âventiuren*), a practice also followed in the *Nibelungenlied.* The chapters fall into three distinct segments. The first, brief segment, *âventiuren* 1–4 (203 stanzas), tells the story of the youthful exploits of the hero Hagen (not the same character as in the *Nibelungenlied*), who is Hilde's father and therefore Kudrun's maternal grandfather. The second segment, *âventiuren* 5–8 (356 stanzas), is organized around the first bridal quest, Hetel's wooing and abduction of Hagen's daughter, Hilde. The third and longest segment, *âventiuren* 9–30 (1,142 stanzas), recounts the story of Kudrun's wooing, abduction, and final triumph.[4]

Kudrun opens with a brief noble lineage that introduces the story's first hero, Hagen. Abducted by a monstrous griffin, which he subsequently slays, Hagen survives for years on a deserted island together with three princesses. Finally rescued, he marries Hilde, one of his fellow captives. King Sigebant abdicates in favor of his son, and Hagen immediately commences dispensing fiefs, marriageable princesses, and justice. In time Hagen and Hilde have one child, a daughter who is also named Hilde.[5] Hagen is a zealous and jealous father, a common figure in medieval legend and folklore. He guards Hilde ferociously, refusing all suitors and even executing their messengers. A number of "normal" bridal wooings are cut brutally short, making necessary the story's first protracted bridal quest and abduction: the story of how Hetel, the king of the Hegelings, wins Hilde. To organize the quest, the scene of the narrative shifts to the court of the active players, Hetel and his kin, who hatch a scheme for tricking Hagen in order to kidnap Hilde. Hetel's messengers—the warriors Horant, Wate, Fruote, Irolt, and Morunc—will sail to Ireland disguised as merchants. Once there, they will lull Hagen and his court into inattention with gifts and lovely wares, then lure Hilde onto their ships

---

4. English translations are from Gibbs and Johnson 1992; their translation of *Kudrun*, abbreviated here as *KU*, is cited by page number. I also follow Gibbs and Johnson in the spellings of personal and place names. Any incidental translation not otherwise identified is my own.

The original text is from *Kudrun* (1965), edited by Bartsch, and revised by Stackmann; this edition, abbreviated here as *K*, is cited by stanza number.

5. See Stackmann's introduction (*Kudrun* 1965, lii–lxxvii) for an excellent discussion of the Germanic sources of the Hilde saga.

and spirit her away. A host of warriors are hidden on a separate cargo ship should push come to shove.

The wily Hegelings succeed, mostly because Horant's magical, seductive singing allows them to bypass Hagen and take Hetel's suit to Hilde directly. Hetel is Hilde's social equal, and she agrees in principle to the match: "If I dared to go against my father, I would gladly follow you away from here" (*KU*, p. 34) [getörste ich vor dem vater mîn, sô wolte ich iu gerne volgen hinnen] (*K*, st. 407). With this tacit consent (although the warriors appear to have been ready to act without it), the Hegeling "merchants" invite the Irish court to the seashore to view their wares, lure Hagen and Hilde to separate ships, and escape with Hilde and her retinue. They sail to the outer reaches of Hetel's kingdom, where seven days later Hetel greets them joyfully. However, an enraged Hagen has pursued the abductors, and he catches up with them the day after the reunion. A vicious battle ensues: after Hagen has wounded Hetel and himself has been wounded by Wate, Hilde begs Hetel to rescue her father from Wate. Hetel intercedes, the two sides make peace, and Hagen gives his consent to the marriage of Hetel and Hilde, who depart for Hetel's kingdom accompanied by Hildeburc, the Queen Mother Hilde's companion both during and after their sojourn on the desert island. Back home in Ireland, Hagen reports to his wife that "he could not have arranged a better marriage for his daughter" (*KU*, p. 47) [er kunde zuo niemen sîn tohter baz bewenden] (*K*, st. 560), and the Queen Mother assents: "All my senses, my heart, and my mind rejoice that things have gone so well for our daughter" (*KU*, p. 47) [daz uns mit unser tohter sô wol gelungen ist, / des freunt sich mîne sinne, daz herze mit dem muote] (*K*, st. 561).

We turn now to Kudrun. Fully three times longer than her mother's story, the story of Kudrun's wooing, abduction, captivity, and rescue expands on the repertoire of images, themes, and narrative structures introduced in the first two parts of the poem. Kudrun's story, like her mother's, is structured according to the narrative model of the bridal quest. No fewer than three young noblemen seek to gain Kudrun's hand in marriage. The first, Sifrit, king of Garadie and Morland, is turned away. The second suitor, Hartmuot of Normandy, is egged on by his mother, Gerlint, and given support by his weak-willed father, Ludewic. Hartmuot sends messengers to Hetel's court, where his suit is dismissed by Hilde on the grounds that Hartmuot's father owes fealty to Hilde's father, Hagen. Hartmuot's family is thus, by her reckoning, of lower status than Kudrun's. After some years, a disguised Hartmuot pays a second visit to Hetel's court himself and secretly declares his love to Kudrun. Kudrun, however, turns him down, and Hartmuot flees back to Normandy, where he makes preparations for war. In the meantime, a third suitor, Herwic, king of Seeland, gathers an army and attacks Hetel's kingdom. In much the same fashion as the struggle between Hilde's father, Hagen, and her then suitor, Hetel, the ensuing combat between Hetel and Herwic proves Herwic's mettle (Hilde even anticipates, approvingly, this kind of "test" when Herwic arrives). A truce is declared, and Herwic, whose valiant fighting has won the admiration of both Kudrun and her mother, is allowed to woo Kudrun himself. Kudrun says yes, and the marriage ceremony takes place. Before the marriage is consummated, however, Herwic departs, having granted Hilde's request that Kudrun be left in her care for one year, because "she wanted to prepare her daughter better for her role as his queen" (*KU*, p. 58) [Hilde sprach zem künige, si woltes zuo der krône baz bereiten], (*K*, st. 666).[6]

But trouble is ahead. The rejected rival Sifrit launches a series of attacks on Herwic's territories. Hard-pressed, Herwic sends messengers to ask for his father-in-law's aid in repelling the invaders. Hetel defers to Kudrun in the decision to render aid to Herwic: "Whatever she commands shall be done" (*KU*, p. 60) [swaz sô diu gebiutet, daz sol allez sîn] (*K*, st. 680). Kudrun couches her plea for his support in terms of defending her *own* territory: "My losses will be overwhelming unless your warriors lend their willing hands to help my friends" (*KU*, p. 60) [mîn schade wirt alze grôz, ez enwellen dîne degene mit williclîchen henden helfen mînen friunden] (*K*, st. 686). An army is assembled, and Hetel, accompanied by Wate, Horant, Morunc, and his son Ortwin, hurries off to do battle in Seeland. Now the second suitor, Hartmuot, seizes the opportunity to renew his suit with force. Informed by his spies that the Hegeling warriors are occupied elsewhere, he and his father sail with an army to Hilde's castle. When Hilde and Kudrun again disdainfully turn down the offer of marriage Hartmuot's messengers bring to them—this time backed up by the threat of violence should Kudrun refuse—Hartmuot attacks. In spite of Hilde's valiant defense, Hartmuot by force carries away Kudrun and sixty-two ladies, including the companion Hildeburc. Hilde immediately sends word of these disasters to Hetel and Herwic, who make peace with

6. There has been some debate among scholars about whether at this point Kudrun is married or merely engaged to Herwic. Loerzer (1971) links the structural repetitions of courtship and marriage in *Kudrun* to legal history. He presents legal aspects of the marriage ceremony performed between Kudrun and Herwic, emphasizing Kudrun's consent and arguing convincingly that it is a binding marriage (1971, 122–31). Further, the text indicates that Kudrun considers herself married during the entire ordeal that follows her kidnapping; she resists Hartmuot's advances on the grounds that she is already Herwic's wife. See also Herlihy on *consensus non concubitus:* "In a series of decretals, pope Alexander III (1159–1189) endorsed Lombard's analysis and affirmed that the spoken consent of the eligible partners alone rendered the marriage valid and binding" (1985, 80–81).

Sifrit, enlist his support, and rush after the men of Normandy. The two armies meet on an island, Wülpensant, but after a day of terrible fighting, in which Ludewic kills Hetel, neither side emerges as victor. That night Hartmuot and Ludewic flee with their captives to Normandy; the devastated Hegeling armies are unable to follow them.[7]

Kudrun's sufferings are only beginning. As the ships approach Normandy, Ludewic renews the offer of marriage; when Kudrun refuses, Ludewic tosses her overboard, and only Hartmuot's quick action saves her from drowning. Gerlint arranges a magnificant reception, but Kudrun refuses her welcoming kiss and rejects Gerlint's petitions on behalf of her son. The frustrated Hartmuot turns Kudrun over to the care of his mother, whose task it becomes to effect Kudrun's consent. The narrator leaves no doubt as to Gerlint's role in the story: she is called "she-devil" (*tiuvelinne, K*, st. 738, 996), "evil" (*übele,* st. 1188), and "she-wolf" (*wülpinne,* st. 1015, 1203). Gerlint begins by separating Kudrun from her retinue and setting all of the captive women to the lowest tasks: tending the fires, combing and spinning flax. When three and a half years of this treatment bring about no change in Kudrun's attitude, Gerlint commands Kudrun to act as maid, dusting with her hair, sweeping, and tending the fire. When nine years have passed, and Kudrun still refuses marriage, Hartmuot threatens rape, but in the face of Kudrun's defiance backs down from carrying out his threat. As punishment, Kudrun is set to doing the washing, summer and winter, until a total of fourteen years have passed.

In fourteen years a new generation of warriors has reached maturity in Hegelingen. Hilde is at last able to raise and equip a new army, which sets sail under the leadership of Herwic. Meanwhile in Normandy, the laundress Kudrun is visited by a heavenly messenger, a bird that brings her news of her relatives and her imminent rescue. Kudrun's first question is: "Does my mother still live?" (*KU,* p. 104) [lebet noch Hilde?] (*K,* st. 1171–72). The next day, Herwic and Ortwin, who are acting as scouts, find Kudrun and her faithful companion, Hildeburc, washing at the seashore, and a touching recognition scene soon follows. The men return to the army, while Kudrun returns to Gerlint's castle with a load of unwashed linens. Furious, Gerlint sets out to whip Kudrun, who now craftily agrees to marry Hartmuot. Her ladies, at last all reunited with her, express dismay at this turn of events. In response, Kudrun laughs for the first time in her fourteen years of captivity. Gerlint rightly interprets this laugh as a sign that Kudrun is up to no good, but her warning to Hartmuot goes un-

7. *Kudrun* supplies a reason for this defeat. In their haste to chase after Hartmuot, the Hegelings had stolen the vessels being used by pilgrims. Their defeat is punishment for this sacrilege.

heeded. Kudrun orders the ladies to bolt the door to their chamber and announces, "Today I kissed my husband Herwic and my brother Ortwin" (*KU*, p. 117) [Ich hân geküsset hiute Herwige mînen man/und Ortwîn mînen bruoder] (*K*, st. 1332).

The next morning the climactic battle takes place in front of the fortress, with the women watching from the battlements. Herwic kills Ludewic; Hartmuot saves Kudrun from the sword of one of Gerlint's knights; Kudrun sees to it that Wate spares Hartmuot, who is then taken captive; Kudrun saves Hartmuot's sister, Ortrun, from Wate's rage, but not Gerlint, whom Wate decapitates. Hilde's victorious army returns to Hegelingen with the exiles and their captors. Coached by Kudrun, Hilde makes peace with Ortrun and Hartmuot and arranges the crowning of Kudrun as Herwic's queen, with a grand celebration to follow. During these festivities, Kudrun negotiates three marriages: Kudrun's brother Ortwin marries Hartmuot's sister Ortrun; Hartmuot marries Kudrun's loyal companion, Hildeburc; and Sifrit marries Herwic's unnamed sister. With this interlocking series of marriages undergirding the alliances of former enemies, peace is assured.

The Bridal Quest

In the *Nibelungenlied*, when Kriemhild actively employs wealth and authority in order to exact vengeance, her mother represents a notion of conventional, passive femininity against which we can measure how far Kriemhild has strayed from the norm. Kudrun, in contrast, matures into a stern but fair judge and peacemaker, with two strong, contrasting mother figures: a strong-willed yet exemplary biological mother, Hilde, and an equally strong-willed but demonic foster mother, Gerlint. Kudrun is positioned narratively between these two mothers, one good and one evil, in a way that complicates issues such as the socialization of daughters by mothers, the repudiation of mothers by daughters, and the use and abuse of power by noblewomen. Using the mother-daughter material, *Kudrun* presents a unique picture of continuity across female generations.

Continuity between the birth mother, Hilde, and the daughter, Kudrun, is established in the first instance by means of a narrative device scholars have dubbed the "wooing expedition" or the "bridal quest." In his introduction Stackmann (1965, xix) defines the bridal quest and its variation, the bridal abduction, as follows: "Ein junger Fürst, unterstützt von treuen Männern, erringt nach allerhand Abenteuern eine Frau, die ihm unter höfischen Ehren angetraut wird" [A young prince, assisted by loyal vassals, wins a woman following all sorts of adventures, and the woman is

then married to him with courtly honors].[8] Varied repetitions ("vari-
ierende Wiederholung") of the bridal quest function as the organizational
skeleton of *Kudrun*'s plot (1965, xix). The very first bridal quest in *Kudrun*
is an unproblematic wooing sequence that follows immediately upon the
Queen Mother's advice to Sigebant, Hagen's father. It represents a kind of
compressed, generic model of a bridal quest (this one unproblematic), a
model that will be rewritten in a number of ways before the epic is
through.[9]

> He [Sigebant] gave orders that the finest noblewoman be wooed on his be-
> half. She lived in Norway, and his kinsmen supported him eagerly in his
> suit. She was betrothed to him, so we are told, and a great many beautiful
> maidens and seven hundred sturdy men from Scotland constituted her ret-
> inue. (*KU*, p. 7)

> der hiez im werben eine die besten von den rîchen,
> diu saz in Norwæge. des hulfen im sîne mâge vlîziclîchen.

> Si wart im gemahelet, alsô ist uns geseit.
> dô wart ir hovegesinde vil manic schœniu meit
> und siben hundert recken von Frideschotten lande.
> die fuoren mit ir gerne, wan si den jungen künic wol erkanden. (*K*, st. 8–9)

In the bridal quest story, gender roles are clearly assigned. Stackmann's
description, which tells the bridal quest story from the perspective of the
male actors, makes this clear: men act, while women become the sought-
after objects of exchange between patrilineal dynasties, a passive role
reflecting some aspects of the position to which real noblewomen were
consigned in the Realpolitik of late medieval marriage politics.[10] Yet it is
possible to summarize the bridal quest story from the perspective of the
female actors. To paraphrase Stackmann, with an inversion of genders: A
young woman, acting completely alone or with a single confidante,

8. The bridal quest was a popular narrative device in medieval German literature; many
stories are either built around it or contain one or more bridal quests, for example, *König
Rother* (c. 1150), *Ortnit* (c. 1220), *Orendel* (c. 1200), and the *Nibelungenlied*. See also Pearson
1992.

9. Even Hagen's abduction by the griffin can be read as a grotesque variation on the
bridal quest, in which the griffin's quest to find food for its young functions similarly to
the parent's quest to find a suitable partner for his or her child. Thus, the adult griffin is the
parent, Hagen the desirable "love" object, the baby griffin the child in need of a spouse.
The proposed union is of course a heinous mismatch, inverting the mastery of human over
beast.

10. On this aspect of the poem, see Nolte 1985, 26–33.

chooses a husband, experiences all sorts of adventures, and is at last married to him with courtly honors. It will not escape the reader's notice that inverting the gender of the protagonist has the unexpected effect of making the bridal quest sound like a romance (Wailes 1983), and it is precisely this inversion that the *Kudrun* poet has undertaken.

The longest bridal quests of the story, the one that leads to Hilde's marriage and the one that leads to Kudrun's marriage, are narrated from the point of view of both the male and the female protagonists. This perspectival doubling has the effect of making room in the story for women's agency. It transforms *Kudrun* from a story in which men are actors and women merely valuable objects into a story that tells us about women's choices as they act within a political and social system that depends on their multiple family allegiances. The story of Hilde's abduction and marriage demonstrates the power of such a transformation. Like the virgins Kriemhild and Lavina, Princess Hilde is strictly guarded, and her most intimate relationship appears to be with her mother. The few glimpses we are given of mother and daughter together show us a companionable and unproblematic relationship. Hilde's situation as an heiress guarded fiercely by her father reflects a female passivity, immobility, and inaction that is enforced by a vigilant paternal overlord. The key term here is *enforced.* The passivity to which Hilde is consigned at this stage in her life is never construed as a reflection of her "nature"; it is rather a function of her status as a highborn heiress. Under enormous constraints, Hilde takes a number of momentous actions undermining her father's authority: she smuggles the messengers in and out of her chambers, she agrees to Hetel's suit, and she consents to the abduction. Nowhere does the text pass a negative judgment on Hilde for these choices (the motif of the magical seduction wrought by Horant's singing may serve in part to excuse Hilde's defiance of her father's authority by making her subject to an overwhelming, magical force outside of anyone's control). Rather, the text implies that Hagen's aversion to allowing Hilde to marry is extreme. Having received a proposal of marriage from a man who is socially her equal, Hilde is justified in taking active steps to assist Hetel's warriors in wresting her free of excessive paternal control.

Kudrun makes creative use of the bridal quest in another way: it tells the story of both mother and daughter according to this single pattern, recounting first the bridal quest that leads to the marriage of the mother, Hilde, and subsequently the story of the bridal quest and marriage of Hilde's daughter, Kudrun. This repetition of the bridal quest model across two succeeding generations is reserved for mother and daughter; though a number of the male characters undertake bridal quests, it is never repeated for a father and his son. For mother and daughter, however, the bridal quest signals a special continuity between women, because it predicts how each generation of women will proceed from one stage of life to the next. It posits certain stations in the life of a young noblewoman (secluded childhood, choice of spouse) that both mother and daughter must pass through in order to progress to the position of queen. The bridal quest produces a kind of narrative pattern that traces a female protagonist's movement from daughter to wife. The bridal quest in *Kudrun* is transformed into a shared story of female maturation. Configured as mother-daughter story, *Kudrun* revisits the bridal quest as a matrix of female biography.

The Politics of Kinship

The bridal quest in *Kudrun* emphasizes the extent to which, for a woman, the movement to a new stage of life signals the acquisition of greater agency and authority. The bridal quest ends in marriage, which the bridal quest defines as an integral part of secular lordship. Yet the politics of marriage is also the politics of lineage. For both male and female protagonists in *Kudrun*, winning a marital partner of high rank not only marks the generational transfer of political power but is also a visible sign of the status of one's kin and one's lineage. The politics of kinship is central to *Kudrun*. Hilde and Kudrun actively assert Kudrun's agnatic *and* cognate descent. By doing so, they represent noblewomen using their multiple family allegiances to defend their claims to power and their right to determine their own kinship alliances.

Of primary importance for the European nobility of the High Middle Ages was agnatic (patrilineal) lineage, descent traced through the father. In *Kudrun*, for example, the notion of an illustrious patrilineal dynasty is introduced at the story's outset with the figure of Kudrun's maternal great-great-grandfather, Ger, the ruler of Ireland. Ger's death in the first lines of the narrative permits the immediate succession of his son, Sigebant, who will in turn produce as an heir the hero of part 1, Hagen. This quick succession of father-son relationships—Hagen is born in stanza 22—evokes a world where dynastic patrilineage, which in David Herlihy's words "traces its descent through the male back to a known founder" (1985, 82), is the preeminent source of family prestige and power. Linked to the "rise of feudal principalities" (Herlihy 1985, 92) and to the increasingly intimate connection between family identity and fixed property, this sense of lineage began emerging in the great noble houses of France in the eleventh century and was firmly in place in the German-speaking territories by the time *Kudrun* was written. The dynastic patrilineage opening *Kudrun* signals authority.

Yet, as Herlihy reminds us, patrilineality was not the only means of or-

5. A visiting prince clasping the hand of the princess he admires as family and retainers from both noble households look on. This courtly scene could well illustrate the many receptions and presentations in *Kudrun*, particularly if we see in the older, female figure in the foreground the princess's mother. From the *Nibelungenlied*, Berlin, Staatsbibliothek zu Berlin Preußischer Kulturbesitz, ms. germ. fol. 855, f. 17v. Courtesy of the Staatsbibliothek zu Berlin Preußischer Kulturbesitz, Handschriftenabteilung.

dering family descent and kindred relations in feudal Europe. The pre-eminence of the agnatic kin did not so much displace as overlay earlier, bilineal descent systems, in which the nobility traced their descent through both paternal (agnatic) and maternal (cognate) kin. The continued coexistence of these potentially conflicting systems of establishing family relationships is born out by the mother-daughter material in *Kudrun*. In the narrative, the generational alignment shifts over time from father-son to father-daughter to mother-daughter arrangements, thus slipping from agnatic to cognate relations. Yet the story constructs these relationships as belonging to the same lineage. Indeed, the assumption upon which the entire epic rests—that Kudrun is the heir of her valiant mother's heroic father in both kin and character—suggests the continued existence of a bilineal kinship network and its overlap with a more strictly agnatic lineage structure. The two systems of kinship stand, of course, in a power relationship to each other, with agnatic descent favored over cognate and sons favored over daughters. Yet in *Kudrun* bilineal descent is, if not flourishing, still present as an alternate system; kinship is established on the basis of either, or both, paternal and maternal descent.

Kudrun's heroics assert her claim to be Hagen's kin.[11] What this seemingly obvious point glosses over, however, is that Kudrun's relationship to her mother, Hilde, and her maternal grandfather, Hagen, is, in kinship terms, a cognate relationship. In medieval Europe cognate relations were of secondary importance, because descent was traced through paternal kin. That is to say, patrilineality prevailed in many legal, economic, and political matters. Kudrun is not even an heiress, because she has a living brother. Yet this story glorifies maternal kin relations, insisting that like agnatic kin they, too, represent socially binding and politically valid kindred ties. *Kudrun* stages a veiled struggle between the notions of patrilineality and bilineality in which the notion of bilineality wins out not by replacing patrilineality but by asserting its own validity alongside it.[12]

We examine first the kindred status of Kudrun's mother, Hilde. Hilde is Hagen's only child. Having a daughter as heir means that a woman, not a man, will carry on Ger's lineage, an impossibility in strictly agnatic, father-son, terms. Yet in *Kudrun*'s terms Hilde clearly carries on her father's line. As her story begins, Hagen is moved into the role of the dy-

11. Campbell discusses the connection between Kudrun and Hagen in terms of the *Kudrun* author's concern with what Campbell calls "protective leadership" (1978, 285–89) and "productive leadership" (298–302).

12. In the following paragraphs I am also arguing against Hoffmann's thesis that the question of Kudrun's social status is unimportant (1967, 105–106).

nastic founder, supplanting Ger, who is mentioned for the last time when Hilde is first mentioned to Hetel:

He [Morunc] spoke: "Her name is Hilde and she is from Ireland. Her father is Hagen, a kinsman of King Ger." (*KU*, p. 19)

er [Môrunc] sprach: "si heizet Hilde und ist ûz Irlant. ir vater heizet Hagene und ist daz Gêren künne." (*K*, st. 212)

From this point on, Hilde is repeatedly called "the child of Hagen" or "the daughter of Hagen"; only twice is she "Hetel's wife."[13] In one of the epic's pivotal moments, Hilde herself defines her status and that of her children through their descent from Hagen when she (not her husband) rejects Hartmuot's suit for Kudrun on the basis of Hartmuot's inferior social status as a vassal of her father, Hagen:

Then Queen Hilde spoke: "How could she be his consort? His father [Ludewic] holds one hundred and three cities in Gardie in fief from my father Hagen. It would not be fitting for any relatives of mine to receive fiefs from Ludewic's hand." (*KU*, p. 51)

Dô sprach diu frouwe Hilde: "wie læge si im bî?
ez lêch mîn vater Hagene hundert unde drî
sînem vater bürge dâ ze Garadîne.
diu lêhen næmen übele von Ludewîges hende die mâge mîne." (*K*, st. 610)

Hilde's assertion of superior rank, based on her father's status, is supported by both her husband and her enemies. Hartmuot is not good enough for Kudrun. This confirms what Ludewic has prophesied in his deliberations with Hartmuot and Gerlint a few strophes earlier: "The Hegelings are proud people, and I don't expect that Kudrun's relatives think we are good enough for them" (*KU*, p. 50) [daz volc ist übermüete: Kûdrûnen mâgen wæne sî wir smæhe] (*K*, st. 593).[14] Although Gerlint and

13. To enumerate: "des wilden Hagenen tohter" (*K*, st. 226, 250, 252, 381); "hagenen tohter" (*K*, st. 456, 573); "des wilden Hagenen kinde" (*K*, st. 566); "daz Hagenen kint" (*K*, st. 933); "Hetelen wîp" (*K*, st. 765, 788).

14. The phrase "Kudrun's relatives" (*Kûdrûnen mâge*) does not distinguish between cognate and agnate descent. Ludewic also refers to Hilde's voyage from Ireland and the defeat of Hagen by Hetel. Thus both Kudrun's maternal lineage (Hilde and Hagen) and her proud and audacious (*übermüete*) paternal lineage figure in Ludwic's speech, a speech that only serves to remind Hartmuot of the honor Hetel won by marrying Hilde, thus spurring Hartmuot on to attempt the same for himself: "Lady Hilde was crowned by mighty Hetel, and this was indeed an honor for the Hegelings" (*KU*, p. 46) [gekroenet wart frou Hilde: daz was den Hegelingen gar ein êre] (*K*, st. 547).

Hartmuot ignore Ludewic's protest, it both confirms Kudrun's superior status and casts that status as a part of her appeal. Later, Hetel explains the rejection of Hartmuot in the same terms that Hilde had used: "I knew that he, the King of Normandy, held his land in fief from Hagen" (*KU*, p. 72) [wol weste ich daz in lêch, / dem künige ûz Ormanîe, Hagene sîn lant] (*K*, st. 819).

Like her mother, Kudrun is fully aware that she is Hartmuot's social superior. Upon her forced arrival in Normandy, she says so clearly when she rejects Hartmuot's suit on any terms: "Even if his family were equal to mine so that he could marry me, I'd die before I'd take him as my husband" (*KU*, p. 86) [im wære ez von dem vater geslaht, daz er mich solte minnen, / den lîp wil ich verliesen, ê ich in ze friunde welle gewinnen] (*K*, st. 959). The reader is not allowed to forget that Kudrun's high birth derives from the descent she traces through her mother to Hagen. Kudrun is "kin of Hagen" at six dramatic and pivotal moments in the story. She is indirectly called this by her mother in stanza 610, quoted above. Hartmuot calls her "kin of Hagen" (daz Hagenen künne, *K*, st. 614) during his first unsuccessful courtship. After Hartmuot's threat to rape her, Kudrun calls *herself* "kin of Hagen" when she taunts Hartmuot with the conviction that his peers will not recognize such a union as a legitimate marriage: "for when other noblemen came to hear of it, they would declare that Hagen's granddaughter was a concubine in Hartmuot's land" (*KU*, p. 92) [ez spræchen and er fürsten, sô si des hôrten mære, / daz daz Hagenen künne in Hartmuotes lande kebese wære] (*K*, st. 1030). This assertion of kindred status is particularly forceful because Kudrun is telling Hartmuot that *only* a proper marriage, based on her consent, will win him common recognition of the elevation of his family's status that he seeks through this marriage (Miklautsch 1991, 122–23). Further, the narrator calls Kudrun "Hagen's kin" twice (st. 1270, 1281) in the scene in which Kudrun, knowing that rescue is near, baits Gerlint into threatening a whipping, and in the same scene Kudrun herself, without explicitly referring to Hagen, boasts to Gerlint that her status is superior to Gerlint's own: "I am certainly of higher birth than you and all your kinsmen put together" (*KU*, p. 113) [jâ bin ich verre tiurer danne ir mit iuwern mâgen] (*K*, st. 1279). And finally, Kudrun says of herself in the last recognition scene: "I am called Kudrun, and I belong to Hagen's family" (*KU*, p. 131) [ich heize Kûdrûn, und bin daz Hagenen künne] (*K*, st. 1486).

Kudrun is not only called "Hagen's kin." She is also defined paternally: as "Hetel's child" or "Hetel's daughter" (six times, either by the narrator or by Gerlint); "Wate's kin" (once); and "maid from Hegelingen" (four times, once by Kudrun herself). Far and away the most common designation for Kudrun is, however, "Hilde's daughter" or "Hilde's child," which occurs more than twenty times.[15] It is the mother-daughter connection that is to remain foremost in the mind of the reader, a connection that, among other things, serves to uphold and sustain Kudrun's status as "kin of Hagen." The subtle difference between Hilde and Kudrun as "kin of Hagen" is of course that Hilde is defined in terms of her distinguished paternal lineage, which skips one paternal ancestor (Hagen's father, Sigebant) in order to establish a lineage that reaches back to Hilde's great-grandfather, Ger. In being called "kin of Hagen," however, Kudrun is defined in terms of her distinguished maternal lineage, since Hagen is Kudrun's maternal grandfather. The lineage founder in both cases is, and remains, a man, but a daughter—in this case, Hilde—can function as a "node" through which descent is traced. In other words, although—technically speaking—the purely agnatic line of descent from Ger has died out in Hilde's generation, *Kudrun* does not seem to recognize this; in Hagen's daughter's daughter, Kudrun, Ger's line lives on.[16] The mother-daughter connection validates Kudrun's claim to construct her own pedigree in a bilineal fashion.

The assumption upon which the entire epic rests—that Kudrun is Hagen's heir in both kin and character—suggests the continued existence of a bilineal kinship network and its overlap with a more strictly agnatic lineage structure. While cognatic relationships show up very vaguely in Hetel's kin as well (the avunculate tie between a man and his sister's son is given special recognition), the most interesting example of the coexis-

15. Following is a list of these ephithets, with speakers indicated. *Hetelen tohter* (Hetel's daughter): *K,* st. 587 (narrator); 1015 (Gerlint); 1030 (narrator). *Heteln kint* (Hetel's child): *K,* st. 970, 1000 (Gerlint); 1525 (narrator). *Dez alten Waten künne* (the kin of old Wate): *K,* st. 1307 (narrator). *Diu maget von Hegelinge* (the maid of Hegeling): *K,* st. 1242 (Kudrun herself); st. 1019, 1327, 1533 *(ûz Hegelinge lant dem Hilden kinde)* (narrator). *Hilden tohter* (Hilde's daughter): *K,* st. 740 (Hartmuot); 977 (narrator); 1052 (Gerlint); 1289 (Hartmuot's messenger); 1473, 1510 (narrator). *Hilden kint* (Hilde's child): *K,* st. 1511 (Wate); 1516, 1533 (narrator). The formula *Dô sprach diu Hilden tohter* (then Hilde's daughter spoke): *K,* st. 959, 1178, 1199, 1233, 1268, 1330, 1482, 1517, 1632, 1651, 1653.

Campbell, following Hoffmann, states that stanza 959 represents the first occurrence of "Hilde's daughter", but this is incorrect (Campbell 1978, 284, citing Hoffmann 1967, 161). The phrase first appears in stanza 740 as a part of Hartmuot's speech.

My discussion of epithets in *Kudrun* is by no means exhaustive. Campbell's interesting discussion of the use of the adjective *hêr* (most noble, exalted), for example, supports my conclusions (Campbell 1978, 246–50).

16. Ortwin is, in fact, never once called "Hagen's kin," although as Kudrun's brother he clearly *is* Hagen's kin.

tence of potentially competing lines of descent is Kudrun herself.[17] In three separate, dramatically charged moments, Kudrun identifies herself either as "kin of Hagen" (twice) or as "maid of Hegeling": when threated with rape ("kin of Hagen," st. 1030); when testing her rescuers ("maid of Hegeling," st. 1242); and in the final recognition scene ("kin of Hagen," st. 1486). Although one is a cognate relationship (her maternal grandfather), and the other an agnate relationship (her father), both designations rely on male relations to locate Kudrun within family structures. Further, the entire third part of the epic hinges on Kudrun's insistence that she is Herwic's wife. I noted above that the most frequent appellation for Kudrun, usually used by the narrator but also employed by other characters, is "Hilde's daughter," but nowhere does Kudrun use this designation herself. Her self-reference as "maid of Hegeling" is necessary to discover whether or not the knights who have approached her are in fact her relatives. Her self-references as "kin of Hagen" are made in situations when she is being humiliated or intimidated by her captors. They draw on socially dominant family terminology—on the most overtly powerful *male* kin of the family networks available to her, her maternal grandfather—in order for her to assert her worth.

Yet the phrase "Hilde's daughter" recurs throughout Kudrun's story, with clearly positive connotations. It continually reminds us of Hilde's existence, of the fact that Hilde is Kudrun's connection to "the kin of Hagen." Women mediate between competing kinship systems, yet at the same time they have a powerful interest in asserting their understanding of what those kindred networks represent. The mother-daughter relationship, which appears to be legally, economically, and socially peripheral in the calculation of descent, becomes in *Kudrun* the center of generational continuity. "Hilde's daughter" identifies the familial connection between Kudrun and her mother as a crucial source of the knowledge and the strength Kudrun summons to defy her captors.

17. In contrast to Hilde and Kudrun, the exact degrees and terms of relatedness among Hetel and his kin are never disclosed. We learn that Wate has been foster father to Hetel on the basis of an unspecified tie of kinship; later Wate is mentioned as Ortwin's foster father as well (st. 574). We learn that Horant, king of Denmark, is Wate's "sister's son" (*swester kint*) (st. 206), and that the nameless chamberlain who discovers Horant and Morunc in young Queen Hilde's room is Horant's cousin: "my father and his mother were brother and sister" (*KU*, p. 35) [mîn vater und sîn muoter / diu wâren eines vater kint] (*K*, st. 414). Later we are told that Horant's mother was Hetel's sister (st. 1112). This information, gleaned from various places in the text and nowhere presented as a coherent whole, yields a family tree that would appear to be inaccurate, since it makes Hetel and Wate brothers. What it does prove is that the *Kudrun* poet is not interested in establishing a coherent lineage for Hetel. Herwic's lineage is similarly murky.

The Birth Mother: Hilde

The struggle over Kudrun shows that for the feudal aristocracy, marriage was viewed as a event that could advance or diminish an entire kindred's political fortunes and social rank. What *Kudrun* emphasizes is how dynamic, how changeable, and how contestable issues of lineage were, and how women's multiple family allegiances situated them at the nexus of these controversies. *Kudrun* also show us—from two points of view, that of Gerlint and that of Hilde—how powerful women manage this struggle. Gerlint's quest to advance her family's fortune is coded by the text as illegitimate. Represented according to the stereotype of a disorderly woman, she demonstrates for the reader the abuse of authority. Hilde, on the other hand, supplies the reader with a positive model of female authority. Nevertheless, Kudrun must interact and learn from them both. *Kudrun* thus links the politics of lineage with the issue of mothers' upbringing, fostering, and socialization of their daughters in the widest sense, the education into gender roles of human beings born noble and female.

Hilde provides a positive example of a noblewoman's use of power. According to Ian Campbell's survey of older scholarship, Hilde was often regarded with disapproval, a reading that Campbell's work goes far to correct (1978, 222–40). Indeed, it is hard to discover a basis for the powerfully negative bias that scholars have brought to their interpretations of this powerful woman ruler. Aside from her breach of paternal authority in eloping with Hetel, Hilde handles the considerable power that falls to her after her marriage in exemplary fashion. She knows the value of her lineage and its history; she is valiant, though unsuccessful, in the defense of Kudrun during Hartmuot's siege of the fortress; once widowed, she uses her wealth to endow religious establishments; she raises an army to avenge her husband's death and to rescue her daughter (an army that the text unambiguously designates as hers through phrases such as "Hilde's ships," "Hilde's followers," and "Hilde's banner");[18] she agrees, after some initial resistance, to her daughter's peace plans; and, in an act that harks back to Sigebant's surrender of power to Hagen, she graciously passes to Kudrun the authority to negotiate the marriages that will secure the newly won peace.

18. I count at least eleven instances of such designations: *die Hilden kiele* (Hilde's boats): *K*, st. 1106; *daz Hilden her* (Hilde's army): *K*, st. 1126; *daz Hilden ingesinde* (Hilde's followers): *K*, st. 1344, 1386; *die Hilden friunde* (Hilde's relatives): *K*, st. 1547; *daz Hilden zeichen* (Hilde's banner): *K*, st. 1353, 1392, 394, 1416, 1421, 1548.

The prominence of Hilde's role as an example of a well-situated and shrewd noblewoman who draws knowledge, power, and authority from both the circumstances of her birth and the circumstances of her marriage has made it easy to overlook the contrast between *Kudrun's* rote clarification of inheritance and investiture in the case of the male heirs and its silence on the same issue for Hilde. In the cases of Sigebant, Hagen, Hetel, and even Hartmuot, *Kudrun* explicitly tells us that the son succeeds his father as ruler and takes over his patrimony, treating this as a completely unexceptional issue that is resolved in simple statements such as "in time he became powerful in the lands of his father, King Sigebant" (*KU*, p. 15) [sît wart er gewaltic in sînes vater Sigebandes landen] (*K*, st. 163). In contrast, Hagen continues to rule his own lands after Hilde's marriage. Nevertheless, as his only child, Hilde stands to inherit her father's lands and authority after his death. Historically, this would have made her a prize within a patrilineal system if her father's realm passed to her children through her, as was commonly the case in twelfth- and thirteenth-century Europe, including Germany (Duby 1980). Yet Hagen's death is not even mentioned, although the fact that he is not summoned to aid in Kudrun's rescue presumably indicates that he is decreased.

The epic leaves entirely unexplained what happens to Hagen's territories. There are various possibilities. Do they pass to a different male relative, a collateral line of Ger? Or does this inheritance pass, as was just suggested, to Hilde, her spouse, or her children? If so, does Hilde rule Ireland alone, after the manner of many noble marriages in the early Middle Ages, in which the spouses' territories and properties are not combined into a single, economic and political unit, but rather maintained as strictly separate entities? Or does Hetel assume overlordship over them? We are simply not told. Instead, the text characterizes Hilde's political rule in two historically significant areas—the assertion of prominent kinship alliances and the right and duty of a widow to exercise regency. Hilde administers Hetel's kingdoms after his premature death, she raises the expeditionary force to free Kudrun, she is deferred to as supreme ruler upon the force's victorious return, she transfers certain aspects of seigneurial power to Kudrun after Kudrun is crowned Herwic's queen. Thus, though her status vis-à-vis Hagen's territories is uncertain, at the end of the epic she is shown transferring power to her daughter, much as Sigebant transferred power to Hagen.

The historical record suggests that the issues of noblewomen's agency as rulers and their control over family wealth were salient ones in feudal Europe. Patrilineal inheritance patterns set out to limit women's inheritance rights, and inheritance battles among aristocratic families over daughters' rights attest to the fact that women's share of economic and political power brought to the fore *competing* claims of law and custom, inheritance and kin. In separate articles, the historians John Freed (1990) and Ute-Monica Schwob (1982) argue that women of the Austrian aristocracy wielded more influence than has been generally acknowledged. Each of them also shows that in Austria, as in feudal Europe generally, noblewomen's agency tends to become visible in two specific situations: when the woman comes from an important and/or wealthy birth family, often of higher station than her husband; and when a woman is widowed. Schwob makes it clear that noblewomen's claims to inheritance and station could be contested, and that often only a fortunate combination of circumstances (influence, wealth, age and sex of children, important kinship connections through birth or marriage) determined whether or not a noblewoman could assert in practice rights that may have been hers in theory. Perhaps *Kudrun* is silent on this economic and political issue because it would have been controversial. Avoiding such contentious matters, *Kudrun* concentrates instead on displaying Hilde's abilities as a ruler. In sum, *Kudrun,* promoting the bilineal kinship system as a way of securing women's political and social standing, celebrates Hilde's political abilities but does not address how problematic politically the economics of her position may well have been.[19]

It has become a commonplace in scholarship that Hilde's most important legacy to her daughter, Kudrun, is the disposition to make peace. After her elopement, Hilde halts the battle between her father and husband, thus bringing about peaceful coexistence, just as her daughter negotiates between warring factions three marriages that end the epic. Both these actions achieve peace; because they are negotiated by women, scholars have argued that the epic constructs them as feminine political acts in a positive sense. Winder McConnell, for instance, concludes that this peacemaking, carried out by women, provides an "alternative vision of society": "Revenge is by no means eradicated, but it is kept within bounds, and the primary exponents of this moderating stance are, in every instance, women" (1988, 98). Thus McConnell argues that the *Kudrun* poet advances a vision of politics based on women's innate abilities to make peace. The contrast between powerful women peacefully settling

---

19. The story's silence on this issue might be explained as a function of the story's origins in legendary material. Such an argument might contend that Hilde's rule is anachronistic, reflecting a disappearing cultural memory of a time when noblewomen wielded more power. This could be called the "remnants of matriarchy" argument. However likely that may be (and I am dubious of such claims), there is historical evidence that women's place in kinship systems and their inheritance rights were still of considerable importance at the time and place when *Kudrun* was written.

certain disputes in *Kudrun* and a powerful woman vengefully fueling the fires of war in the *Nibelungenlied* is often cited as evidence supporting this reading.[20] And indeed, Kudrun both carries out and improves upon her mother's legacy when she at epic's end reconciles the warring parties without further bloodshed.

The flaw in this interpretation has to do with viewing *women* as being particularly suited to the tasks of peacemaking.[21] There is a prominent counterexample within the story: Gerlint. Further, negotiating peace and negotiating marriage were by no means viewed in feudal Europe as belonging to some sort of "feminine sphere." On the contrary, both functions belonged within the purview of powerful men, as is shown in many passages in the *Nibelungenlied,* for example. Although fighting in battle was a male prerogative (or obligation), both the *Nibelungenlied* and *Kudrun* show us that women as well as men were expected to be able to manage the political business of warfare. The dichotomy of equating women with peace and men with war breaks down; both peace and war belong to the political sphere that involves competently wielding the public authority of political office. This office—in feudal terms *lordship*—is traditionally filled by male nobles. We must modify the peacemaking thesis. What connects Kudrun and her mother, Hilde, is their ability to fill a male role successfully. When Kudrun pacifies her mother and negotiates the final marriages, she establishes her effectiveness in carrying out the functions of male authority. The widow Hilde has done the same by successfully managing her husband's kingdom as well as raising and equipping the army that rescues Kudrun. Kudrun and Hilde do not bring some special but undefined "feminine" quality to their task; they demonstrate their ability, based not on stereotypical gender characteristics but

20. Gibbs and Johnson sum up the contrasts between Kriemhild and Kudrun nicely in their observation that the two poems "offer contrasting modes of action taken by two women in response to the injustices they have suffered; one ends in terrible revenge, the other in reconciliation" (1992, xiii). That *Kudrun* answers peacefully back to Kriemhild's violent redressing of her wrongs in the *Nibelungenlied* has long been a commonplace of scholarship. For classic statements of this thesis, see Hoffmann 1967 and 1976 and Kuhn 1976b. Challenges to this position have come from Campbell (1978) and Nolte (1985).

21. Nolte models his discussion of the difference between male and female ways of being on Oskar Negt and Alexander Kluge, *Geschichte und Eigensinn.* Nolte argues that Kudrun's work represents counterproduction, which stands for the principle of production, i.e., the principle of the concrete ("Ihre Arbeit ist Gegenproduktion, sie steht für das Produktions- bzw. Konkretionsprinzip," 1985, 56). This concept of work overcomes the principle of war and abstraction ("Kriegs- und Abstraktionsprinzip," 56) represented by Wate and the Hegelings as well as by Hartmuot and Gerlint. Nolte also relies on a notion of female solidarity and cooperation as being instrumental in peacemaking (55, 61).

on class allegiance, to intelligently fill public, political, traditionally male roles.

The Foster Mother: Gerlint

Kudrun lives up to Hilde's example. Her mother has provided a model of how to function proficiently in the public, male role of overlord, and she has followed it. Yet Kudrun's story has an added layer of complexity—her struggle with her foster mother, Gerlint. Gerlint assumes prominence as a mother figure in two ways. The first is that she aspires to be, and acts as, Kudrun's mother-in-law, although the marriage to her son, Hartmuot, never takes place. The second is that in this capacity as affinal kin (i.e., kin by marriage) to Kudrun, she takes over the custodial role traditionally enacted by foster parents in medieval literature.[22] Gerlint's fosterage of Kudrun is, of course, never intentionally sought out by Kudrun's family, yet her birth mother has seen the need for Kudrun's further education. After the marriage of Herwic and Kudrun, Hilde asks for an extra year to "prepare Kudrun for the crown" (*KU*, p. 58) [zuo der krône baz bereiten] (*K*, st. 666). Hilde feels that her daughter needs to be taught how to act as a queen; it is one thing for a noblewoman to acquire a position of power through marriage, but it is another thing to wield the authority of lordship. Clearly, Hilde intends to undertake this maternal transfer of knowledge herself. Events, however, provide Kudrun with a different teacher, a foster mother who differs from Hilde not so much in her position and influence as in her attitude toward Kudrun.

The narrative treats Kudrun's years under Gerlint's authority as a period of socialization and education (Wailes 1983, 358). The vocabulary of instruction is repeatedly used to inaugurate this phase of Kudrun's story; in addition to the verb *ziehen*, meaning to bring up or to train (*K*, st. 993; 1015) and the related noun form *zühte*, here meaning tutelage (*K*, st. 995), the verb *lêren* (to teach) is used by Hartmuot when he gives Kudrun over to Gerlint's care: "Madam, you are to instruct her kindly" (*KU*, p. 89) [frouwe, ir sult si güetlîchen lêren] (*K*, st. 994).[23]

---

22. In stanza 576 we are told that Kudrun was sent by her father, Hetel, to be raised by his closest kin in "Tenelande" (Denmark), which is ruled by Horant, but nothing more is made of this circumstance.

23. Hartmuot repeatedly admonishes his mother to "treat her [Kudrun] kindly" (sîn güetlich phlegen, *K*, st. 1001) and to "educate her, using moderation" (ir ziehet si in der mâze, *K*, st. 1003).

However, Gerlint ignores Hartmuot's directive for kind treatment of Kudrun. She removes Kudrun from her retinue, demeans her by requiring that she perform a series of ever more humiliating menial tasks, and finally threatens her with physical violence. Though she is not truly a stepmother, Gerlint's treatment of Kudrun may well qualify her as the first example of an "evil stepmother" in German literature—Gerlint, forcing Kudrun to sweep and dust with her hair, is much like the evil stepmother in fairy tales. Unlike fairy tale cruelty, however, Gerlint's threats and punishments are clearly and carefully embedded in a set of material, social, and political concerns.[24] Gerlint is a noblewoman ambitious for the advancement of her son. She has initially connived with Hartmuot to press his suit for Kudrun (Ludewic is not consulted but merely informed of their decision); she encourages Hartmuot in his kidnapping scheme, and when their fortunes are reversed and their castle attacked by Hilde's armies, she attempts to act as military leader by telling Hartmuot what to do (st. 1378–86). Most significantly, Gerlint exploits the quasi-parental authority she enjoys to deprive Kudrun of the rights of her birth station and to force upon her the duties of a lower social class.

The narrative of socialization is thus bound up with political concerns. Gerlint's fosterage is a continual struggle between Gerlint and Kudrun in which Gerlint disputes and Kudrun asserts the social superiority of Kudrun's lineage over Hartmuot's. Gerlint fosters Kudrun through humiliation by class (in medieval terms, estate), making Kudrun occupy a lower-class position and function in lower-class roles. Gerlint uses Kudrun as a servant, and Kudrun knows that marrying Hartmuot would raise her out of the demeaning position into which Gerlint has forced her. The marriage to Hartmuot would then represent a public reclaiming of Kudrun's noble birth status. The fact that Kudrun has acted as a servant before such a marriage might even conveniently mask the fact that the proposed union is below Kudrun's station.

Hilde's rejection of Hartmuot as Kudrun's suitor signals that his family is of lower status than hers—the vassal, Hartmuot, should not marry Kudrun, the kin of his overlord. In Hilde's eyes, in Kudrun's eyes, and, it seems, in the eyes of the narrator, this hypogamous marriage exchange (one in which the wife-taker is of lower status than the wife-giver, i.e., the

---

24. Arguing that Gerlint's latent motivation for tormenting Kudrun is jealousy, Nolte goes on to interpret this jealousy psychologically, as a reflex of Gerlint's unconscious, in which Kudrun disturbs an incestuous mother/son relationship (1985, 46–49).

man is marrying "up") is to be resisted.[25] Yet the lowering of the wife's status raises the husband's. For Gerlint, the advance up the social hierarchy that such a marriage represents is precisely what makes it so attractive, for Kudrun's high status and her acclaimed kin remain two of the most important aspects of her allure.[26] Gerlint's strategy, then, must aim at subtly redefining Kudrun's estate status. Gerlint does not so much want to change Kudrun's estate status as to blur it enough so that the marriage marking the redefinition of her own family's status can take place.

Gerlint goes about blurring the differences in rank between her kin and Hilde's by attempting to establish her own readings of kin hierarchies. Gerlint has already asserted that Hartmuot is Kudrun's equal (*KU*, p. 89; *K*, st. 988), an opinion no other character appears to share with her. She prefers to call Kudrun "Hetel's child," an appellation that appears six times in the narrative and is used only by the narrator (st. 587, 1031, 1525) and by Gerlint herself (st. 970, 1000, 1015). Since Hetel has been killed by Ludewic much earlier (*KU*, p. 79; *K*, st. 880), Gerlint's choice of this kinship designation for Kudrun is both cruel and strategic. It not only reminds Kudrun of Hetel's death but is also a tactic for establishing a different set of power relations. First, Gerlint stresses Kudrun's paternal

25. No one objects at the end of the epic when Kudrun arranges a marriage between Ortwin, her brother (and Hagen's grandson), and Ortrun, Hartmuot's sister, who is the daughter of Ludewic, Hagen's vassal. Ortrun's status may even be further compromised because she is a captive. Yet while the families are the same, this second union represents a hypergamous marriage, in which the wife-taker's family is of higher status than the wife-giver's. The fact that Ortwin can marry Ortrun without a murmur about his potential loss of status for "marrying down" underscores, perhaps, what Kudrun and Hilde seem to have been stressing all along, namely, that a woman's social standing is more threatened by a mesalliance than a man's.

Freed's fascinating study (1995) of the marriage politics of the medieval nobility in the archdiocese of Salzburg throws an interesting regional light on the problems and strategies of marrying 'up' or 'down' in the social hierarchy. In this territory, the problem of noble marriages was complicated by the fact that many wealthy and influential noble families (ministerials, *ministeriales*) retained their servile status into the fourteenth century, while the number of free noble families slowly declined. Yet marriages took place between the free nobility and the ministerial lords. The need for such marriages and "the disjunction between the ministerials' legal condition and their social status as the de facto nobility of southeastern Germany" (1995, 276) may well have created formidable strains for the thirteenth century Salzburg nobility regarding changes in legal and social status owing to marriage.

26. When Hartmuot refers to Kudrun as *daz Hagenen künne* (*K*, st. 614), he acknowledges her superior status, which is of course part of what makes her attractive. After Kudrun is his captive, he states that he is *Herwic's* equal (*K* s. 1048), i.e., the equal of the man Kudrun has accepted in marriage. This argument is different from asserting his equality with Kudrun.

lineage because Ludewic (Hartmuot's father) and Hetel (Kudrun's father) seem to share a similar rank—there are no issues of vassalage establishing clear rank differences between them. In this version of Kudrun's lineage, Hartmuot and Kudrun are equals in rank. Second, Gerlint's use of "Hetel's child" places Kudrun within the paternal lineage that has been almost destroyed in the battle of Wülpensant. Calling Kudrun "Hetel's child" thus implies that she is virtually an orphan. Gerlint does finally drop the designation "Hetel's child" and call Kudrun "Hilde's daughter" (st. 1052, when she reduces Kudrun to a laundress). At this point Kudrun has endured nine years of abuse in captivity, and Gerlint's switch from "Hetel's daughter" to "Hilde's daughter" can be read as a recognition—whether grudging or inadvertent—of Kudrun's heroic qualities. Fourteen years into the ordeal, when Kudrun feigns consent to the marriage, Gerlint changes her kin terminology yet again, enveloping Kudrun in the folds of her own kin by addressing Kudrun as "my dear daughter" (*KU*, p. 116) [liebiu tohter mîn] (*K*, st. 1315), and raising her to regal status by calling her "the queen" six stanzas later (*KU*, p. 117; *K*, st. 1321). "Queen" is the final term Gerlint uses to address Kudrun when she begs her in vain for protection from Wate's wrath (*KU*, p. 134; *K*, st. 1516). Kudrun's steady ascent in Gerlint's kinship terms for her—from orphan to queen—marks the stages of her victory over Gerlint.

Yet Gerlint's contradictory reorderings of kin and estate hierarchies do not bring about the end she desires, the marriage of Hartmuot and Kudrun. Gerlint's stubborn abuse is successful, however, in strengthening Kudrun's unyielding sense of her own worth. Kudrun's tutoring by her inflexible mother-in-law fosters not her compliance but her resistance. Kudrun's defence of her status as Herwic's wife depends on the birthright of superior nobility and celebrated maternal kindred represented by "Hagen's kin." Kudrun's steadfast rejection of compromise on the issue of her estate and marital status is what makes her heroic.

Kudrun's Heroics

It is not in an atmosphere of goodwill and kindness that Kudrun can learn what she needs to know about being a powerful woman in a man's world, but rather in the grueling school of deprivation, degradation, and humiliation. The interruption of Herwic's bridal quest—for fourteen years—opens up a narrative space in which allusions to the conventions of the saint's legend can introduce another rhetoric of gender to the story. The testing of Kudrun by Gerlint elaborates a new set of virtues that *Kudrun* constructs as particularly appropriate for women. With Gerlint playing the part of the unrepentant and merciless goader (a stock part in the narrative of the saint's legend), the text borrows from the repertoire of female virtues represented in saints' and martyrs' lives—steadfast resistance, strength through patience—to cast Kudrun in a new role, that of long-enduring, but ultimately triumphant, innocent sufferer.[27]

The struggle between Gerlint and Kudrun, then, introduces a rhetoric of suffering that counterpoints the political and socially grounded rhetoric of the bridal quest and the heroic epic. To put it simply, these two rhetorics mark out a dichotomy of action and patience, aspects that correspond to the epic's understanding of the male and female spheres. This is not to say that the story aligns its female characters in any simplistic way with passivity—indeed, my point all along has been that *Kudrun* is about demonstrating women's ability to manage affairs brilliantly and actively in the male realm. Nor do I wish to imply that suffering is a femininized quality, an assertion clearly at odds with medieval Christian Europe's understanding of the spiritual significance of suffering for the attainment of salvation. However, in order for *Kudrun* to highlight the ways in which women can and do act in the conventionally male sphere, it has to establish the conventional parameters of female and male spheres. *Kudrun* maintains one crucial boundary between men and women: bearing arms and fighting wars is done only by men; patient resistance and the patient endurance of suffering belong only to women. Aggression distinguishes men from women; the Gerlint-Kudrun episode introduces and elaborates the corollary notion that the ability to endure suffering distinguishes women from men.

Hilde assumed that Kudrun needed more training before becoming queen; I have argued that Kudrun receives that training during her years with Gerlint. What Kudrun must be trained in is how to suffer. Before Kudrun can speak for male authority, she must undergo a process of socialization that forces her to practice a set of virtuous behaviors that reinforce conventional notions of female conduct. Kudrun prevails as the kind of hero who must *suffer* abuse (even though she leavens her captivity with violent rebukes of Hartmuot): that is to say, she must endure and, in so enduring, triumph. Gerlint's testing celebrates Kudrun's capacity for suffering, or—perhaps better put—Kudrun's heroism consists of the capacity to *choose* patience. The hardships Kudrun endures demonstrate her strength and heroism. The paradox is that since Gerlint and Hartmuot have made Kudrun an offer of marriage, Kudrun must choose the "rewards" of humiliation in order to maintain and secure the superior social status that

27. See Cazelles 1991. For a modern perspective, see Weigel 1983. On medieval noblewomen's interest in saints' lives, see Bumke 1979.

her lineage grants her. Kudrun courageously refuses the social identity being thrust upon her and insists on the definition of her place and rank she has learned from her biological mother. Kudrun's tenacious resistance to Gerlint's brutal fostering doubly ensures the justice of Kudrun's claim to her superior social status as Hilde's daughter and Hagen's grand-daughter. By linking the heroic code with the saint's life, *Kudrun* establishes a new category for female behavior in which patience and endurance are *active* modes of existence.

In one sense, then, the heroine, Kudrun, excels in both the male and female spheres, embodying positive aspects of both. By anyone's standards, she is exemplary. However, the fact that Kudrun's *imitatio* of saintly suffering precedes her emergence as a representative of male authority suggests a second interpretation: Kudrun's induction into an exemplary, female suffering is a necessary precondition for her emergence as a representative of male authority. In order to avoid the lowered social status as Hartmuot's wife being offered her in Gerlint's household, Kudrun can only choose a different status, one that is simultaneously more demeaning, because it degrades her to the function of servant, and more ennobling, because it elevates her to the status of martyr and hero. For fourteen years Kudrun endures in this conventional model of female suffering. Her capacity to sustain such deprivation proves her worthy of her birthright. Only when these lessons of femininity have been learned, however, can Kudrun rule—as a woman—in justice and peace. Kudrun must have experiences within the conventional female sphere before she can act as a just and shrewd ruler.

Kudrun implies that it is necessary to maintain—indeed, celebrate— a conventional definition of women as more able to endure suffering than men, even when women can and must occupy positions of public power and authority. In this context, Gerlint is not only Kudrun's teacher, but also her antithesis, embodying the sort of overreaching and over-ambitious female ruler Kudrun should not become. Kudrun's confrontation with and overcoming of this disorderly mother is thus a necessary precondition for her identification with the orderly one.[28] The story of Kudrun's passage into adulthood requires both mother figures. Hilde is Kudrun's legitimate mother both socially and politically. Yet Gerlint,

28. Again I disagree with Hoffmann, who argues that Kudrun stands in an antithetical relation to Hilde: "Sie steht in einer doppelten Antithese: in einer solchen gegen das Nibelungenlied (Kriemhilt) und in einer solchen innerhalb der 'Kudrun' selbst, nämlich gegen ihre Mutter Hilde" [She stands in a double antithesis, first in one vis-à-vis the Nibelungenlied (Kriemhild) and second in one vis-à-vis the epic *Kudrun* itself, namely, her mother Hilde] (1967, 81). I argue that the evidence for identification and continuity between Kudrun and Hilde as types is much stronger.

the "illegitimate" mother, is necessary in this text's construction of femininity. Gerlint's cruel fostering and her negative example are prerequisites
for Kudrun's formation as a politically responsible woman. Here one is
certainly reminded of psychoanalytic theories of development, which
postulate that the creation of an "evil" or monstrous parental figure preserves the "good" one inviolate (Nolte 1985). In *Kudrun* Gerlint's monstrousness allows Hilde to remain exemplary—there are apparently some
lessons in the patriarchal social order that no daughter can learn from an
exemplary mother. In *Kudrun*'s contrasting mother-daughter stories, Kudrun learns to emulate Hilde as an exemplary queen, but her degradation
at the hands of Gerlint teaches her the resisting patience that signals an
exemplary woman. Hilde supplies both the heroic birthright and an exemplary model of female rule, while Gerlint's testing teaches Kudrun endurance, even obstinacy, an inflexibility that both confirms and asserts
Kudrun's place in the maternal lineage of heroic noblemen and exemplary noblewomen.

Yet what is most unusual about *Kudrun* is not the struggle of the exemplary daughter with her "unruly" foster mother. The repudiation of a
powerful, disorderly mother figure by a more compliant daughter often
forms the basis of the daughter's induction into the patriarcal order, as we
have seen in the *Eneasroman*. What is unusual about *Kudrun* is rather the
existence of the exemplary mother figure, holding and wielding power
in a constructive and just manner, who passes that power to her daughter, allowing—indeed, insisting—that her daughter claim authority and
power. In the peaceful transfer of power across generations that marks the
ending of the epic, a powerful mother is followed by her powerful daughter, whose rule provides them both with ample scope for demonstrating
their political acumen.

That Kudrun has learned her lessons well is shown at epic's end. Kudrun arranges three marriages, casting a net of alliances in order to ensure
peace. The couples she brings together are her onetime suitor and present
ally, Sifrit, and her unnamed sister-in-law; her brother, Ortwin, and Gerlint's daughter, Ortrun; and her kidnapper, Harmuot, and her faithful
companion, Hildeburc. The marriage between Hartmuot and Hildeburc
has always vexed scholars because Hildeburc, who began the narrative as
a captive on the griffin island with Hagen, must be at least sixty years old
at the time of this marriage. Hildeburc's advanced age is usually inter-
preted as some sort of mistake or oversight: a drastic example of the
shortcomings of the poet's style; an example of typical heroic style, which
is unconcerned with such mundane details; or an indication that the one
version of *Kudrun* we possess represents a draft, not a finished work. But
there may be a rather simple interpretation that takes this marriage at face
value and reconciles Hildeburc's age with Kudrun's political intentions.

Because of Hildeburc's advanced age, she and Hartmuot will have no children. If Hartmuot dies without issue, his territories will pass to his nearest relation, his sister, Ortrun, and her children by Ortwin, Kudrun's brother. Hartmuot's lands then will pass from the overlordship of Hagen's kin into their patrimony. The marriage of Hartmuot and Hildeburc is, in this light, the shrewdest political action that Kudrun undertakes, for it is reconquest—a legal, peaceful act of political annexation.

Kudrun combines the best of both mothers. She assimilates Hilde's power and authority, and her fourteen years of humiliation in Gerlint's care ensure her devotion to using that power and authority to maintain the social order. She overcomes Gerlint in their match of obstinacy, and in the process proves she is truly "Hagen's kin" because her heroic endurance shores up the bilineal-based kinship claim she and her mother have advanced. Yet *Kudrun*'s message is not one of radical change but of radical continuity. *Kudrun* is socially conservative insofar as its heroines insist on the rigidity of social hierarchies, but the confrontation between Kudrun and Gerlint betrays the fluidity of hierarchies based on kinship networks. In *Kudrun* the heroine can and must assert how her kindred identity is to be constructed. Not all women are just, as the example of Gerlint shows. *Kudrun* argues, however, that women can learn to become just rulers who use their multiple family allegiances to maintain the social order. In showing a mother and a daughter actively and politically asserting their kinship alliance with each other, *Kudrun* affirms generational continuity between women in a manner that is unique in medieval German literature.

❦ 4 ❦

"In This She Takes after Me"

Queen Isolde and Princess Isolde in
Gottfried von Straßburg's Tristan und Isolde

> Zehn Tage nach ihrem Tode war sie im Traum plötzlich
> wieder da. Als hätte jemand gerufen, zog es mich
> zum Fenster der früheren Wohnung. Auf der Straße
> winkten vier Typen aus einem zerbeulten VW
> einer drückte dabei auf die Hupe. So ungefähr
> sahen die berliner Freunde vor fünf Jahren aus.
> Da winkt vom Rücksitz auch eine Frau:
> meine Mutter.
> —Ursula Krechel, "Meine Mutter" (1977, 5)[1]

BOTH THE ARTHURIAN ROMANCES and the Tristan stories belong to what Jehan Bodel (c. 1165–1210) in his *Chanson des Saisnes* called *li conte de Bretaigne* (l. 9), the "Breton stories," which derived from the lore and legends of the Celtic language regions on both sides of the English Channel.[2] In the Breton stories, heroines play numerous roles: they can be sorceresses, mothers of great men, ladies who inspire or vex the hero, attendants who counsel and assist another lady. Only rarely, however, are they daughters of mothers or mothers of daughters. In the Arthurian tradition, many heroines have no parents at all (Lunete and Laudine in *Iwein*); some have only fathers or male guardians (Condwîrâmûrs in Wolfram's

---

1. Ten days after her death she suddenly, in a dream, / reappeared. As if someone had called out, I was drawn / to the window of our former apartment. On the street / four fellows were waving from a dented VW / one of them was honking the horn. That's more or less / how my friends in Berlin looked five years ago. / Then, from the backseat, a woman also waves: / my mother.

2. Jehan Bodel contrasts the *conte de Bretaigne* with the *conte* or *matieres de France*, which correspond to the genre of the *chansons de geste,* and with the *matieres de Rome,* which correspond to the stories from the ancient world (Bodel 1989, ll. 1–10). The *Eneasroman* belongs to the last category.

Parzival; Queen Guinevere); some have active fathers and passive, ghost-like mother figures whose function is subsumed by the appellative "mother-of-noble-birth" (Enite in *Erec;* Obîe and Obilôt, daughters of King Lyppaut, in *Parzival,* book 7). These heroines appear to be freed from maternal influence, detached from any sort of female lineage. They function in an imaginary world that assigns to men the transmission of knowledge, status, and pedigree across time. The Arthurian heroine ensures the continuity of the male line even as she ennobles and enriches it, while remaining without female ancestors or descendants. Her accomplishments most often culminate in a relationship with a male hero, be he lover, spouse, or son. Assimilated into the hero's story, she is dispossessed of female inheritance.[3]

But the *conte de Bretagne* also contained mother-daughter stories, particularly in the tale of Tristan and Isolde.[4] The Tristan material, which is of Celtic origin, was certainly circulating in Old French literature by the middle of the twelfth century and was known throughout much of Europe by the end of that century.[5] In the Continental versions of this legendary story of adulterous love, the daughter's destiny is both prepared and altered by a gift from her mother, the love potion. Of the earliest surviving Tristan epics, however, only the Middle High German version by Gottfried von Straßburg, *Tristan und Isolde* (c. 1210–1215), elaborates the portions of the story where the mother-daughter plot appears. This situation is doubtless due to the fragmentary state of the surviving Old French epics; both Béroul's *Tristan* (c. 1170–1191) and the *Roman de Tristan* by Thomas d'Angleterre (c. 1172–1175), are extant only in fragments that, as bad luck would have it, record episodes following Tristan and Isolde's sharing of the love potion, when Isolde's mother has already been left behind in Ireland.[6] None of these fragments contains the mother-daughter story, though it seems virtually certain that the full version of Thomas's *Roman de Tristan* did, since it is Gottfried's source. Gottfried's detailed account of the mother-daughter story is unique in the German Tristan tradition as well. Eilhart of Oberg's *Tristrant* (c. 1170 or 1185–1190), which predates Gottfried and relies on a version of the Tristan material related

3. For a groundbreaking study of women's roles in medieval literature, see Ferrante 1975; on women in the Arthurian sphere in particular, see 119–20. This study treats mostly Latin and French literature.

4. The *Lai de Fresne* by Marie de France (fl. c. 1160–1190) is another mother-daughter story; for an interpretation, see Freeman 1988.

5. On Tristan in the Old French tradition, see Zink 1995, 59–61. On Tristan in the German tradition, see Stein 1984.

6. For the Old French texts, see Payen 1989.

to Béroul's sources, assigns *all* of Queen Isolde's actions, with the exception of brewing and bestowing the love potion, to Princess Isolde. The queen is not even named.[7]

Summary of *Tristan und Isolde*

Gottfried's *Tristan* opens by recounting the tragic love story of Tristan's parents, Rivalîn, lord of Parmenîe, a territory in France, and Blanchefleur, sister of King Mark of Cornwall. Gottfried then tells of Tristan's boyhood and youthful exploits, culminating in his arrival at King Mark's court and the unwed Mark's adoption of his nephew, Tristan, as his heir. Tristan kills in a legal duel the Irish champion, Morold, who has for years been collecting cruel tribute (the sons of Mark's highest nobles) from Mark's kingdom in the name of his lord, the husband of Morold's sister, King Gurmun of Ireland. Wounded in this battle by Morold's poisoned sword, Tristan uses disguise and trickery to gain entrance to Gurmun's household as the artist, Tantris. Morold's sister, Queen Isolde, cures him and keeps him on as a tutor to her daughter, Princess Isolde. Upon Tristan's return to Cornwall, Mark decides to woo Princess Isolde, the daughter of his archenemy, and Tristan is sent to Ireland to win the bride. On this second Irish journey, Tristan's true identity as her brother's killer is discovered by Princess Isolde and her mother, but the queen makes peace with Tristan, the marriage between Mark and Princess Isolde is arranged, and Tristan and Isolde depart for Cornwall (the particulars of this part of the plot are recounted in detail below).

The sea voyage brings the fateful event: sharing by accident the love potion prepared by Queen Isolde and intended for King Mark and Princess Isolde on their wedding night, Tristan and Isolde fall deeply in love. Upon their return to Cornwall, the marriage between Mark and Isolde takes place, but the lovers continually plot and intrigue to be together, ably assisted by Isolde's cousin, confidant, and lady-in-waiting,

7. For an edition of Eilhart, see Buschinger 1976. For an English translation of Eilhart, see Thomas 1978.

Many studies comparing the figures in the Old French and German traditions exist. On the female figures in particular, see Deist 1986 and Mälzer 1991.

Gottfried's version, too, is a fragment; it breaks off as Tristan is contemplating marriage to Isolde-White-Hand. Two medieval German continuations exist, both based on Eilhart. The continuations are of interest primarily as interpretations of Gottfried's work, because both continuers read *Tristan* as the hero's tragedy, for whose fall Isolde, as temptress, is to blame. For an anthology offering a panoramic view of the medieval Tristan stories, see Buschinger and Spiewok 1991.

Brangaene, who has accompanied her from Ireland. Torn between trust and suspicion, King Mark counterschemes either to trap the lovers or to prove their innocence. At length, Tristan returns to France, where he marries the sister of a companion, Isolde-White-Hand, whose chief virtue is that her name reminds Tristan of his true love. Gottfried's epic breaks off immediately before this marriage takes place.

In Thomas's version (Gottfried's source), Tristan bitterly regrets the marriage to Isolde-White-Hand and does not consummate it. Isolde, who is still in Cornwall, suffers deeply. She and Brangaene quarrel bitterly, and Tristan's infrequent visits, in disguise, bring little happiness. Then Tristan is severely wounded in France. The local physicians cannot cure him, so he sends for Isolde, who is a healer. But his wife, Isolde-White-Hand, overhears the bedridden Tristan's instructions that the returning ship should hoist white sails if Isolde is on board and black if she is not. When the white-sailed ship is sighted, she tells Tristan that its sails are black. Declaring his unceasing love for Isolde, Tristan dies. Upon disembarking, Isolde hears the cries of lamentation and the tolling of the church bells. She rushes to her dead lover's chamber, embraces his corpse, and dies.

The Education of the Daughter

The mother-daughter story in Gottfried's *Tristan* is developed at great length and culminates in the gift of the love potion. Both mother and daughter are named Isolde. The daughter, Princess Isolde (also known as Isolde the Blonde, or Fair Isolde), is Gurmun and Isolde's only child, selected to become the bride of King Mark, Ireland's archenemy and the ruler of Cornwall, but fated to become the lover of Mark's nephew, Tristan. The mother, Queen Isolde, the sister of the Irish champion Morold (killed by Tristan in battle), is the wise and respected spouse of Ireland's ruler, King Gurmun. The political and social order of the fictional world within which these characters move is congruent with what historians tell us about the organization of kinship and political power in the northern European aristocracy of the twelfth and thirteenth centuries. Marriage was often used instrumentally, as a tool for securing political alliances while keeping wealth, influence, and power within the noble class. The primary bearers of this function were noblewomen, who upon marriage normally left their natal family and entered the households of their husbands.[8] Such a dynastic marriage of convenience between King Mark and

8. For a feminist interpretation of representations of women in late medieval literature based on a structuralist view that sees noble women as objects of exchange between patrilineal families, see Fisher and Halley 1989, 1–17.

Princess Isolde is the premise for the plot of *Tristan*. The plot (that is, the erotic love between Tristan and Isolde), however, comes about because the arranged marriage goes awry, and it does so because Tristan, not Mark, shares with Princess Isolde a love potion that is her mother's gift.

Queen Isolde is depicted as a powerful, knowledgeable, and intelligent woman. Her knowledge of government and diplomacy places her alongside other powerful fictional queens (the queen in the *Eneasroman*, Kriemhild, Hilde, Kudrun, Gerlint), all of whom, in their own right, wield considerable political influence, whether for good or for evil. Moreover, Queen Isolde is an herbalist and physician second to none, a woman whose skills as a healer are augmented by the occult powers made manifest in her clairvoyant dreams and in the love potion. Because these realms of knowledge are conventionally associated in fiction with (magical) female power, her command of them aligns Queen Isolde with the sorceresses who hold sway without male consorts on the margins of Arthur's world.[9] By being placed at the side of a man, however, Queen Isolde is transferred out of the realm of fairies, myth, and magic, the realm to which all-powerful sorceresses are assigned, and into the realm of historical time or patriarchy in a way that diminishes her power. For this sorceress-queen is also a mother who has one child, her cherished daughter, Princess Isolde, to whom she has taught, as the unfolding epic makes clear, many of her skills, but whom she must nevertheless relinquish in marriage—finally and dramatically—to the patriarchal world.

Mothers educate their daughters and guide them into marriage. In brewing the love potion, Queen Isolde is preparing Princess Isolde to fulfill her role in a political system in which alliances are secured through marriage. Her actions parallel those of the queen in the *Eneasroman*, who intends her conversation about love with her daughter, Lavinia, to prepare the way for Lavinia's marriage to Turnus, the queen's favorite. Queen Isolde's actions might also be compared with Hilde's wish to spend a year preparing her daughter, Kudrun, for queenship. In each case, though the motivations and outcomes are different, we recognize the general parameters of a familiar convention about mothers and daughters briefly explored in the introduction to this book. Mothers, through their instructions or through their acts, fashion a notion of female identity for their daughters that depends on becoming an attractive and compliant object of male desire. According to Trude Ehlert, "[Alle Lehren der Mutter] zielen also darauf ab, die Frau zu einem problemlosen Glied der Gesellschaft und einem Instrument der Selbstperfektionierung des

---

9. On the figure of Queen Isolde as a healing woman, see Meister 1990, 1–31.

Mannes zu machen, das sich nur auf diese Gesellschaft und auf den Mann hin ausrichtet" [All the mother's teachings are thus intended to make woman a member of society who causes no problems, an instrument for men to use in perfecting themselves, one that is oriented exclusively toward society and men] (1986, 61). As a notion of total compliance in society's expectations of women, Ehlert's "instrumental function" (1986, 44) often functions as a dominant ideological frame for the development of a mother-daughter story. In the story of adulterous love in *Tristan und Isolde*, however, as in other medieval mother-daughter stories, woman's instrumental function can also become a convention to be defied and a model to be subverted.

When inculcating woman's "instrumental function," the mother seems to reproduce in her daughter the same kind of female identity that the mother herself has acted out, or is in the process of acting out. The goal of the mother's instruction is for the daughter to adopt and fulfill her mother's teachings, in other words, for the daughter to replicate her mother, to become her mother—for Isolde to become . . . Isolde. From the perspective of replication, the mother-daughter relationship is set up to act out a concept of femininity that guarantees continuity at the expense of distinct identities. In such a mother-daughter relationship, change is not supposed to take place, for only when daughters become like their mothers can all women be alike. Yet an ambiguity arises when the notion that all women are similar is linked with the mother-daughter relationship, because the concept of familial generations—mothers and daughters—introduces to that relationship a notion of change over time. Thus the mother-daughter relationship implicitly proposes a female history, which implies change, even as the ideological frame of woman's instrumental function proposes a static notion of female identity, which implies lack of change.

These dilemmas of similarity and dissimilarity between women are given a unique valence by the mother-daughter motif, which shapes them into dilemmas of continuity and disruption. The mother-daughter stories discussed so far move between such contradictory poles in manifold ways. In the *Eneasroman*, the queen forcefully pursues a marriage for Lavinia that may well have brought with it political advantages for mother and daughter. However, her attempt to reproduce in her daughter a politically astute self-awareness is negated by the text's dominant ideological framework of romantic love, which finds its culminating expression in Lavinia's marriage to Aeneas. In the *Nibelungenlied*, Uote encourages Kriemhild to believe that Kriemhild's life as wife and widow will follow the same, uneventful course as Uote's own life, an assurance of similarity that the text undermines with great virtuosity. In *Kudrun*, the positive continuity of leadership and courage between Hilde and Kudrun is guaranteed only after Kudrun has proved that she will not be like Gerlint.

In *Tristan und Isolde*, the likeness between Queen Isolde and Princess Isolde is already suggested by their shared name. In this chapter I shall argue that the continuity between mother and daughter is symbolized by the love potion and that this continuity is both affirmed and disrupted. The gift of the love potion might seem to suggest that Queen Isolde bequeaths to her daughter an almost perfect compliance in woman's instrumental function, as if by means of love Princess Isolde can be enabled to conform perfectly to society's demands on her. However, if we take seriously the notion that Queen Isolde seeks through the love potion to bequeath to her daughter a role and identity that is similar to the role and identity she herself is acting out, we must look more closely to see what that role and identity actually comprise. Paying close attention to the figure of Queen Isolde adds a political dimension to the mother's gift; we see that for Queen Isolde love has provided access to political power. These are some of the aspects of continuity symbolized by the love potion. Of course, as the story is played out, the love potion causes the life of the daughter to take a very different course from the life of the mother, because the love between Tristan and Isolde interferes with Isolde's instrumental function. Yet this disruption, too, may be considered a part of the maternal legacy.

Queen Isolde's Example: How a Noblewoman Wields Political Power

The epic shows Queen Isolde as both an exemplary mother and an exemplary ruler.[10] During Tristan's first stay in Ireland, Queen Isolde demonstrates her exceptional skills as a healer by curing the venomous wound that Morold had inflicted on Tristan—without knowing, of course, that she has saved the life of her brother's killer. She also recognizes Tristan-Tantris's extraordinary artistic gifts and keeps him on to instruct Princess Isolde, showing the attention to her child's upbringing that was, in medieval Europe, traditionally a maternal concern.[11] During Tristan's

10. Not all scholars view the queen in a positive light. For example, Hugo Bekker compares Queen Isolde (together with Brangaene) to the cowardly and intriguing barons at Mark's court, though he later calls her "prudent" (1987, 163) and a "true believer in the bond of married love" (1987, 164) for having brewed the love potion. Belkker's view of Queen Isolde as a scheming, conventional, yet somehow judicious woman who plays a negligible role in political affairs is not supported by my reading.

11. On medieval motherhood, see Atkinson 1991. On the medieval use of the image of St. Anne as a wise mother instructing her daughter, the Virgin Mary, see Sheingorn 1993.

second stay in Ireland, Queen Isolde is called upon to prove her maternal devotion in a series of events that also—and not coincidentally—demonstrate her political skill, her mettle, and her resolve.

Tristan arrives in Ireland to find that King Gurmun has promised Princess Isolde in marriage to the man who can slay a dragon that is devastating the countryside. After killing the dragon and cutting out its tongue, Tristan is overcome by the dragon's poison and falls into a deep stupor. An ambitious Irish seneschal, long enamored of Princess Isolde, comes upon the dead dragon, cuts off its head, and swaggers back to court, where he gleefully announces that he has won the princess. Both Princess Isolde and her mother forcefully reject a humiliating match with an upstart subordinate as an alliance below Princess Isolde's worth, but the king, judicially bound by his vow and the evidence, is powerless to prevent it. Under these somber and threatening circumstances, it falls to Queen Isolde, ably assisted by Brangaene, to save her daughter.

Using her occult powers, the queen summons a dream that reveals to her the true circumstances of the dragon slaying; she organizes the search for the wounded hero, which is carried out together with Brangaene and Princess Isolde; she again heals Tristan, near death. The women recognize Tristan as Tantris, Isolde's former tutor. These events happen secretly, known only to the queen, the princess, and Brangaene. It also falls to Queen Isolde, however, to orchestrate a public repudiation of the seneschal using the knowledge that the true dragon slayer has been found.

The scenes in which Queen Isolde successfully carries out the plan of repudiating the false dragon slayer present a critical examination of the range, the limits, and the dependencies of the power of a wise and well-respected queen.[12] They thus provide testimony on the role Queen Isolde attempts to secure for her daughter through the love potion. They also show the queen publicly asserting the continuity between mother and daughter. The queen carries out her plan in two segments, the first private and the second public. King Gurmun has set a date for a public hearing to adjudicate the seneschal's claim, and he has summoned his neighbors, vassals, and kin to take part and to advise him. When they are assembled, he seeks their counsel, summons the queen, takes her aside, and privately confers with her. Revealing that she knows the truth, the queen comforts and reassures him, and then she tells him how to proceed: he should

12. Classen, arguing that Gurmun is a passive and weak king, and Queen Isolde is "in control of the governmental affairs" (1989, 81), contends that this situation reflects "a literary model of matriarchy which . . . clearly reflected historical reality of the earlier and high Middle Ages" (86). Far from supporting Classen's claim that Queen Isolde enjoys supreme power, my reading of the text reveals that power's very real limitations and dependencies.

6. Top band: Queen Isolde, Princess Isolde, and Brangaene on horseback, discovering the decapitated dragon. Middle: The women, flanked by a retainer, pulling the armed and unconscious Tristan out of the pond and then (right) riding away. Bottom: Tristan sitting in a bathtub. The scroll reads "Tristan sat in the bath. 'Lady, alas, what is this?'" [tristran in dem bade saz frŏwe owe waz ist daz]. To Tristan's right stands Princess Isolde (*ysot* written on her arm) who, having recognized Tantris as Tristan, her uncle's murderer, now raises his sword to strike him dead. Simultaneously, Princess Isolde looks over her shoulder at her mother, Queen Isolde, (wearing a crown over which is written *regina* [queen], who stands behind her and restrains the blow by grabbing hold of the sword blade. In the final sequence, two women (Princess Isolde and Brangaene?) converse. Gottfried von Straßurg, *Tristan und Isolde*. Munich, Bayerische Staatsbibliothek, cgm 51, 67v (mid-thirteenth century). Courtesy of the Bayerische Staatsbibliothek.

calmly summon the assembly, affirm without fear that he will keep his vow, wait for the two Isoldes to arrive, allow the seneschal to set forth his demand, and then turn things over to her by ordering her to speak.

> When you command me, then I will speak for you, for Isolde, and for myself.

> sô gebietet mir'z, sô spriche ich
> vür iuch, vür Isôt und vür mich.[13] (ll. 9753–54)

Evidently this scheme suits the king, and evidently he trusts his wife, for although the queen tells him no more, he proceeds as she has privately advised. The narrative now advances to the public hearing. As the crowd whispers, Queen Isolde and Princess Isolde enter the palace, greet the assembled noblemen, and take their places beside the king. Before the assembly the seneschal asserts that his love for Princess Isolde has caused him to risk his life to slay the dragon. Brandishing the dragon's head as evidence, he demands the princess as his rightful reward. At this point the queen interrupts and throws down the gauntlet, forthrightly accusing the seneschal of deceit. The seneschal attempts to head off this dangerous intervention by demanding that the king speak for himself. The king does speak, but only to follow the plan his wife has laid out and formally turn the proceedings over to her.

> "Seneschal," said the queen, "the man who desires such a rich reward as my daughter, Isolde, without having earned it, truly, he covets too much." "Egad," said the seneschal, "Lady, you are acting badly; why are you saying this? My lord, who is to decide this matter, can surely speak perfectly well for himself. Let him speak and reply to me." The king spoke: "Lady, speak, for yourself, for Isolde and for me!" "With thanks, Lord, I shall do so."

> "truhsaeze" sprach diu künigîn
> "der alsô rîlîchen solt,
> als mîn tohter ist, Isôlt,
> ungedienet haben wil,
> entriuwen des ist alze vil."
> "ei" sprach der truhsaeze dô
> "vrouwe, ir tuot übel, wie redet ir sô?
> mîn hêrre, der ez enden sol,

---

13. Hereinafter, citations refer to the line numbers from Gottfried von Straßburg, 1984. All translations are my own. I have consulted the excellent English translation by Hatto (1960).

der kan doch selbe sprechen wol.
der spreche und antwürte mir."
der künec sprach: "vrouwe, sprechet ir
vür iuch, vür Isôt und vür mich!"
"genâde hêrre, daz tuon ich." (ll. 9820–32)

In the ensuing confrontation between truth and deception, conventional notions of femininity and masculinity become weapons in the struggle. The seneschal deploys conventional notions of masculinity on his own behalf when he parades as a dragon-slaying he-man. He also deploys misogynist conventions when he wonders aloud why the queen is speaking instead of the king; his remark not only attacks the queen's public authority and implies that as an important man he should not have to deal with a woman but also may even suggest that a king should not allow a mere woman to speak for him. The queen, then, must defend her right and authority as a woman to publicly represent the king and to bindingly arbitrate a case in which she has located all the evidence. She begins by rejecting the seneschal's claim while sarcastically praising his masculinity:

> Seneschal, your affections are pure and good; truly, you show manly resolve. You are certainly worth a good woman. . . . Yet you have claimed for yourself a deed and a courageousness of which you are entirely innocent, so it has been whispered to me.

> "truhsaeze, dîne minne
> die sint lûter unde guot
> und hâst sô menlîchen muot.
> du bist wol guotes wîbes wert.
> . . . .
> du hâst dir selbem ûf geleit
> eine tât und eine manheit,
> der dû mit alle unschuldic bist,
> als ez mir zuo gerûnet ist." (ll. 9834–37, 9841–44)

When Princess Isolde seconds her mother's rejection of the seneschal's suit, he declares how much he worships her and how much he has risked on her account. (This show of devotion strikingly recalls the self-abasement in love practiced as a privileged enactment of masculinity by the courtly love poets of both the Old French and the Middle High German schools. The seneschal has already played another conventional masculine role, that of the dragon-slaying warrior.) Yet Princess Isolde rejects

him again. At that, the seneschal turns face and launches into a misogynist diatribe on the fickleness and contrariness of women:

"Yes" said the other, "I know full well that you act just like all other women.
You are all created alike, alike in nature and in spirit: you always believe evil
is good, and good you always believe to be evil. This nature is strong in all
of you. You have got it backwards in every way. . . . You love that which
hates you and hate that which loves you. How can you think like that?
How can it be that you love the opposite of things so strongly, something
we see in you so often?"

> "Jâ" sprach der ander "ich weiz wol,
> ir tuot vil rehte als elliu wîp.
> ir sît alle alsô gelîp,
> alsô g'artet unde gemuot:
> iuch dunket ie daz arge guot,
> daz guote dunket iuch ie arc.
> diu art ist an iu allen starc.
> ir sît verkêret alle wîs
>
> . . . .
>
> ir minnet, daz iuch hazzet;
> ir hazzet, daz iuch minnet.
> wie sît ir sus gesinnet,
> wie minnet ir sô harte
> der dinge widerwarte,
> daz man der sô vil an iu siht!" (ll. 9866–74, 9880–85)

The seneschal's behavior mimics the misognistic flip-flop between
worshiping women and vilifying them that, feminists argue, lies at the
heart of courtly love poetry.[14] Queen Isolde herself implies as much a few
lines later when she taunts the seneschal by saying that he has set forth
his misogynist arguments "just like a lady's knight should" [rehte alse ein
vrouwen ritter sol] (l. 9905). The entire scene may well be a deliberate
send-up of the superficial and fickle notions of courtly love, which will be
further diminished through implicit contrast with the soon-to-be-ignited
erotic passion and loyalty shared by Tristan and Isolde.[15] In any case, the
rejection of the seneschal by mother and daughter also hinges on the issue of hierarchy. In addition to being a coward and a boaster, the
seneschal is in his social standing so much lower than Princess Isolde that

14. See, for example, Burns 1985.
15. For an account of the scholarly controversies surrounding Gottfried's attitudes towards courtly love poetry and a differing account of this scene, see Dietz 1974, 61–72.

he is an unworthy partner for her. Just as in *Kudrun*, in which Hilde and her daughter, Kudrun, rejected a marriage of Kudrun with Hartmuot on the grounds of his inferior rank, so Queen Isolde works mightily to avoid a union for her daughter that would join her with a man of much lower station.

With his attack on the woman he supposedly adores, Princess Isolde, the seneschal introduces conventional notions of femininity to the trial scene. In his speeches, these conventions become misogynist utterances. Not only does the seneschal name as typically feminine the traits of contrariness and fickleness, he asserts that they are shared by all women. Though ostensibly aimed at Princess Isolde, this statement about traits common to all women also renews the seneschal's attack on the queen's political authority, for it impugns her ability to act wisely and judiciously—solely on the grounds that she is a woman. The queen counters this attack with great shrewdness. She takes up the seneschal's rhetoric and agrees with the conventional traits he assigns to women. She argues, however, that men, too, can act like women, and points to the seneschal himself as an example. In sum, the queen attacks the seneschal by openly faulting him for being effeminate.

"Seneschal, your arguments are forceful and shrewd, when one regards them shrewdly. They sound as if they had been thought up secretly by women in their chambers. Furthermore, you have put them forth just like a true lady's knight. You know women's ways too well. You have advanced too far in that, and it has robbed you of your manly nature."

"truhsaeze, dîne sinne
die sint starc unde spaehe,
der spaehe an sinnen saehe.
si habent dem gelîchen schîn,
als sî ze kemenâten sîn
in der vrouwen tougenheit bedâht.
dar zuo hâstû si vür brâht
rehte alse ein vrouwen ritter sol.
du weist der vrouwen art ze wol.
du bist dar în ze verre komen.
es hât dir der manne art benomen." (ll. 9898–9908)

It is the seneschal's contrariness—by his own definition a womanly trait—that betrays his effeminancy, continues the queen. The seneschal should leave such things to women like herself and reassert his manhood by no longer desiring someone who does not desire him, namely, Princess

Isolde. The queen laces her speeches with puns that question the seneschal's masculinity: in her opening speech, when she says that he deserves a good woman, the phrase she uses can also mean that he has the same worth as a good woman ("du bist wol guotes wîbes wert," l. 9837). Given the sarcastic tone of the above speech, calling the seneschal a lady's knight ("rehte alse ein vrouwen ritter sol," l. 9905) implies not only that he is a lady's knight but also that he is a lady's man and even a ladylike knight. Goading the seneschal by quoting his own words back at him, the queen spurns his advances to Princess Isolde in her own name:

> "You have bound the ways of women too tightly to your rope. You love that which hates you; you wish for that which does not wish for you. . . . She [Princess Isolde] is indifferent to many a man who desires her greatly and among those you are in first place. She takes after me in that. I never cared for you, either. I know Princess Isolde feels the same way; in this she takes after me."

> "du hâst die selben vrouwen site
> sêre an dîn seil gevazzet:
> du minnest, daz dich hazzet;
> du wilt, daz dich niht enwil.
> . . . .
> ir ist der vil unmaere,
> dem sî doch vil liep waere,
> der dû ze hant der êrste bist.
> daz selbe ir von mir g'artet ist.
> ich selbe enwart dir ouch nie holt.
> ich weiz wol, alse entuot Isolt:
> ez ist ir g'artet von mir." (ll. 9912–15; 9931–37)

The queen has taken up the notion that all women are alike and turned it against the seneschal. If women can be defined by their contrariness, then, on the basis of his actions, the seneschal is a woman, too. Generalizations about women include him. It is only in the specific case of forcefully rejecting the seneschal's suit that the queen clearly asserts the similarity of women—not of all women, to be sure, but of mother and daughter. Twice the queen repeats virtually word-for-word the same phrase: in her dislike of you, Princess Isolde takes after me. To say this, the queen uses the phrase *ir ist g'artet* that was introduced by the seneschal himself in his first diatribe against women (l. 9869). The meanings of the noun *art* from which the verb derives range from "innate quality, nature, essence" to "origin, descent, birth."[16] In the ideology of nobility of the twelfth and thirteenth centuries, these meanings existed on

16. On the usage of the term *art*, see Schwietering 1961.

a continuum; an aristocratic lineage's possession of wealth, privilege, and political power, for example, was believed to rest on inborn qualities of the lineage that raised it above other classes. Nevertheless, the seneschal intends primarily the first set of meanings; he is talking about qualities belonging to all women. The queen, however, links her use of the phrase with the mother-daughter lineage, as if to say that in this matter, Princess Isolde demonstrates that she is truly Queen Isolde's descendant. By so doing, the queen evokes those connotations of *art* that indicate not so much the feminine nature of mother and daughter as the fact that their likes and dislikes derive from their royal origins. The seneschal argues from the perspective of sexual difference; the queen argues from the perspective of what we call *class*, but what in medieval terms should be called *estate*.

The seneschal, then, argues from the perspective of essences; the queen argues from the perspective of estate and from the perspective of actions. Men, the queen asserts, can imitate women, though in the seneschal's case this redounds to his disadvantage; by analogy, women can also emulate men, and there is no reason to think that they cannot do so well. The queen does not argue this point; rather, she proves it through her actions in the public hearing itself. Her verbal prowess in steering towards truth a legal process that is being abused by a swindler is a consummate demonstration of her skill as a ruler. His misogynistic utterance rebounds on the seneschal when the queen entices him into making such a convincing display of his own contrariness and deceitfulness that he stands trapped between the virile posture of dragon slayer and lover of women he has claimed for himself and the cowardice and misogyny he shows at the hearing. Every word Queen Isolde speaks, even those where she artfully claims women's frailties for herself, bolsters her right and her ability as a woman to represent political authority.

Queen Isolde has challenged the seneschal to reclaim his manhood by owning up to the truth and by stepping down from his deceitful claim. She has openly established the continuity between her own and Princess Isolde's rejection of him. She now finishes her speech by proclaiming that she knows the identity of the real dragon slayer. Enraged, the seneschal demands the opportunity to fight this unknown challenger, and a combat date is set for three days hence.

In the three-day hiatus between the two public hearings, Princess Isolde discovers that Tantris is, in fact, their enemy, Tristan. Once more Queen Isolde, aided by Brangaene, is the agent who turns potential catastrophe into success. Restraining herself and Princess Isolde from taking revenge on Tristan for being Morold's killer, she learns of Tristan's mission to win Princess Isolde for King Mark, approves of it, and brings about a reconciliation between King Gurmun and Tristan. Queen Isolde comprehends that King Mark's proposal includes not just a way out of a humiliating alliance with the seneschal, not just a truce between former enemies, but also an opportunity for the princess to also achieve rank and privilege commensurate with her own, namely, the status of a queen. In other words, Tristan's proposal, on Mark's behalf, opens up for Princess Isolde the possibility of replicating her mother's destiny, of becoming like her mother, of "living up" to her name.[17]

The second hearing of the seneschal's case proceeds initially very much like the first one; the seneschal addresses the king and is answered by the queen, who summons Tristan. However, Tristan's entrance signals that gender issues have been set aright (the "real man" has appeared) and order has been restored; the king is now fully in charge and takes over the hearing. The queen's last public act is to direct mocking barbs at the seneschal, whose kin, humiliated by his obvious lies, force him to back down in disgrace. Before the assembled nobility, Tristan presents King Mark's suit, and King Gurmun and Tristan negotiate and affirm the marriage settlement between King Mark and Princess Isolde. During this part of the scene, the queen does not speak, although both she and Isolde are still present. Affairs of state are again firmly in the hands of men.

While Tristan makes ready for the return journey to England, Queen Isolde brews the love potion. She entrusts it, along with instructions for its use, to Brangaene, who is to accompany Princess Isolde to Cornwall, and implores Brangaene to look after Princess Isolde well, for "the best part of my life lies with her" [an ir sô lît mîn beste leben] (ll. 11471). With tearful farewells, Princess Isolde departs on the journey that will take her to erotic passion with Tristan and marriage with King Mark. Ireland, King Gurmun, and Queen Isolde recede from the story; mother and daughter will never meet again.

Women's Political Authority and the Love Potion

The possibilities and limits of the queen's power are exemplified in her prominent public role during the seneschal's first hearing. The sequence of events—a private conference of the king and queen followed by her public advocacy—drives the point home that although Queen Isolde may be rich, wise, beautiful, witty, and perceptive, her access to political power is predicated solely on the esteem and love with which her husband the king regards her. She cannot exercise power publicly unless he loves and

17. There is a third Isolde in the story, Tristan's wife, Isolde-White-Hand. On this figure, see Schöning 1989.

trusts her enough to command it. Susan Mosher Stuard locates the historical context for the queen's vulnerability in changes in noblewomen's opportunities for political power during the twelfth and thirteenth centuries (the period of time in which, of course, the many versions of *Tristan und Isolde* were written).

> In the aftermath of this change [the process during the twelfth and thirteenth centuries by which the inheritance of queens was integrated into the crown lands] a queen might still influence a husband or son, and his bureaucracy, or as the surviving parent, she might be trusted with the power of regent during the minority of her son. But neither her office itself nor her inheritance rights and marriage portion sustained her position. Royal women, except those who could claim the right of primogeniture in the event that they had no brothers, lost authority. If they exerted any power at all, they derived it from their intimacy with and access to the reigning king. (Stuard 1987, 163)[18]

Although Gottfried's epic says nothing about Queen Isolde's intentions when she brews the love potion, the argument advanced in the previous pages shows that for a queen's daughter to inherit a queen's power, Queen Isolde must find a suitable mate for her daughter, one who will love and trust her. The love potion is a tool for securing noblewomen's access to political power. Queen Isolde intends not just that love find a place in the arranged marriage between King Mark and Princess Isolde, not just that, as Hugo Kuhn has pointed out, love cement the political alliance between Ireland and Cornwall (1976a, 163–64), but that a queen's political skills and political interests can be expressed in her daughter's marriage. In other words, this epic is not simply about erotic love or simply about male power struggles. It is also about a noblewoman's knowledge of her limited access to political power and about her manipulation of the resources available to her in order to secure recognition of her authority, her legitimated right to power.

The mother's gift of the love potion means that while acquiescing in her daughter's (and her own) instrumental function, Queen Isolde still desires to give her daughter a measure of control over it. For, as is shown by the paradox of Queen Isolde's first exchange with her husband, when she orders him in private to command her in public, Queen Isolde knows

---

18. Facinger 1968 analyzes queenship as an office in her important study of Capetian queens. See Parsons 1993 for a study of Plantagenet queens, and Shadis (1994, 1996) on the patronage of queens.

that for powerful women the rule of love and the exercise of public power are inextricably linked.

What Queen Isolde appears to want for her daughter is a love that ensures the stability of patriarchal society. The love potion is intended to guarantee not just that Princess Isolde experience love but, more important, that she be able to wield legitimate political authority in her arranged marriage. However, the mother's promise miscarries calamitously: not Mark and Isolde, but Tristan and Isolde drink the potion and become bound to each other through an erotic love, characterized by cycles of pain and pleasure, that will last until (indeed, bring about) their deaths. Queen Isolde's gift seeks a replication, for Princess Isolde, of Queen Isolde's life as a woman who strategically deploys normative conventions of femininity, such as wifely obedience, without overturning them. Yet the magical agent that was to have ensured this replication becomes instead a violent agent that shatters the maternal legacy, replacing it with a fate that could not be more different from Queen Isolde's. Princess Isolde never bears children. Princess Isolde is not honored and loved by a trusting husband but, rather, alternately tyrannized and petted by a suspicious and jealous husband, King Mark. Princess Isolde is neither consulted in private nor given any public authority but, rather, repeatedly tested and even forced to submit to a public ordeal. Her life makes a sham of wifely obedience, of women's subordination to their husbands. For her, private deceits and public denial become necessary so that she and Tristan can maintain and endure their passion. Princess Isolde experiences love as a force that is irreconcilable with the normative social and sexual order. Love has become the solvent that threatens to erode the substance of patriarchy.

The Mother's Gift

The love potion is the gift of a loving mother to her cherished daughter. The mother intends it to shore up the daughter's power and authority as a ruler in her new existence. She gives it in hope that it will aid her daughter in establishing a way of life that resembles the mother's own. With the love potion Queen Isolde seeks to bestow upon Princess Isolde the gift of continuity between mother and daughter, imagined as the replication of a particular kind of access to political authority. In many ways, as we have seen, such a simple continuity does not come to pass. On the contrary: the effect of the potion is disruptive, undermining Princess Isolde's position at court and making her the target of suspicion and intrigue. Yet the disruptive force unleashed by the love potion is not only destructive[19] but also transformative. With it, women's pursuit of power through love is transformed into an erotic love that insistently lays bare the elemental contradictions in the social order with which it remains fundamentally incompatible. Queen Isolde's ambition to harness this potentially disruptive power in order to secure her daughter's political authority may have failed, but her gift retains its transformative power and becomes a subversive force.

The subversive force of the love potion must also be seen as a part of the mother's gift, as an aspect of the mother-daughter relationship. The love potion subverts Princess Isolde's instrumental function and liberates her from the law of wifely obedience. Isolde and Tristan experience the incompatibility of love and social roles. Their love disrupts the existing social order, exposes the hypocrisy and weakness of Mark's court, and in the scene of Isolde's ordeal even dislodges the hierarchies of law and divine justice.

The transformative effects of the love potion reverberate even in the narrative organization of the Tristan story. In the world before the love potion, events are ordered as a progression towards a goal (which is the potion itself); afterwards, the meetings and partings of the lovers are the story's events. These episodes share an internal ordering as repetitive cycles that oscillate between separation and union, suspicion and certainty, denial and affirmation, pain and pleasure. The sequence in which they appear in the narrative, however, has little internal development. In this sense, the narrative organization of these episodes is bewitchingly arbitrary and random: they belong in no particular order and could be rearranged in various ways. And indeed, although the various medieval versions of the Tristan legend agree on the sequence of events leading up to the love potion, the events following it are presented in different sequences in the many different versions (Stein 1984, 365). Progression towards an ending reenters the narrative only during the final scenes, when Tristan and Isolde must die.[20]

Most importantly, the subversive effects of the love potion do not altogether disrupt the continuity between mother and daughter, although the love potion does separate Princess Isolde from the way of life her mother

---

19. In referring to Thomas's version, Ferrante writes: "The woman Tristan loves incarnates the destructive force of love, the all-consuming passion that excludes any other ties. She unleashes the destructive impulse in him, the death-wish, bringing on the surrender of a noble spirit to a passion that must kill him" (1975, 93).

20. This conclusion is based on other versions of the story, because Gottfried's *Tristan* breaks off before the marriage of Tristan and Isolde-White-Hand.

wished to bestow upon her. Princess Isolde never has the loving marriage that ensures her authority, but her character traits make her more and more resemble her mother. Although their outward lives differ, the likeness between mother and daughter increases as the epic unfolds. Joan Ferrante makes rhetorical use of this resemblance between mother and daughter when, in discussing the relationship of Princess Isolde and Tristan in Thomas's version, she repeatedly summons the image of Queen Isolde: "In a way, she [Princess Isolde] draws him [Tristan] to her by magic (the poison on Morolt's sword comes from her mother); she gives him new life (her mother cures him of that wound and later of the dragon's poison); and she awakens him to the passion of love (the love-potion, too, comes from her mother)" (1975, 93). Princess Isolde learns to manipulate language and rhetoric with the same skill and shrewdness her mother showed against the seneschal. She masters one precarious situation after another by drawing on resolve, cunning, and intelligence that resemble her mother's, even though Princess Isolde uses her strength and wit to defy the conventions her mother embodied. In the end, Princess Isolde is, like her mother before her, a master healer, and like her mother the only person with the skill and knowledge to cure Tristan after all learned medicine has failed. Her mother's powers and knowledge are truly her own.

In the story of Tristan and Isolde, erotic love is not only the source of pleasure and enduring attachment but also the source of abiding grief, sorrow, and pain. Perhaps this duality, too, is a part of the maternal legacy, a piece of the continuity between mother and daughter. In the first half of the story, Queen Isolde expresses her devotion to her daughter: "To me nothing has ever been as dear as you" [mir wart nie niht sô liep sô duo] (ll. 10296). We are told that King Gurmun cherishes Queen Isolde and we are shown that Queen Isolde respects her husband, but we learn of Queen Isolde's feelings only with regard to her daughter. Perhaps her love for her child surpasses her love for her husband. Yet the attachment between mother and daughter is ended as a living and growing relationship when Princess Isolde departs Ireland. Queen Isolde and Princess Isolde are separated from each other irrevocably. We learn that on the journey to Cornwall, Princess Isolde weeps and mourns, feeling abandoned and bereft. Her sense of abandonment as she sails to her new life in a way prefigures Tristan's sense of abandonment as he dies. Princess Isolde will never be reunited with her mother, nor will Tristan be reunited with Isolde. This is great pain indeed.

We learn nothing of what Queen Isolde feels as her daughter departs; it is left for us to imagine. Let us imagine then that the loss of this beloved child, the knowledge of having to abandon her, is a kind of death; that having to give up this daughter, completely and utterly, to her patriarchal role is the source of fierce and permanent sorrow; that the love potion is a kind of compensatory gift, a gift that seeks to recompense the daughter for the loss of the mother and that carries with it the strength of the mother's devotion and the force of her grief. One is reminded of Adrienne Rich's words: "The loss of the daughter to the mother, the mother to the daughter, is the essential female tragedy" (Rich 1986, 237). Perhaps these losses, these multiple abandonments, live on in the suffering Tristan and Isolde experience as a part of love. Their sorrow in love might then be no more and no less than a transmuted form of Queen Isolde's grief at having to surrender her child to the patriarchal order so that mother and daughter may survive.

A Historical Epilogue

In the medieval world, the ration of power a mother could bequeath to her daughter seems modest at best. In fact, we know very little about the lives of ordinary medieval mothers and daughters; the historical record is too paltry, the documents too sparse, much evidence lost, and much, much more never written down. But fragments of knowledge surface. For example, there is the testimony of Béatrice de Planissoles, a member of the minor nobility in France, who was interrogated by the bishop of Pamiers, Jacques Fournier, on a charge of heresy in 1320 (some one hundred years after Gottfried's *Tristan* was written) in the village of Montaillou (Duvernoy 1978, 1:260–90). Her words entangle the mother-daughter bond with the sphere of secrets also mastered by Queen Isolde: magic and subversion.[21] They also tell us from what a love potion, such as the one Queen Isolde brewed for her daughter Isolde, could be made.

---

21. On medieval magic, see Kieckhefer, who notes in passing that "while there is no reason to think that women alone practiced magic, both pagan and Christian writers ascribed it primarily to them" (1990, 39). The mother-daughter-magic nexus resurfaces often in Kieckhefer's book (81–82, 192).

However, we must be careful not to confuse medieval bias with medieval reality. Kieckhefer reminds us that "a particularly important element in the stereotype of the witch was the centrality of women. . . . This bias may owe something to the role of women as popular healers with herbs and charms, but there is no reason to think that women had a monopoly on these or other forms of magic. . . . Ultimately the vulnerability of women in this context must be seen as a corollary to the precarious position women held in late medieval society (and, for that matter, in almost every society through history)" (197–98). On erotic magic, see Kieckhefer 1991.

Béatrice has been shown some "very suspect things" (Geary 1992, 202) that were found among her possessions. After confirming that these things belong to her she explains the origin and function of each in turn. About a cloth stained with blood she says:

> "These clothes stained with blood are from the menstrual blood of my daughter Philippa and because this baptized Jew [a woman] had told me that if I kept some of her first blood and that I gave it to her husband or to another man to drink he would never be interested in another woman" (Confession of Béatrice, widow of Othon de Lagleize of Dalou, from the inquisition records of Jacques Fournier, bishop of Pamiers, 1320). (Geary 1992, 202)

Two mothers—one fictional (Queen Isolde, married to a king), and one real (Béatrice de Planissoles, interrogated by the inquisition and convicted of heresy)—have each harnessed the forces of a proscribed realm (the supernatural, the marginalized, the knowledge from an assimilated non-Christian universe as represented by "the baptized Jew") in order to secure for their daughters a measure of autonomy in a male-dominated world. Love, brought about by ingesting menstrual blood, will render a man's economic, legal, and social control of his wife—virtually total control—accessible to her. Béatrice de Planissoles goes even farther than Queen Isolde, for her potion does not bind her daughter, but merely the daughter's spouse or lover. Thus she seeks to give her daughter the gift of control over the only "commodity" she possesses in patriarchy: her sexuality, her desirability, her instrumental function.

In curbing the potential adultery of her husband, Philippa may possibly strengthen marriage, both the institution and her own; yet, in gaining power over her husband, she weakens and subverts the medieval convention of male rule and female subordination in marriage. Philippa's power over her husband may make her complicitous in upholding marriage, the social institution that represented the destiny of virtually all well-connected medieval women and symbolized the hope of economic and social security for women poor in goods and kin. Yet Philippa's control over her husband promises her agency in her marriage, some rein to do as she pleases. It restores to her a measure of independence in a social institution that insists on her dependency. This independence can also be read as a form of "marriage resistance" smuggled into the institution of marriage.[22]

Perhaps in a world where the parameters for women's choices fol-

22. The term "marriage resistance" is borrowed from Adrienne Rich (1983, 157).

lowed economic, social, and cultural lines differing from our own, the boundaries between complicity, collaboration, and resistance should be redrawn. What matter that the voices of these women are brought to us by men? Before us flashes one of those rare moments in medieval history, a moment that illuminates what Adrienne Rich calls the "double-life" of women. For a second the veil in which recorded history shrouds so much of medieval women's lives is rent and we glimpse truths that can only be discerned as shadows: the shadows of women's embattled and subversive knowledge of their oppression; their collusion and resistance in the struggle for empowerment; their love for one another.

5

"If Men Desire You, Then You Are Worthy"

The Didactic Mother-Daughter Poem Die Winsbeckin

Das Thema startet
Zum Thema Gesellschaft—
ISOLDES STECHENDER BLICK

Anna ist 20, Isolde ist 40
Isolde minus 20 ist Anna
Isolde minus Anna ist zwanzig
Isolde plus Anna ist Isolde
Anna plus x ist y
. . .
Anna Isolde Gesell Gesell
Anna Isoldes Mutterschaft, Gesellschaft
Isolde Annas Vaterland, Schaft
—Elke Erb, "Das Thema startet" (1985, 66–67)[1]

AN ANONYMOUS mother-daughter exchange about aristocratic love that belongs to the genre of didactic poetry (*Lehrdichtung*), *Die Winsbeckin* appears in manuscripts together with an anonymous, father-son didactic poem entitled *Der Winsbecke*. The titles scholars use for these poems are found only in the Codex Manesse (Heidelberg cpg 848). The title of *Der Winsbecke* in manuscript Tübingen mgf 474 reads: "This book is called valuable counsel" [Ditze bûch heizzet der wertlich rat]; The title of *Die Winsbeckin* in manuscript Copenhagen 662, 8° reads: "This is the mother's

---

1. The topic starts / On the topic of society— / ISOLDE'S PIERCING GAZE / / Anna is 20, Isolde is 40 / Isolde minus 20 is Anna / Isolde minus Anna is twenty / Isolde plus Anna is Isolde / Anna plus x is y / / Anna Isolde fellow fellow / Anna Isolde's motherhood, society / Isolde Anna's fatherland, shaft.

teaching" [Ditz ist der mûter ler].[2] Because of the courtliness of the poems and their allusions to classical texts of medieval German courtly literature (for example, the Arthurian epics *Parzival* and *Iwein*), the poems are sometimes dated to c. 1210–1220, but the question of dating them with any certainty is a vexed one.[3] The first half of the thirteenth century seems likely.

Die Winsbeckin depicts an aristocratic mother teaching her daughter about sexuality, love, and honor. In the forty-five stanzas of the poem in Albert Leitzmann's standard edition (1962), this tutelage takes place as a dialogue between mother and daughter, with the mother speaking twenty-five stanzas and the daughter twenty. This lively give-and-take revisits a number of issues discussed in previous chapters, foremost among them the notion of women's collusion in or resistance to their instrumental function. In *Die Winsbeckin*, the mother's teachings suggest that woman's happiness comes from creating herself as a perfect object for male desire, not from getting or doing what she, as a subject, might want. The mother inculcates in her daughter a set of rules and norms for instrumentalizing herself. The mother thus collaborates in the construction of an other-directed definition of woman as the object of male desire.

Yet an argument that focuses on the mother's authority, which is underwritten by her conformity to patriarchal expectations, may overlook the resistance encoded in the daughter's objections. My reading follows the hints of alternatives that surface in the daughter's resistance to her mother's lessons, which, I argue, is both defined and subtly devalued by means of humor.[4] This humor is chiefly conveyed in two ways. First,

2. The original meaning of the titles *Die Winsbeckin* and *Der Winsbecke* in the Codex Manesse is obscure: it is now impossible to determine whether these designations referred to an author or a place or the fictional characters themselves. A manuscript closely related to the Codex Manesse, Stuttgart cod. HB XIII.1 (known as the *Weingartner* or *Stuttgarter Liederhandschrift* now in the Württembergische Landesbibliothek) leaves both poems untitled. For a list of manuscripts and pertinent bibliography see the standard edition by Leitzmann, revised by Reiffenstein (1962, vi–x; xix–xx). The Codex Manesse is in the Heidelberger Universitätsbibliothek, Tübingen mgf 474 is in the Tübingen Universitätsbibliothek, and Copenhagen 622, 8° is in Det Kongelige Bibliotek.

3. Kuhn gives these dates in his article in the first edition of the *Verfasserlexikon* (1953a, 1013). Ehlert (1985, 47) follows Kuhn. In his recent volume of *Geschichte der deutschen Literatur im hohen Mittelalter*, Bumke does not assign a date (1990, 333–34). Behr argues that while frequent echoes of Wolfram von Eschenbach firm up the *terminus post quem* 1210, there is no clear reason for a breakoff date of 1220: the firmest evidence for the *terminus ante quem*, dates from the 1290s (1985, 379).

4. To support my reading of *Die Winsbeckin* as a didactic poem that employs elements of comedy, I cite Kuhn, who called *Die Winsbeckin* "diese Parodie des "Winsbecken" ins Feminine" (*Der Winsbecke* parodied in the feminine) (1953b, 1016). Kuhn does not explore or explain what he means by parodic or which aspects of the text he views as being parodic.

a comic effect is evoked by the poem's gradual dismantling of the stereotypes of the experienced, rational mother and the innocent, emotional daughter. Second, humor manifests itself in the daughter's utterances, which typically display a comic rift between literal and rhetorical levels of meaning. Finally, by paying attention to the discord between the mother's teachings and the daughter's responses in *Die Winsbeckin*, my reading also explores the issues of continuity and discontinuity, or similarity and dissimilarity, between mothers and daughters.

To make these aspects of *Die Winsbeckin* more visible, I also briefly discuss *Die Winsbeckin's* male-voiced counterpart, *Der Winsbecke*. In Leitzmann's standard edition (1962), *Der Winsbecke* is made up of eighty stanzas that are divided into two parts. The first fifty-six stanzas are called *"das alte Gedicht"* (the Old Poem), which is a monologue by the aristocratic father, who advises his son on courtly behavior. The second twenty-four stanzas are called *"die Fortsetzungen"* (the Continuations). A block of six stanzas at the beginning of this part is spoken by the son, who rejects his father's worldly values and advocates a life of piety. In the remaining eighteen stanzas the father enthusiastically endorses a religious way of life. The division of the poem into these two parts has long been accepted by scholars; recently, however, Hans-Joachim Behr has argued persuasively on codicological and stylistic grounds for accepting all eighty verses as a unified poem, a practice I follow here (1985, 379).

Scholars believe that *Der Winsbecke* provided the model for *Die Winsbeckin*, in terms of the stanzaic form and in terms of didactic content. The poems are complementary in other ways, most notably in the largely stereotypical gender roles they depict. For example, *Der Winsbecke* discusses many practical deeds and actions, while *Die Winsbeckin* chiefly explores an inner, emotional world. Trude Ehlert has shown that these two texts talk about women and men in a way that preserves a traditional understanding of gender relations as separate spheres that are ordered hierarchically (1985). Suzanne Barth follows this line of argumentation and ties it into the poem's emphasis on the daughter learning self-restraint, a motif medieval conduct literature traditionally directed at aristocratic girls, which here serves to further the daughter's subordination to a courtly ideology defined from a male perspective (1994, 75–84). The female sphere complements the male sphere and is subordinate to it. The expected subordination of women to men is a part of the ideology of love constructed in *Die Winsbeckin*. Yet at the same time, the daughter's voice bears witness to the contradictions and resistances that pressed upon patriarchal discourse about women.

The Male-Voiced Counterpart

The father-son poem *Der Winsbecke* explicitly explores male authority. The first fifty-six stanzas are a monologue spoken by the noble father. Addressing his son, the father instructs him on the exemplary fulfillment of various civic, masculine roles. Generalized precepts on various worldly topics for seemly behavior are presented in these stanzas: knighthood *(Ritterlehre)*, weaponry *(Waffenlehre)*, courtly behavior *(Hoflehre)*, household management and etiquette *(Hauslehre)*, and also, briefly, love *(Minnelehre)*.[5] This completes the "Old Poem." In the "Continuations," the son takes the floor, briefly but commandingly advocating a religious way of life *(WE, st. 57–61, 64)*.[6] Moved by his inexperienced son's piety, the father renounces the world in eighteen verses addressed to God *(WE, st. 62–63, 65–80)* and delivered in the form of a prayer-like confession: "I make my confession here to you" [ich tuon hie mîne bîhte dir] *(WE, st. 77, l.1)*. In the last stanza (st. 80) the father puts into action the plan formulated by the son in stanza 61, forgiving his enemies, freeing his serfs, renouncing his tariffs, and founding a home *(Spitâl)* for the poor, to which he and his only *(eingeboren, st. 80, l.9)* son will retreat.

Within aristocratic circles, prestige and reputation are vital issues for both sexes. Male and female virtue share the notion that honor is the highest good in society, but the ethic of honor is constructed differently for men and for women. *Der Winsbecke* constructs honor as a set of rules codifying moral actions in the outside world. Such a code of honor also holds for the religious segment, in so far as the quest for spiritual forgiveness follows the analogy of a vassal establishing honorable relations with his lord, and involves a number of practical activities (building a hospital, freeing serfs) that bear material witness to the vassal's contrition. The construction of honor for these noblemen also testifies to the fact that they perform in a diverse and wide-ranging world of kin, court, and church; in *Die Winsbeckin,* however, the noblewomen's world is narrow, entirely focused on dealing with social consequences of love as sexual passion, which is defined in terms of male desire.

The etiquette and protocol of polite, courtly speech—how one talks, to whom one talks, and how one is talked about—are central concerns for

---

5. According to Ehlert's tally, nine of *Der Winsbecke's* first fifty-six verses deal with worldly love *(Minne)*, which is little more than a sixth of the poem. Since the twenty-four additional verses of the "Continuations" do not discuss worldly love at all, their addition further diminishes the thematic importance of love. In *Die Winsbeckin,* thirty-three of forty-five stanzas deal directly with love (1985, 55).

6. All citations are from Leitzmann 1962. *Der Winsbenke* is abbreviated as *WE* and cited by stanza and line. All translations are my own.

the aristocratic father in *Der Winsbecke* as well as for the aristocratic mother in *Die Winsbeckin*. Yet the self is understood in *Der Winsbecke* as a subject acting on society through men's capacity to take action in order to ensure prestige. Men are granted agency in the pursuit of a good reputation, whether in the secular world or in the spiritual one that transcends it. They act upon the world as well as in reaction to it. In contrast, as we shall see, mother and daughter in *Die Winsbeckin* are acted upon. Their power of agency is limited to actively shaping themselves into virtuous objects. To be talked about and looked at as an embodiment of modesty comprises a woman's honor. The historical record demonstrates the many ways in which medieval noblewomen strove to actively shape their worlds, but nothing hints of this in *Die Winsbeckin*. The mother constructs an ideology of love in which a woman's range of possible action is largely confined to imposing self-control and restraint upon herself. This self-restraint and modesty is the largest component of female honor. Women do not act; instead, they react. By conforming to this model of honorable passivity, the mother suggests that the daughter take up the paradoxical position that is a commonplace in medieval depictions of women: a woman is granted the status of self, of subject, only when she acts as an object.

The Mother-Daughter Dialogue

A reading of the poem shows the essential themes: the ideology of love as male desire and the objectification of women, the issue of comedy, and the continuity and discontinuity between mother and daughter. The aristocratic mother, characterized positively as a "womanly woman" (ein wîplîch wîp) (*WI*, st. 1, 1. 1) in the poem's only narrative insertion, opens the poem by warmly asserting her love for her daughter and her intention to instruct her on how to preserve womanly honor and reputation ("dîn lop wîplîch"), *WI*, st. 3, 1. 6).[7] In reply, the daughter proclaims her obedience to her mother and God (st. 2) and her intention to avoid false pride; the woman who becomes the topic of dishonorable talk, she asserts, will have difficulty acquitting herself again ("müelich si sich verrihtet wider") (*WI*, st. 4, 1. 10).

Mother and daughter often return to the notion, implicit in what the daughter has just said, that women establish themselves socially not as speaking subjects, but rather as the objects of other people's speech. The

7. All citations are from Leitzmann 1962. *Die Winsbeckin* is abbreviated as *WI* and cited by stanza and line. All translations are my own.

following examples make the importance of public approbation clear: "For this the best people will thank you," spoken by the mother [des sagent dir die besten danc] (*WI*, st. 11, l. 5); "Winning the praise of worthy people is something I will always pursue," spoken by the daughter [daz ich der werden lop bejage, / dâ wil ick immer jagen nâch] (*WI*, st. 16, ll. 1–2); "Thus you earn the approval of worthy people," spoken by the mother [sô dienestû der werden gruoz] (*WI*, st. 29, l. 7). In stanza 5 the mother connects this concern with reputation to a generalized and stereotypical set of courtly ideals for women:

> Dear child, you should be in good spirits, and yet still conduct yourself in a well-bred manner, for then your prestige will be worthy of the best people and your garland of roses will suit you well.

> Trût kint, dû solt sîn hôchgemuot,
> dar under doch in zühten leben,
> sô wirt dîn lop den besten guot
> und stêt dîn rôsenkranz dir eben. (*WI*, st. 5, ll. 1–4).

Stanza 5 presents a catalogue of courtly virtues: refined high-spiritedness *(hôchgemuot)*; living in a genteel fashion *(in zühten leben)*; honor *(êre)*; moderation *(mâze)*. However, a good standing at court means not just learning the rules for proper behavior; it also means learning the rules for how one should be perceived by others. Recalling in the closing lines of stanza 5 a stereotype of courtly poetry, the mother tempers her ideals with practical advice:

> Don't cast too many wild glances when cunning spies are about you.

> schiuz wilder blicke niht ze vil,
> dâ lôse merker bî dir sîn. (*WI*, st. 5, ll. 9–10)

After being asked to spell out what "wild glances" are, the mother explains that they are the "roaming" eyes that indicate a restless mind, and that results from immoderation. She counsels that averted eyes are best. Heartily agreeing, the daughter speculates that youth often misguides young noblewomen. The mother reminds her daughter that a modest woman's reputation is established by others. This stanza reminds us of the behavioral constraints that the notion of womanly honor placed upon women. An honorable woman does not speak; she is spoken well of. She does not watch, but instead looks away. She neither seeks eye contact nor surveys her world but instead veils her own glance in order to present herself as the modest object of other people's looks. Such counsel is commonplace in advice to noblewomen (Bumke 1986, 470–72). A woman's agency is limited to actively restraining herself as she strives to make herself into a passive object.

After a short, affectionate exchange of mutual praise, the daughter abruptly asks to change the subject, and the mother does so (*WI*, st. 12). The mother's tutelage now turns to sex: living up to society's norms will awaken in men sexual desire.

> Beloved daughter, be even-tempered, so that heart and mind attend to self-control. Be constant and good-hearted, then you will be blessed by well-born people. If you can rise in virtue, then many a worthy man will lie with you in his dreams. If you are to grow old with good fortune (together with the beauty you already possess), then the forest will be laid waste on your account.

> Wis, liebiu tohter, wolgemuot,
> daz doch der zuht die sinne phlegen.
> wis staeter site, von herzen guot,
> sô hâstû guoter liute segen.
> mahtû die tugent ûf gewegen,
> dir wirt von manegen werden man
> mit wûnschen nâhen bî gelegen.
> soltû mit sælden werden alt
> zuo der schoene, die dû hâst,
> durch dich verswendet wirt der walt. (*WI*, st. 13, ll. 1–10)

The notion of desire presented here is clearly identified with men's sexual appetites; love is male desire that a woman attracts and excites by displaying exemplary passivity in the face of male action. The stanza's closing image of a forest being laid waste in knightly tournaments because of the daughter's beauty and modesty sustains the idea of male active desire fueled by exemplary passive feminine beauty. The eloquent rhyme scheme *segen/ûf gewegen/bîgelegen* (blessing/move towards/lie with), expressing that blessings are the way to bed, reinforces the message that socially sanctioned, demure, virtuous, asexual feminine conduct arouses male lust.

The next stanza records the first moment when the daughter's voice breaks the poem's didactic tone in a humorous way. The daughter's previous responses to her mother's teachings have been respectful and compliant, but now she is indignant. Vehemently rejecting the idea that male lust reflects any honor back upon her, and at the same time asserting her intention to remain virtuous, she replies:

Mother, is this supposed to honor me, that someone fancies a roll in the hay with me? My mind and senses can't believe that this might actually be true. . . . I do not wish to be held responsible if someone desires to tumble me on the grass.

> Sol, muoter, mir daz êre sîn,
> ob man mîn wünschet ûf ein strô?
> es ahtent niht die sinne mîn,
> daz im von wârheit sî alsô.
> . . . .
> ich wil dar an unschuldic sîn,
> ob man mich wûnschet ûf daz gras. (*WI*, st. 14, ll. 1–4, 9–10)

The daughter's indignant rejection of sexuality (here equated with male lust) places her in a category of femininity already familiar from previous chapters: the innocent, virginal daughter. Her response resembles Kriemhild's outright repudiation of love in the *Nibelungenlied*. As in the *Eneasroman*, when Lavinia asks how she can live without her heart, the daughter's resistance to her social role as a desirable object is converted to comedy. The representation of the daughter's innocence is designed to entertain the reader. In the case of *Die Winsbeckin*, this is carried out by means of the daughter's anger and her use of uncourtly images drawn from the peasant sphere ("a roll in the hay," "tumble me in the grass"), which contradict the demure behavior and modest speech that, as the mother has been explaining, are expected of a lady at court. As we saw previously with Lavinia and Kriemhild, the daughter's response is hyperbolic; resistance and exaggeration, apparently, go hand in hand.

From the perspective of the mother, the daughter in *Die Winsbeckin* has a lot to learn. Her mode of expression and her imagery are too frank; she must learn to moderate her feelings and express herself in the euphemisms of the courtly sphere. Like her counterparts in the *Eneasroman* and the *Nibelungenlied*, the mother brings the perspective of experience to the mother-daughter exchange. In *Die Winsbeckin*, the mother answers her daughter's question in the affirmative: to be lusted after *does* increase a woman's honor. To correct and educate her daughter, the mother reaffirms the link between male desire and societal approval.

If men often think of you and desire you, then you are worthy.

> so man gedenket ofte an dich
> und wünschet dîn, sô bistû wert. (*WI*, st. 15, ll. 9–10)

The mother's reply redirects the mother-daughter exchange away from the daughter's implicit critique of sexual relations at court and towards the daughter's display of anger and her use of uncourtly language. In a manner similar to that of Lavinia and Kriemhild, the daughter now expresses a measure of compliance with her mother that stops short of outright agreement. Deferring to her mother, the daughter stipulates only that her future husband be an honorable man:

> Any man can desire me but the one to whom my garland is granted he must be squarely steadfast.

> ein ieglîch man mac wünschen mîn:
> swem aber mîn schapel werden sol,
> der muoz vil wol gevieret sîn. (*WI*, st. 16, ll. 8–10)

Mother and daughter continue their discussion of desire and the proper management of its social consequences by taking up the problem of seduction. The daughter has stated that secret, "lowly" love (whether by "lowly" she refers to a cross-class marriage or to erotic passion is at first unclear) causes scandal and torment; she will love only a steadfast man (*gevieret*, *WI*, st. 16. l. 10). But the problem, says the mother, is how to identify steadfast men among the hordes who speak sweet words (*WI*, st. 16–17). In a run of three stanzas, the daughter proudly proclaims her faith in her own ability to avoid seducers' snares. She will be guided by her knowledge of how these things were done according to the "good old ways" (in alten siten, *WI*, st. 20, 1. 1); then men asked for love decorously, carrying women tenderly in their hearts, while women either said no with good manners or said yes with so much sense that they never had cause to lament (*WI*, st. 18–20).

Perhaps the daughter has been reading too much, for she has obviously paraphrased the roles of poet-lover and lofty lady that govern so many courtly love poems (one thinks particularly of the work of the poet Reinmar of Hagenau). From the mother's perspective, however, such an allusion is not sophisticated, but naïvely overconfident. Having viewed the daughter's notion of sexual relations at court as too realistic, the mother now views the daughter's notions of what sexual relations at court used to be and should be again as too literary and naïve. The mother apparently feels that the daughter's speech only demonstrates her immaturity and vulnerability. She counters it by introducing a new concept of love, which now appears in the guise of a transcendental, extrasocietal, coercive force that strikes men and women equally (*WI*, st. 21).

The mother's authoritative role is underscored in the next stanzas, as she works out for her daughter some of the consequences of this notion of a kind of love that does not seduce but rather compels. She teaches that this love is invincible, that only God can protect one from it (*WI*, st. 22–23), that it has addictive qualities, and that practicing virtue is the only defense if it overpowers one (*WI*, st. 25). During these speeches the mother also gives it a name: she calls it *hôhiu minne* or "lofty love" (*WI*, st. 25, l. 8), a term originating in courtly love poetry. By using the terminology of the courtly love lyric, the mother has effectively appropriated the literary, courtly sphere upon which the daughter based her resistance. Yet this new notion of love is also cast as a natural force; it comes from outside of the human sphere. In introducing such a notion to underwrite her exposition of what society expects of women, the mother suggests that the social is natural. The notion of coercive, transcendental love thus also underwrites the position of object that the mother insists is the only appropriate role for the daughter. We should also note that the mother's notion of love is in no way original; in its salient features, it recasts the ideology of love that we heard the queen expounding in great detail to Lavinia in the *Eneasroman*.

At first, the daughter continues to challenge her mother's teaching. She stubbornly asserts that she is personally untouched by love, immune to its lure, and that she would rather die than love. She also suggests that her mother's teachings betray experience of love. Such a suggestion might imply criticism, but it also seems to propose a new basis for the mother-daughter exchange, in which the mother would share with her daughter her personal memories (*WI*, st. 24). However, the mother pointedly refuses to discuss her experiences, and it is at this point that the daughter's resistance begins to falter (*WI*, st. 25). She has been shaken, it would appear, by her mother's description of the coercive and violent nature of lofty love, for her speech links her pledge of compliance with the fear of violence and with the fear of losing her mother's affection.

> Would you not still love me, if love compels my mind and senses and does so by force? I don't want to despair, so reveal your will to me, and I will serve you always.

> bin ich dir deste lieber iht,
> ob minne twinget mînen sin
> und von gewalte daz geschiht?
> ich wil niht in dem zwîvel sîn:
> nû tuo mir dînen willen schîn,
> daz diene ich immer umbe dich. (*WI*, st. 26, ll. 1–6).

The daughter's response makes explicit the implied violence in the mother's explanations; the rape imagery is unmistakable. Further, it makes clear the daughter's dependence on her mother, for the daughter complies out of fear that lofty love might cause her to forfeit her mother's love. This leads the daughter to further statements that highlight the centrality of the mother's desire in the daughter's self-fashioning. Not only does the daughter assert that any honor she attains will in fact truly belong to the mother ("gevar ich wol, diu êre ist dîn," *WI*, st. 26, l. 7). She also tells the mother that she has decided to accept as satisfactory *(guot)* those aspects of herself that please the mother (*WI*, st. 26, ll. 8–10). This is an extraordinarily clear statement of socialization: the fear of the loss of maternal love induces compliance, while identity is shaped (consciously, one should add) by amplifing those aspects of oneself that please the mother. The daughter asserts in every way the continuity between herself and her mother.

To her daughter's assertions the mother responds by returning to her lessons on virtue: when coercive love strikes, the daughter should direct her love towards an honorable man, but she should not give in to him (*WI*, st. 27). The daughter must renounce the role of subject in love and acknowledge her vulnerability as its object. Alluding to the Fifth Commandment, the daughter again ardently promises to obey her mother and suggests a remedy should the strength of coercive love awaken her disobedience.

> Dearest mother, then I desire if you should see the results of such love in me, that you tie me up with ropes.

> > vil liebiu muoter, sô ger ich,
> > ob dû die volge sehest an mir,
> > daz dû mit riemen bindest mich. (*WI*, st. 28, ll. 7–10)

In asking to be tied up, the daughter asks that her status as object be literalized. Exaggeration again provides the occasion for humor; the daughter has taken the loss of self-control implied in the notion of all-powerful love too literally. This moment of comedy both highlights and masks the violence of love and its virtually complete objectification of the daughter, by interpreting her fear of coercion (whether by human or supernatural forces) as laughable. Again, the mother responds by recasting the daughter's literalism in abstract terms. She introduces the concept of *huote* (physical or moral guardianship, being chaperoned or watched over) to the poem, which she elaborates over three stanzas (*WI*, st. 29–32). Refusing the role of her daughter's chaperone, the mother instead advocates that the daughter exchange the wish for literal bonds with the allegorical bonds of the self-imposed guardianship of constancy.[8] Finally, in stanza 33, she praises her daughter's virtue.

The daughter responds by returning to the topic she introduced in stanza 26, maternal and filial love. She now affirms the reciprocity of their mutual affection: just as the mother carries her daughter in her heart, so the daughter's heart is full of love for her mother (*WI*, st. 34, ll. 1–6). She then returns to the lesson at hand by inquiring further into the nature of sexual love, *Minne* (*WI*, st. 34, ll. 8–10). Ovid called love Venus, says the mother, and it is a kind of spirit or ghost (*WI*, st. 35). The daughter now introduces a new problem to the discussion: that *Minne* causes people to love across class boundaries, thus breaking down social categories (*WI*, st. 36). It is a strange God who causes such behavior, she claims, and it would be better if the highborn desired the highborn and the lowly the lowly (*WI*, st. 36, ll. 8–10).[9]

The mother's reaction to this rudimentary social critique of *Minne* is to insist that love elevates whoever embraces it, that it is a sovereign force not subject even to royalty, and that it ignores the weak-minded (*swachen muot*, *WI*, st. 37, l. 6) and the lowly (*der nidern*, *WI*, st. 37, l. 10) altogether. In other words, the mother narrows her definition of *Minne* so that it cannot include anyone beyond her estate; for her, *Minne* is a class-bound phenomenon. But this explanation does not assuage the daughter, who

8. The mother elaborates on the difference between guarding women and trusting them to watch over themselves. The former she advocates only for inexperienced, ignorant women who do not look after their honor themselves. She also alludes to male abuses of *huote*: not only is the counsel of friends absolutely necessary, but guardianship based on suspicion or jealousy (*kranken wân*) harms women's honor. It is worthless, she says. Her words hint, nevertheless, at the mistreatment and abuse of power to which medieval women were exposed.

9. The issue of class was already raised by the daughter in stanza 16, when she talks about the weak or lowborn (*den swachen*, *WI*, st. 16, l.2) and lowly or sensual passion (*schwacher heimlîch*, *WI*, st. 16, l.6). *Swach*, which I translate as "lowly," may refer to class as well as a weakness for sensuality. Since the ideology of desire produced in this poem links low birth with greater sensuality, the distinction may be moot. The terminology mother and daughter use in stanzas 36–44 is "low" (*nider*) and "high" (*hôh*). These are also "code" words in the courtly love lyric that usually stand for "sensual" love and "ennobling" love, respectively. The later, *hôhiu minne*, was already introduced by the mother in stanza 25. The dichotomy of low and high love is emblematized in Walther von der Vogelweide's famous lines: "Low love is the name of the kind that weakens one so that one (or: the body) strives for inferior love: this love hurts in an unpraiseworthy manner. High love inspires mind and spirit to ascend towards lofty nobility" (*nideriu minne heizet diu sô schwachet / daz der lîp nâch kranker liebe ringet: / diu minne tuot unlobelîche wê. / hôhiu minne reizet unde machet / daz der muot nâch hôher wirde ûf swinget*, L 47, 5–9). (The standard scholarly notation for Walther's poetry refers to the page and line numbers of Lachmann's edition).

returns to the threat of violence inherent in the mother's conception of love. Such love would do her violent harm (*si tœte mir gewalt*, *WI*, st. 38, l. 1) if it forced her to love in a manner that would compromise her honor. She asks to be taught how to be compelled toward honor. That the daughter's reaction is spoken completely from the point of view of being the object of love (and even her suggested solution remains within that perspective) is underscored by her insistent use of images of violence and capture. Yet by skeptically questioning the mother's precepts, the daughter continues to resist.

In response, the mother changes her definitions of "high" and "low," which now refer to virtue and vice in love, respectively. Again she assures her daughter that *Minne* is incompatible with anything "lowly" (*WI*, st. 39). That such reasoning contradicts the mother's earlier claims of *Minne*'s universal power does not escape the daughter's notice. Expressing skepticism based on experience, she returns to the issue of "high" and "low" love in a way that conflates the issues of class and vice. Though but a child in years, she has heard and seen enough intrigues to know that such love causes dishonor and hardly deserves her loyalty. In her words:

Love ought not allow a lowborn heart of jaded virtue to desire above itself, nor should it allow highborn lovers to succeed among the lowly.

> si sol niht lâzen hôhe gern
> ein nider herze tugende kranc
> und hôhe minner nider gewern. (*WI*, st. 40, ll. 8–10).

To this the mother replies that love and dishonor are antithetical, for curiosity, not love, is to blame for dishonorable behavior (*WI*, st. 41).

The dissonance between class-bound and ethically bound notions of love is addressed by mother and daughter in different ways. The mother simply denies that love is anything other than an aristocratic, virtuous force. The daughter, on the other hand, is aware of the contradictions in the mother's teaching. For her, love is a transgressive force. It blurs the boundaries between highborn and lowly both in social and in moral terms. Both mother and daughter wish to reconcile love with honor. The mother does so formalistically, by defining *Minne* so that any dishonorable passion does not belong to it. Thus she preserves her notions of nobility and honor intact. The daughter is unwilling to deny the evidence of her experience. To her, the reconciliation of love and honor is a fragile and embattled thing. She believes that love is a potential threat to the aristocratic self-fashioning advocated by her mother.

It is important to note that this disagreement between mother and daughter restates in some measure the opposing modes of the literal and the abstract/rhetorical that they have come to represent. The daughter's knowledge of experienced reality, in which lovers in fact often act dishonorably, is coherent with the literalism of her previous speeches. In the earlier examples ("a roll in the hay," "tie me up with ropes"), the daughter's literalism was humorous. These last challenges, however, are more serious, for they signal a skepticism that undermines the very basis of the mother's notion of love.

For the daughter, love is the site of contradiction; for the mother, love is the site of harmony. The mother cheerfully constructs an ideology of love that banishes any evidence of its social contradictions. Her answers have repeatedly recast the daughter's objections—at times according to a principle whereby the literal is recast in symbolic terms (from real ropes to inner vigilance), at times according to a principle whereby the literal is systematically abstracted out of the domain of love. We come to see that the mother is largely demonstrating how to *talk* about love. Her ideology of love is a rhetoric of love.

At this point, the daughter resigns herself to accepting her mother's word. If love possesses the laudable ways your mouth *(dîn munt)* claims, says the daughter (always a literalist), it would be wrong to continue struggling against it. She asks that her mother teach her the rules for the school of love (*WI*, st. 42). In a reply of three stanzas, the mother supplies three general rules of love for women (*WI*, st. 43–45). First, an honorable woman does not envy other honorable women. Second, an honorable woman avoids those who speak ill of others, seeks out the company of the wise, and speaks properly herself. And

> The third rule teaches us that we should be courteous and even-tempered, completely without malice, completely without anger, with womanly ways and womanly goodness, and at the same time wise in virtue.

> > Diu dritte regel uns lêret, daz
> > wir sîn in zühten wolgemuot,
> > gar âne nît, gar âne haz,
> > wîplicher site, wîplîchen guot,
> > dar under tugentlîchen vruot. (*WI*, st. 45. ll. 1–5)

In the closing, the mother returns to the requirements for the embodiment of perfect womanhood that were already set out in stanza 13. Yet the struggle between the literal and the abstract, between experience and rhetoric, that runs through the poem has smuggled itself into the last image used by the mother to evoke the ideal of an honorable, virtuous woman.

If we follow this advice steadfastly, then the guardianship of good fortune will cover us, so that no storm can dirty us: We go to bed with honor and we proceed into the day without a veil.

> sîn wir dem râte stæte bî,
> sô decket uns der sælden huot,
> daz uns kein weter selwen mac:
> mit êren wir ze bette gên
> und âne sloiger and den tac. (*WI*, st. 45, ll. 6–10)

The cyclical imagery of rest and motion, day and night suggests the enduring quality of "unsullied" female virtue. The mother intends to say that modesty and virtue secure an honorable reputation for women. Yet on a literal level the imagery she chooses offers up a sexualized female body, bedded by night and unveiled by day. This image connects back to the mother's teaching that modest behavior arouses men. The image of the sexually available female body suggests that even when women adopt virtuous ways, they remain within the economy of male desire, and that the fundamental purpose of female virtue is to make women sexually available to men.

Comic Elements

The daughter's challenges and her resistance to her mother's teachings introduce an irony and ambiguity that expose the fissures in the patriarchal conventions of female identity. In *Die Winsbeckin* the mother's message is that women are to accommodate themselves to their instrumental function vis-à-vis men. Modesty and virtue ensure women's honor, and both men and the force of love desire only virtuous women. The daughter also aspires to maintain her honor. She reacts strongly to the loss of control and agency that she must experience in an economy of love that gives her only one role: that of object. Though she never claims a position as desiring subject, her reactions hint that she believes that she can shape and inhabit a feminine identity that, however reactive, is nonetheless free of (male) sexuality. In such reactions, the daughter hints at female self-definition and self-determination, matters which the test may treat comically but which it cannot erase. When the mother teaches that even modest female behavior excites male lust, she renders the daughter's concerns utopian, but she cannot remove her daughter's insistence on a different perspective.

The differing perspectives of mother and daughter give rise to an exploration of love that is replete with comic elements. Only *Die Winsbeckin* contains humor; there is nothing to laugh about in *Der Winsbecke*, which is unrelentingly serious—indeed, preachy—in tone. In great measure, the humor in *Die Winsbeckin* is achieved through creating a split between the speaker and her message, a disparity that is left to the audience to decode. I earlier discussed the humorous qualities of the daughter's indignant rejection of male lust (*WI*, st. 14) and of her timorous request for physical restraints should love overwhelm her (*WI*, st. 28). A further example can be found in the daughter's repeated assertions that she does not condone the force of love but instead spurns it—a reaction of comic blindness. The daughter's repeated avowals of immunity from love are hyperbolic, and this exaggeration is enacted at the level of the text, for this is the only time in the entire poem when the daughter speaks *three* consecutive stanzas (*WI*, st. 18–20). That is to say, she protests too much. We are asked to believe that her resistance demonstrates only that the conclusions she has drawn from her not inconsiderable knowledge of the world are wrong; she is denying the poem's "truth" (so enthusiastically enacted by her mother) that the subversive power of love will capture her as well. As we have seen, such resistance and exaggeration characterize the daughter throughout the poem. Her self-divided speech repeatedly achieves an effect it does not (from her point of view) intend—laughter. Such dividedness is a critical feature of how *Die Winsbeckin* establishes its conception of womanly virtue and desirability, a dividedness that comes about in the tensions between intended and actual messages, between literal and symbolic levels of meaning, between people's social experiences of love and an idealizing rhetoric of it.

The mother is also a comic figure acting out the clash of these polarities. The bearer of courtly values, she is nevertheless constructed as a tease, who has personal knowledge of *Minne* to which she alludes but which she will not divulge. The self-proclaimed authority on female modesty, she is nonetheless made to express herself in imagery that exposes the bodiliness of women for all to see. She proclaims herself an expert on male desire and human passion, yet she alleges that these tumultuous forces respect the social order. Nor are her choices of role models for her daughter above suspicion. In stanza 11 she asks her daughter to emulate the lady-in-waiting, Lûnete, from the Arthurian romance *Iwein*, who "counseled her widowed mistress to marry her husband's murderer, Iwein, as the best possible guarantee of her crown and country" (Mustard and Passage 1961, 434), advice that is cited by the author Wolfram von Eschenbach in *Parzival* as being opportunistic, hasty, and fickle.[10]

---

10. Wolfram von Eschenbach, *Parzival*, 253, 10–14 and 436, 4–10. In both instances, Wolfram compares this inconstancy and haste unfavorably to his character Sigûne's unwavering fidelity even after her lover's death.

Die Winsbeckin and, to an even greater extent, *Der Winsbecke* contain repeated echoes of and allusions to Wolfram's work.

As in the *Eneasroman*, the stereotypes of experienced mother and innocent daughter are invoked, only to be progressively dismantled as the
poem proceeds. By the end of *Die Winsbeckin*, it is unclear which of the
women is the more knowledgeable, which more naïve. Together, mother
and daughter seem one person in a before-and-after depiction illustrating
the omnipotence of desire: the daughter enacts the "before" state of innocence, which is ignorance, while the mother enacts the "after" state of experience, which is delusion.

Dialogue, Authority, and Gender

The status of the speaking mother and the speaking daughter is paradoxical, contradictory. Neither is in control of the meanings her utterances
create. The comic dimensions of their speech suggest that it is difficult for
women to maintain control of their reputation for modesty and honor
even as the mother's message strenuously insists on the necessity of it.
This double-talk is congruent with the dialogue form chosen for *Die Winsbeckin*, which is, in effect, dividedness in action, dividedness translated
into form.[11] It is the banter between the women—the daughter's insistent
questions and the mother's incomplete answers, the daughter's outbursts
and the mother's corrections—that makes the clash of meanings a part of
the poem. The dialogue is really a comic debate.

In contrast, *Der Winsbecke* is dominated by the father, whose monologue (st. 1–56, 62–63, 65–80) is only briefly (though decisively) inter-
rupted and redirected by the son. The monologue form chosen for *Der
Winsbecke* buttresses the poem's ambition to speak earnestly of truth. A
monologue spoken by the father is also the form adopted in the popular,
didactic, rhymed-couplet text known as *Der deutsche Cato*, a translation of
a collection of Latin rules for moral living widely represented in German
compilation manuscripts.[12]

The choice of form—monologue for father and son versus dialogue for
mother and daughter—is related to the issues of authority and gender.
The father's voice is an authoritative voice; it holds forth without interruption. Even the surviving parodies of *Der Winsbecke* and *Der deutsche
Cato* repeat the use of a monologue by the father.[13] Although in *Der Winsbecke* the son in his role as the divinely inspired innocent formulates the

---

11. Glier is to my knowledge the first to point out the significance of this stylistic choice
(1971, 33–35).

12. For an edition of *Der deutsche Cato*, see Zarncke 1852. On the transmission and use of
the text, see Henkel 1988 and Westphal 1933, 42–48.

13. The parody of *Der Winsbecke* appears in Leitzmann 1962, 67–71, and that of *Der
deutsche Cato* in Zarncke 1852, 144–53.

religious ethic that will replace the father's worldly code, his wisdom can best be given binding form through the mouthpiece of the father. In contrast, in *Die Winsbeckin* the authority of both the mother's experience and the daughter's innocence is undermined, as we have seen, by the comic give-and-take of the dialogue form.

The undercutting of female authority is significant in view of the fact that *Der Winsbecke* grants authority to the male speakers precisely because of parental experience and filial innocence. The father is a wise (and, in the end, contrite) man of the world; the son is an innocent whose lack of worldly knowledge guarantees the excellence of his spiritual advice. Father and son are constructed not as self-divided but rather as unified speakers. Nobility, authority, worldly and spiritual virtue all reinforce one another. Who father and son are, what they express, what they intend, and what they teach are one; the speaking male subject and his message present a unified whole in which each guarantees the integrity of the other. Exchanging one doctrine for another does not blur or modify the male speakers' identities; the son remains the divinely inspired innocent, and the father becomes a penitent and wise man of the world. In the end, father and son share one road but remain two types.

This is not the case for mother and daughter in *Die Winsbeckin*. As we have seen above, a clear demarcation between the stereotypes of experienced mother and innocent daughter is not reinforced but blurred. The comic debate in which mother and daughter engage tends to merge these two stereotypes. The daughter's resistance, presented as comedy born of ignorance, ridicules the struggle for a different destiny, making it seem all the more illusory. Yet her experience of the world has been sufficient for her challenges to reveal the abstracted and idealized basis of the mother's advice. These challenges in turn undermine the authority out of which the mother presents her knowledge. Nevertheless, the mother's advice proposes that the daughter follow in her mother's footsteps in the "school of love." The daughter is supposed to make herself a copy of her mother.

The poem's emphasis on desire masks the fact that, for heterosexually active medieval women, the spheres of sexuality and procreativity (conception and birthing) overlapped.[14] Doubtless the daughter will herself soon become a mother. Although *Die Winsbeckin* contains no instructions about motherhood (the birth, rearing, and education of children), it is not too far-fetched to supply this dimension to our interpretation of the poem, especially since it is precisely the cycle of procreativity that is broken in *Der Winsbecke* when father and son enter their spiritual retreat. Yet mother and daughter remain in the world, where the daughter, with the advent of sex-

14. For an excellent, succint statement of different views of medieval women's sexuality, see Green 1990.

7. *Die Winsbeckin.* The lively conversation between the mother (seated) and her daughter (standing) is indicated by their hand gestures. From the Codex Manesse, dated to the first third of the fourteenth century. Heidelberg, Universitätsbibliothek, cod. pal. germ. 848, f. 217r. Courtesy of the Universitätsbibliothek Heidelberg.

8. *Der Winsbecke*. The father speaks while his son listens. Heidelberg, Universitätsbibliothek, cod. pal. germ. 848, f. 213r. Courtesy of the Universitätsbibliothek Heidelberg.

ual maturity, may well come to share her mother's worldly destiny: motherhood. This movement towards continuity and similarity is prefigured in the blurring of types enacted in the poem. The differences between mother and daughter are already unstable, and they may well be undone by the daughter's experience of sex and motherhood. For all of the comic dissonances separating mother from daughter (and, indeed, each from herself), their types tend to merge and the daughter's fate may duplicate the mother's. The potential polarity of the stereotypes of experienced mother and innocent daughter is revealed instead to be stages of a woman's life, places on a continuum. Mother and daughter are fundamentally similar; the distinction between them is blurred and temporary.

The father-son pair insists on distinct identities even while maintaining connection; the mother-daughter pair insists on likeness even while playing with separateness. The gender difference between these male and female generational pairs is corroborated by the illustrations that accompany the poems in the *Codex Manesse* (see Figures 7 and 8). The gestures of father and son indicate their distinct roles: the father talking (using an explanatory gesture in which the index finger of the right hand touches a finger of the left hand), the son listening (indicated by his folded hands). Their clothing and appearance also separate them. The father's dress—rich robes, with fur collar and sleeve lining, as well as a hat—signal his status as a wealthy and prominent nobleman, while the son's plain, high-collared garment represents a simple, generic version of noble dress. Mother and daughter, however, are much more closely matched. They are both using the speech gesture, so their body postures mirror each other's. Richly dressed, mother and daughter are clothed similarly; the mother's mantle is lined (perhaps with fur), the daughter wears a full dress covered by a tunic lined in a third fabric. Both women's clothing has gold collars and cuffs. While the father-son and mother-daughter pairs both use details of hair and headdress to indicate age, there are also subtle distinctions based on gender. The father's beard and grey hair signify wisdom and age; the women's headdresses indicate differences in both age and sexual status, the mother wearing the wimple of a married noblewoman, the daughter the garland and free-flowing hair of a noble virgin. The son's curls, held in place by a young nobleman's garland, probably signal only his youth. The only significant iconographic detail these two pairs share is the use of size—parent large, child small—to signal age difference.[15]

15. In a related illumination, *König Tyro von Schotten und Fridebrant sein Sohn,* which uses the same father-son gestures as *Der Winsbecke,* both father and son wear crowns and fur-lined robes, probably because of their perceived status as royalty. Plates of all the miniatures from this manuscript can be found in Walther 1988. Ehlert also dicusses the illustrations (1985, 46).

Mother and daughter act out a concept of femininity that seems to guarantee continuity while playing with separateness. The misogynistic belief inherent in such a concept of femininity—namely, that all women are the same, even those who proclaim their separateness from other women and their differences from one another—is familiar to readers of medieval literature. Mother and daughter struggle against this belief in *Die Winsbeckin,* as they repeatedly attempt to distinguish themselves from those "other" ("dishonorable") women who pay their reputations no heed. Still, the speakers in *Die Winsbeckin* both do and do not succeed in establishing this differentiation. In speaking of modesty, they transgress its boundaries and are accordingly just like those they criticize. Yet they enact a *comedy* of the sameness of all women—a comedy of repeated avowals of mutual affection, harmony, and obedience—in which the speakers hardly ever agree upon anything. Such seeming contradiction may demonstrate how capricious and self-deluded the women are, but it also implies a world in which ambiguity can thrive and in which disagreement is tolerated.

The argument over the possibility of differing identities for women lies at the heart of the different positions on love articulated by mother and daughter. The mother argues from what we might call an essentialist position, naturalizing her teaching that love and passion are a man's game, one that is about domination and subordination. Crucial in making this point is that the mother bring in a notion of coercive love *(Minne)* as a force of nature. This argument naturalizes the mother's construction of *Minne* as a class-specific phenomenon, experienced only by the highborn. In a similar manner, *Minne* shores up the mother's version of the sexual and social inequality between men and women by naturalizing that inequality. The mother's notion of *Minne* captures a gender-driven dynamic of desire as *power* based on natural forces rather than social ones—in which, for women, the "natural" state is one of subordination. Women are the objects of both men's desire and the natural force of love. This statement is also valid when put the other way around: when one is the object of the natural force of love and of male lust, one occupies a feminized position.

By objecting, hesitating, and resisting, the daughter adopts a position that challenges her mother, however circumscribed that challenge may be by the comic reading the text invites us to assume, namely, that such resistance is an ordinary stage of a woman's maturation process. Yet the daughter's challenge goes beyond embodying resistance, for by intellectually challenging her mother's assumptions about the make-up of *Minne,* she unmasks the social and ethical contradictions upon which the mother bases her ideal. The daughter doubts that such a mighty power will gird up the social order as nicely as the mother believes it will. She views

Minne as a subversive force, one that dissolves both social, and by implication, gender hierarchies. She views *Minne* as being dangerous to her, for it will objectify her and molest her, muffle her as a speaking subject and constrict her as an acting subject. By insistently pointing out the contradictions in her mother's teachings on *Minne,* the daughter exposes the gap between human actions and rhetorical idealizations. Her insistence on the distinguishing contradictions hints at a different notion of love, love as a cultural construction. The mother collapses the categories of natural and cultural, but the daughter strives to keep them separate. Further, the daughter's resistance and skepticism imply a contradictory status of women vis-à-vis men—usually his prey and his servant, but before *Minne* his equal, because under *Minne*'s reign they share the feminized status of object. Such equality, however circumscribed, is a paradox that threatens to fracture the gender hierarchy that permits it.

The female speakers in *Die Winsbeckin* seem in any case to be in agreement about one thing. Desire, whether cultural or natural, is a force that works upon women, not a quality that inheres in them. In contrast to the sexually desirous peasant women of the Neidhart poems to be discussed in the next chapter, neither mother nor daughter in *Die Winsbeckin* expresses sexual desires. As aristocratic women, mother and daughter in *Die Winsbeckin* are represented as being exempt from certain medieval beliefs about sexuality, which held that women were earthbound and fleshbound, defined and identified by their weakness for sensuality and the prodigious nature of their sexual drives. Such beliefs are instead projected onto women of the lower classes. In fact, far from assuming that sensuality is innate to women, *Die Winsbeckin* assumes that women must be taught how to inhabit the sociosexual function that is expected of them. With her instructions, the mother is initiating her daughter into the honorable behavior that is expected of her as a noblewoman (Ehlert's "instrumental function"). She assumes that a social female identity is synonymous with sexual identity, and that this sociosexual identity is reactive, shaped in accordance with aristocratic society's (men's) demands on her. In her instructions, the mother fashions a notion of female identity that depends on the female's becoming an attractive and compliant object of male desire. Although in the end the daughter complies, she never endorses her mother's teachings as reflecting any universal or transcendental truth, but merely accepts the necessity of learning rules for conduct that can uphold and justify her social standing as a noblewoman.

Thus aristocratic female identity is implicitly presented as a cultural product, one that is realized through teaching, through education. The mother sees the sexual subordination she teaches as natural, yet it must be learned. The daughter casts doubt on the naturalness of the subordination her mother advocates. She moves towards a position that implies a cultural construction of desire. The daughter's knowledge also threatens to expose the contradictions of aristocratic self-fashioning, but in the end she voluntarily forgoes further questioning in favor of compliance. And yet, though *Die Winsbeckin* may articulate an ideology of womanhood that posits the continuity between all aristocratic women, as *speakers* its mother and daughter enact a connection between women that tolerates and debates differences. Despite their open disagreements, mother and daughter repeatedly affirm their love for each other. The tension in the mother-daughter relationship—between disagreement and mutual affection, between coercion and loving instruction, between skepticism and compliance—is never fully resolved. Instead, it is set aside in favor of a mother-daughter alliance based on aristocratic solidarity.

PART TWO

Common Mothers and Daughters

Sexual Rebellion and Constraint

6

"I Inherited It from You"

The Mother-Daughter Poems of the Neidhart Tradition

Mien mouder dei wol mie geev'n
Ain boer âl met geweld.
Ain boer om met te leev'n
En dat âllain om 't geld.
O nee, o nee, zoo'n rieke boer.
Dei stait ja âltied op de loer.
En dan, en dan, en dan:
Wat dou ik met zoo'n man!
—Anonymous folksong (Kunst 1939, 47)[1]

DURING THE FIRST HALF of the thirteenth century, a poet-composer who called himself Neidhart fashioned a series of comical poems in which a peasant mother and daughter spar over how to respond to a springtime appetite for sex. Neidhart's mother-daughter poems often vary a simple formula: a schematic description of verdant spring (the *Natureingang*) followed by a peasant daughter (sometimes mother) expressing her desire to go dancing with an upper class admirer, the attempts of the mother (sometimes daughter) to restrain her, and the women's subsequent confrontation.[2]

"It is May once again.
Because of the dew,"
spoke a lady,
"flowers and clover blossom.
From the linden tree the nightingale sings

---

1. My mother wants to give me / to a farmer, by force! / A farmer, in order to live with him, / and only because of money. / o no, o no, a rich farmer! / They are always spying and leering. / What then, what then, what then, / What will I do with a man like that?

I thank Hermina Joldersma for sharing this song text with me.

2. There is a long and flourishing folksong tradition of mother-daughter ballads about the choice of a marriage partner. For a fascinating survey of the Yiddish ballad tradition, see Rothstein 1989.

its sweet song.
March was leading the dance:
you can find me with him."

"Daughter, turn your mind
from the dew!
Come here, look,
this is not good news.
Prepare yourself for the cruel winter!
But if you must go,
pay no attention to March's wishes.
Put his speeches behind you!

Anyway, dance so that, no matter what,
if he should deceive you,
at least a cradle
doesn't stand at your feet!
See, then your joy will vanish,
and it just might happen
when you want to go pluck flowers
that a little someone will come crying after you."

"Mother, your worries are a waste of breath.
I don't care
about such troubles:
women have always borne children.
I have no intention of giving up my fun
because of your advice.
Hand me my summer garments:
to hell with the cradle!"

Now listen to what happened next!
They fought
in an uproar.
The mother seized a rake;
the daughter grabbed it where it was thickest,
and right away snatched it
out of the old one's hands.
Then the blows started falling.

They thrashed each other with gusto.
The old one said:
"Such bedlam
I would not have tolerated from you last year.
Alas, now my body is weak

. . . .

Even if you paid March twenty marks,
He would never take you as his wife."[3] (SL 7, st. 1–5a)

Neidhart's poetry appealed widely to medieval audiences, to judge by the twenty-three surviving manuscripts containing his work (Wießner 1984, ix–xv). The popularity of his work can also be determined by the fact that it inspired massive imitation. Using philological criteria, scholars distinguish between a corpus of some seventy poems probably written by Neidhart himself, the so-called authentic poems, and hundreds of verses in Neidhart's style, which were composed in the decades following Neidhart's death.[4] The survival of 341 inauthentic stanzas (alongside only twelve authentic ones) in three early modern printed collections (*Neidhart Fuchs*) testifies to the adaptability and broad appeal of the lyric tradition invented by Neidhart.[5] The mother-daughter formula appears in both the authentic and the inauthentic poems. In total, some thirty poems vary the mother-daughter scheme, enough poems to make it a distinct subgenre of medieval German lyric poetry.[6]

3. All translations are my own. To my knowledge, none of these texts has been previously translated into English. Because of the length of the quotations, the original texts appear in the appendix at the end of the book.

Unless otherwise stated, I have used the standard edition by Wießner (1984) for the authentic Neidhart texts. I also consulted Beyschlag's editions (1975, 1989).

SL stands for *Sommerlied*, "Summer Song," the designation used in the Wießner edition for poems celebrating summer and erotic pleasure. Neidhart also wrote *Winterlieder*, "Winter Songs," which are abbreviated WL. Poems are cited as SL or WL according to this standard terminology. *SL* followed by a number refers to the number of the poem in the standard edition. With one exception (WL 7), all of Neidhart's poems containing mother-daughter stanzas are summer songs.

4. On Neidhart and the Neidhart corpus, see Schweikle 1990. On the question of authenticity, see Simon 1986 and Schweikle 1986.

In this chapter I accept the general scholarly consensus on the question of authentic and inauthentic Neidhart poems. As Schweikle (1986) points out, early editors classified some poems in reliable manuscripts as inauthentic for spurious reasons. By and large, however, the philological and codicological grounds for assigning large numbers of poems to the "Neidhart industry" of the late thirteenth and fourteenth centuries are sound.

5. For editions of *Neidhart Fuchs*, see Bobertag 1885 and Jöst 1980.

6. This number does not include thirteenth-century mother/daughter songs in the Neidhart tradition composed by other poets, such as the following, which appear in Kraus 1978 (abbreviated KLD): Geltar/Gedrut, "der walt und diu heide breit" [The forest and wide heath] (KLD 13); Gotfried von Niefen, "sol ich disen sumer lanc" [Must I all summer long] (KLD 15); Scharpfenberg, "meije, bis du willekommen" [May, welcome to you] (KLD 52); Stamheim, "nu wol ûf, reien fûr den walt" [Step lively and dance at forest's edge] (KLD 55); Ulrich von Winterstetten, "ist iht mêre schoenes" [Nothing is more beautiful] (KLD 59).

On the mother/daughter poems, see Herrmann 1984 and Janssen 1980. For a thorough, feminist analysis of the Neidhartian mother-daughter poems, whose results parallel mine, see Bennewitz 1994.

Mother-Daughter Motifs in Authentic Neidhart Poems

In "Summer Song 7," above, the sexualized continuity between mother and daughter that is a salient feature of the Neidhart and Neidhartian mother-daughter poems as subgenre is not immediately apparent. On the contrary, mother and daughter forcefully assert their differences: the daughter adamantly resists her mother's advice, marking out a position diametrically opposed to her mother's. Yet understanding the opposing roles daughter and mother play is the first step in establishing an argument for the sexualized continuity of mother and daughter, a continuity whose contours are revealed not in the individual poems but rather in the manner in which the entire set of Neidhartian mother-daughter poems transpose and burlesque mother-daughter motifs familiar to the reader from epic texts. Accordingly, I shall focus here on the opposing roles of mother and daughter and on the sexualization of peasant women in the context of Neidhart's poetry before moving on to a discussion of the sexual continuity between mother and daughter.

In "Summary Song 7," the daughter is the first speaker, and the description of the sights, smells, sounds, and feel of spring (blossoming flowers, nightingale, dew) that open the poem are placed in her mouth. Yet the daughter is hardly a disinterested presenter of this spring scene. Rather, her desire to follow "March" to the dance signals that she, too, is a feature of the landscape of spring. The name "March"—both month and boyfriend—also signals the overlap between nature and culture.

There is another equivocal naming practice of the first stanza. In the narrative insertion of line three, the daughter is called "a lady," a highborn woman, although general knowledge of Neidhart's poems as well as the subsequent stanzas of this individual poem make it clear that in fact the daughter is a peasant girl. The use of this appellation could derive from an aspect of the narrative persona Neidhart creates in many spring poems, a narrator who in his pursuit and seduction of peasant girls imbues them with the qualities of ladyhood or promises them ladyhood's material trappings. In any case, the appellation "lady" sets up a marked contrast between the daughter's rather genteel observations and the rustic concerns immediately voiced by her mother. The temporary blurring of class distinctions—a not uncommon device in medieval literature—establishes the poem's comic tone.[7]

The mother's words in stanzas 2 and 3 put the daughter's apparently innocent longings into a rustic perspective. The mother establishes that

---

7. On the interfunctioning of comedy and class in medieval French literature, see Gravdal (1989, 1–19).

"March" is a dangerous and seductive person, that her daughter is not only innocent but shortsighted and naïve, and most importantly, that "dancing" is merely a euphemism for sexual dalliance. In pointing all this out, the mother's role is clearly defined: she represents the voice of experience, convention, and reason. She also makes explicit what was only hinted at in earlier texts, such as *Die Winsbeckin:* sexual activity produces children, and women must then take care of them.

The daughter's subsequent words and actions destroy any notion that she is ladylike in her expressions or sensibilities. Rather, she is headstrong, stubborn, and enthralled by the passion that March (both the season and the man) has awakened in her. Her words and the ensuing fight with her mother establish that the strength of her sexual desire overwhelms reason, convention, and any semblance of polite behavior or respect for her mother's authority. Thus the daughter demonstrates the medieval notion that women are by nature less able than men to govern their sexual appetites (which are, in any case, viewed as being more voracious than men's). The conflict of desire and authority degenerates into a test of physical strength. The first five stanzas of the poem leave the outcome of this struggle uncertain: we do not learn whether the mother succeeds in restraining her unruly daughter. However, stanza 5a, considered by Neidhart's editors to be a later addition to the poem, resolves the issue: the mother's strength is inadequate, and she can only taunt her daughter (who, we can imagine, is striding out the door), with the observation that she may become March's lover but she will never become his wife.

The Sexualization of Peasant Women

"Summer Song 7" provides an example of how Neidhart's mother-daughter poems rehearse and parody familiar mother-daughter motifs, foremost of which is the naïve daughter whose innocence makes her vulnerable and the experienced mother whose authority is weak and ineffectual. In transposing these motifs into a peasant setting, however, the poem creates a fictional space that allows the sexualization of these issues. The noble daughter's innocence arises from her lack of sexual knowledge; she is represented as being so sheltered that she remains untouched by desire. Indeed, the mother in *Die Winsbeckin* counsels her daughter that it is precisely modesty and lack of desire—a kind of exemplary passivity—that will make her attractive to men. Although the noble daughter will doubtless marry and so not remain a virgin, the mother's instructions attempt to preserve in the daughter a virtuous state of wifely chastity. In contrast, the peasant daughter is not innocent of sexual knowledge nor does she lack sexual desire, as "Summer Song 7" makes clear. Rather, she is indifferent to the social consequences of her sexual actions. The peasant daughter is vulnerable precisely because she is sexually desirous and sexually active.

The noble mother draws on her knowledge and experience to guide her daughter. Texts such as the *Eneasroman,* the *Nibelungenlied,* or *Die Winsbeckin* clearly align the mother's knowledge of the social conventions of love with the ideology of aristocratic culture. When the noble mother's authority is undermined in these texts, it is because aspects of her understanding of aristocratic culture—often those regarding women's access to material wealth and the proper scope of their political influence—are in conflict with other textual messages about the nature of nobility. Nevertheless, the discourse of noble love as presented by the noble mother is idealistic and dominated by Ovidian love lore. The *Eneasroman* and the *Winsbeckin* are typical in this regard.

The guardianship of the peasant mother is constructed along similar lines, yet it is ineffectual for other reasons. Like the noble mothers, the peasant mother of the Neidhart poems is charged with the sexual instruction and guardianship of her daughter. She, too, is supposed to guide her daughter into a socially sanctioned marriage. The peasant mother, however, is not concerned with idealizing love lore, Ovidian or otherwise, and her pragmatism is sexually explicit. Instead, she elaborates the material and economic dimensions of the social choice of a marriage partner, as is made clear by the following quotation from "Summer Song 23."

> "Little daughter, don't let yourself be attracted by him!
> Don't get pushy with the knights at the dance.
> They are above you in station,
> little daughter,
> and you alone will bear the damage!
> The reeve's son fancies you." (st. 6)

> "The reeve can go suck his toe for all I care!
> I can handle a proud knight;
> what would I want with a peasant for a husband?
> He could not
> love me the way I want to be loved.
> He will have to do without me." (st. 7)

> "Daughter, you are breaking your promise
> if you reject the son of Herr Kunz, the reeve.
> After all, he has cattle and hogs,
> grain and wine.
> Now do you want to lose all that?
> The reeve's son desires you." (st. 7a)

"Daughter, don't allow yourself to disdain him!
You are too ignorant for this knight's acquaintance,
and it has all your friends and relatives worried.
Many oaths
you swore: Now don't try to deny it,
your desire alone is taking you away from me!"[8] (st. 8)

8. Neidhart poems often show a great deal of variation within the manuscript transmission of individual poems, and this mother-daughter poem is a case in point. It appears in three different manuscripts with three different endings (the original German appears in the appendix). The standard edition, translated above, follows the manuscript Berlin mgf 1062, known as the Riedegger manuscript (Staatsbibliothek zu Berlin Preußischer Kulturbesitz). However, Berlin mgf 1062 does not include stanza 7a ("Daughter, you are breaking your promise . . ."), and after stanza 8 it adds the following stanza:

> "Mother mine, stop nagging!
> For him I will risk my friends and relatives;
> I never concealed my desire from him and
> I want
> the whole world to know it!
> My longing carries me toward Riuwental."
> (SL 23, st. 9)

The Codex Manesse (Heidelberg cpg 484) includes, in rearranged order, all the stanzas except 7a and adds the following stanza:

> The mother grabbed a heavy stick.
> "All right, then, push off! I'm sick of you."
> She knocked her so hard that the whole house rang.
> Everywhere
> she gave her many a swift hard blow
> and packed her off toward Riuwental.
> (SL 23, st. 9a)

Manuscript Berlin mgf 779 follows the same order as manuscript Berlin mgf 1062. It adds stanza 7a as well as the following verses at the end:

> "Little daughter, now what happened to you last night?
> I heard you in the bushes loudly scuffling
> with a proud knight. It's true.
> Bind up your hair!
> He made plenty of hanky panky
> with you: it's completely obvious."

> "Little mother, now don't get so mad!
> A fellow is courting me. It will bring you honor,
> so stop all your worrying.
> Toward Riuwental,
> that's where he's going to set me up,
> where the nightingale sings so fine."
> (SL 23, st. 9b, 9c)

9. Peasant mother (wearing a headdress) and daughter (with free-flowing hair) in lively conversation, as indicated by their hand gestures. Sixteenth century. Woodcut from *Neidhart Fuchs*. Nuremberg, Germanisches Nationalmuseum, Bibl. Inc. 100996. Courtesy of the Germanisches Nationalmuseum.

Through the figure of the peasant mother, the Neidhartian poems cre-ate a discourse about sex and marriage in village life that focuses not on intellectual abstractions about love but rather on social and sexual reali-ties: having sex means having babies; upper-class men exploit peasant girls; peasant boys make good husbands. These mothers are completely pragmatic about the rewards of sexual conformity (marriage to a man who owns livestock and fields) and the consequences of sexual rebellion (a bastard child). Even the pragmatics of disagreement between mother and daughter undergo a burlesque transformation: the differences of opinion exchanged between aristocratic mothers and daughters are trans-lated in the fictive peasant realm into physical blows.

The peasant mother's problem is the strength of her daughter's pas-sion, which makes it virtually impossible for the mother to control the daughter. Because the daughter ignores her mother's words, the mother resorts to physical restraints, such as taking away the daughter's shoes, locking up her dancing clothes, or battering her in an effort to maintain mastery. But what the struggle between mother and daughter shows is that the force of sexual desire is indomitable. It is clear that neither reason nor violence will keep the daughter from blindly following her erotic pas-sion. The mother's guardianship, zealous though it surely is, proves no match for the power of carnal longing. The guardianship of the peasant mother is ineffectual precisely because in this fictional peasant world the strength of female lust makes women deaf to reason and lends them ex-tra vigor in pursuing sexual fulfillment.

Nobles, Peasants, and Parody

Like all of Neidhart's poetry, these mother-daughter poems were writ-ten for and compiled by aristocratic audiences. Their emphasis on peas-ant women's aggression and active sexuality must be viewed not as a reflection of medieval German peasant life but as a parody of medieval aristocratic self-fashioning. As Kathryn Gravdal argues, it was "the insti-tution of knighthood itself that offer[ed] the richest vein of humor to the parodist of twelfth- and thirteenth-century France" (1989, 145). Neid-hart's poetry performs a similar function in medieval German literature. His ouevre can be understood as one long burlesque of knighthood, de-veloped and sustained through the persona of the singer-knight "Neid-hart of Reuenthal," whose poems tell of his forays into the village world, where in the "Summer Songs" he successfully seduces peasant girls and in the "Winter Songs" flees like a sissy before the attacks of the peasant boys.

Neidhart's poetry parodies chivalry and the poet-knight, who seduces country girls, moons after peasant maids, and is scared to death of peasant toughs. Yet Neidhart's effete and fearful chivalric singer moves in a fictive peasant world that stands in complex relation to the courtly culture for which it was created. The peasant world imagined in Neidhart's poems is a place where the veneer of culture is thinner and violence in human relationships surfaces easily, quickly, and often. We have seen an example of this phenomenon in the altercations between mother and daughter in the "Summer Songs." Neidhart's "Winter Songs," too, are replete with physical aggression—fistfights, brawls, mayhem, maimings, all presented with the comic verve of a "Three Stooges" routine. On the one hand, this violent yet comic world is set up to contrast with and highlight the gentility and intellectual sophistication courtly culture attributed to itself. The evidence of medieval history teaches us that among the nobility, too, violence was both frequent and chronic, but Neidhart's poetry disowns such violence by projecting it into a different social class. Those who behave in such rough-and-ready ways are merely peasants. On the other hand, the fictive peasant world in which this violence arises is imbued with extraordinary vitality and vigor. In it the easy recourse to physical force is a sign of potency, and the singer-knight's distaste for fisticuffs makes him less manly than the brash peasant youths and renders him a laughingstock.

What all this signals is a profound ambivalence toward the very gentility that courtly culture was seeking to create and upon which courtly culture built part of its identity. Neidhart's poetry breaks a series of literary, social, and moral rules about courtly culture in the " 'safe' domain of parodic literature" (Gravdal 1989, 144), and thus, through laughter, discharges the anxiety provoked by class transgression. The complex ambiguity regarding the crossing of class boundaries also forms a context for sexualization of peasant mothers and daughters in Neidhart's "Summer Songs." The aggressive sexual desire blindly driving the peasant daughter propels her into the arms of an upper-class lover, the singer-knight. In the "Summer Songs" the singer-knight is almost always successful in the sexual realm, the peasant girls unanimously preferring him to the peasant suitors their mothers have picked out. Thus the irresistible sexual force working on the peasant girl makes her available to noblemen as an object of sexual fantasy—and perhaps also of sexual exploitation. It also creates a powerful excuse for the nobleman's sexual transgression of social boundaries, for the peasant girl is imagined as complicitous in and desirous of this love affair. If the knight is a sexual hunter, then these poems suggest that the prey desires the chase.

Yet the guardian, the peasant mother, views the love affair between the knight and her daughter as class-based, sexual exploitation pure and simple. Because both the aristocratic and the peasant mothers are knowledgeable and experienced in the ways of the world, it is their responsibility to initiate their daughters into the sociosexual conventions for female behavior considered appropriate for their station in life. In both cases, the mother's guardianship of the daughter is described in similar terms; thus, Petra Herrman's description of the peasant mother in the Neidhart poems might also apply to an upper-class mother:

> Die "huote" der Mutter repräsentiert vor allem die gesellschafts-bezogene Forderung nach einer standesgemäßen und materiell gesichter-ten Ehe [footnote omitted]. Damit fungiert sie innerhalb der Fiktion als affirmative Vermittlerin sozialer Realität. Sie ist jedoch nicht nur Instanz negativ besetzter, gesellschaftlicher Tabus and Verbote. Sie ist auch mit Merkmalen versehen, die der Sänger an den jüngeren Mädchen, den Töchtern, positiv wertet: praktisch, handfest, wirklichkeitsnah, d.h. konkret in ihrer Denk- und Handlungsweise. (Herrmann 1984, 121)

> The guardianship (*huote*) of the mother represents above all else the socially instilled wish for a materially secure marriage to someone of equal rank. In this way, she functions as an affirmative mediator of social reality within the fictive realm. She is, however, not merely an instance of negatively inflected social taboos and bans. She is also fitted with features that the singer values positively in the younger maids, the daughters: practical, hands-on, realistic, that is, concrete in her thought and conduct.

The instructions of aristocratic and peasant mothers agree on one point: crossing class lines in the choice of a sexual partner should be avoided at all costs. The aristocratic daughters, however, are shown reaching agreement with their mothers on this point: class solidarity wins out clearly in *Kudrun*, in *Tristan und Isolde*, and in *Die Winsbeckin*. Class alliance is carried through even in the *Eneasroman*, where the daughter repudiates her mother, for one of the epic's points is that the marriage to Aeneas, which the queen believes threatening to Lavinia's status, does not in fact endanger Lavinia's rank but instead further ennobles her. In contrast, the peasant daughter actively oversteps the prohibition against sexual relationships across class lines, and the peasant mother is unable to stop her. Instead, the irresistible lure of sexual fulfillment drives mother and daughter apart, undercuts the mother's authority, and renders fragile any class solidarity mother and daughter might share. The very vigor and sexual vitality believed to characterize the peasant girl make her a traitor to kin and class. There is a certain parallel here to the brawling peasant youths whose raucousness so intimidates the singer-knight, for they, too, are inclined to fight among themselves. Spirited though they are, they also fail in terms of class allegiance, discharging their potential for easy violence against each other rather than against their masters.

Neidhart's mother-daughter poems may also express ambivalence towards the sexual constraints courtly culture imposed on women, a world in which, as the mother in *Die Winsbeckin* reminds us, a woman's honor was the same as her reputation for chastity. Neidhart's poems, in contrast, delight in imagining a world in which women possess great scope of erotic choice and the desire and ability to act on their choices. Neidhart's poems construct this world comically and transpose their images of women actively seeking sexual pleasure into a fictional peasant world, where such notions could be enjoyed without threatening the nobility's claim to greater rational and intellectual resources and noblewomen's claim to greater chastity. Thus Neidhart's mother-daughter poems "signal an ongoing preoccupation with the lines of social class, a preoccupation to which the thirteenth-century audience would have been keenly alive" (Gravdal 1989, 19).

Sexual Continuity between Mother and Daughter

From the preceding section it might appear as though the roles of mother and daughter were fixed according to their age and marital station, with the young, unmarried woman representing sexual desire and social rebellion and with the older, married woman representing sexual restraint and social conformity. Yet, as I mentioned at the beginning of this chapter, this is only partially true. Neidhart's poetry holds fast to creating an opposition between mother and daughter, but it also contains poems in which the roles are reversed and it is the mother who eagerly pursues a lover, the daughter who urges reason and restraint. The interchangeability of the mother-daughter roles makes visible the sexualized continuity between women characterizing Neidhart's poetry, for it represents all peasant women—whether old or young, married or unmarried—as sharing a vigorous sensuality and a lack of self-control in sexual matters. As an illustration, excerpts from two poems containing lascivious, defiant mothers and indignant, socially conformist daughters follow; both are drawn from the corpus of authentic Neidhart poems. First, the beginning of "Summer Song 1":

> An old woman began to leap about
> as high as a young deer: she wanted to pluck flowers.
> "Daughter, hand me my best attire.
> I must dance at the side of a young knight,
> the one who is called 'von Riuwental' ".
> traranuretun traranuriruntundeie.
>
> "Mother, be reasonable!
> He's the sort of knight who doesn't fancy fidelity in love!"
> "Daughter, don't bother me with that.

I know exactly what he offered me.
I am dying for his love."
traranuretun traranuriruntundeie. (SL 1, st. 1–2)

"Summer Song 1" contrasts the daughter's use of the vocabulary of courtly love with the mother's sexual brashness. The daughter refers to fidelity in love with a Middle High German phrase (*stæter minne*) that suggests the complex and highly abstracted code of courtly love poetry. The mother counters this reference to an aristocratic, idealized notion of love with an allusion to the straightforwardly sexual nature of the transaction between herself and the knight: "I know exactly what he offered me." The daughter remains invested in courtly notions of love, but the pragmatic mother is not fooled.

Two stanzas from "Summer Song 17" develop different aspects of the reversed mother-daughter roles. They ridicule the mother's age and underscore the daughter's wholehearted annoyance.

"I'm in charge of you," said the child's mother.
"Hey, let's go together, the two of us, to the linden tree!
In years
I am still a child,
even though the curls
of my hair are grey:
I'll braid them
with silk.
Daughter, where is my headdress?"

"Mother, I have hidden your headdress from you;
it is fitting for a young woman, not an old one,
to wear it on her head
in the crowd.
Who has robbed you
so completely of your wits?
Go to sleep!
Maybe it will be easier for you to dream
of adorning yourself another way!" (SL 17, st. 5–6)

These poems draw on the same repertoire of motifs as the previous Neidhartian mother-daughter poems: the erotically impelled woman's wish to dress up in her best clothes and adorn her hair, the restraining woman's countereffort to hide away the desired attire, the experienced woman's knowledge that the beloved is inconstant, the sexually active woman's intention to throw social norms to the winds. Yet the roles of the sexually active, socially rebellious woman and the sexually restrained, socially conformist woman are tied neither to age nor to marital station. The interchangeability of the mother-daughter roles suggests instead that age and marital status are immaterial to peasant women's active pursuit of erotic fulfillment. Whether old or young, married or unmarried, peasant mothers and daughters are represented in these poems as being eager to yield to their sexual appetites.

As the preceding two excerpts show, the Neidhart poems use the interchangeability of the mother-daughter roles and the commonality of their erotic desire to further burlesque established features of the mother-daughter stereotypes. When the innocent daughter becomes the guardian, she can openly rebuke her mother for behaving irrationally: "Mother, be reasonable!" (SL 1, st. 2). Guardian mothers tend to plead before becoming enraged, presumably on account of their unheeded parental authority; guardian daughters have little personal authority but tend to express a general sense of indignation or even revulsion that their mothers are misbehaving in such outrageous and embarrassing fashion. When the knowledgeable mother actively seeks a lover, she can look foolish, as the grey curls entwined with silken ribbons demonstrate, but her experience can also make her audacious. Innocent daughters tend to believe the improbable promises made by their seducers, driving their commonsensical mothers to distraction; experienced mothers know the score, and still say yes.

Within the context of the individual Neidhart poems, mother and daughter display only differences. It is only within the context of the entire set of "Summer Songs," with their play on the interchangeability of the mother-daughter roles, that the audience can comprehend the essential, sexual similarity represented by peasant mother and daughter. Neidhart's poetry sexualizes peasant mothers and daughters, representing them as being sexually ungovernable, lacking in self-control, and erotically active. In the Neidhart poetry deemed authentic, this sexualized continuity between mother and daughter is not developed as a form of self-understanding. Mother and daughter never articulate a shared notion of what they understand their sexual nature and their sexual protocols to be. On the contrary, peasant mothers and daughters always disagree, forcefully asserting their differences. Yet as a group the "Summer Songs" are designed to show us that peasant mothers and daughters are more alike than they know.

As the previous chapters have shown, the mother-daughter motif suggests a wide range of overlapping themes: the duties of guardianship and instruction, the induction into and defiance of social norms, the tension between innocence and experience and between submissiveness and authority. These themes are masterfully burlesqued in the peasant realm of Neidhart's poetry. Neidhart's use of the mother-daughter motif functions in part as an intertextual device, summoning echoes of the mothers and daughters in epic texts such as the *Eneasroman*, the *Nibelungenlied*, and *Tristan and Isolde*, who were doubtless known to his medieval audiences. In the "Summer Songs," the interchangeability of the mother-daughter roles and the sexual commonality it suggests add a new interpretive dimension to the mother-daughter motif. One could imagine, for example, the sexualization of women being developed through representations of unrelated women, yet Neidhart uses women who are kin, mothers and daughters. In the context of the "Summer Songs," the trope of kinship does double ideological duty. First, it links a whole set of oppositions— old or young, married or unmarried, experienced or foolish, sexually restrained or sexually wanton—closely together by summoning notions of generational change and familial authority to explain them. Second, the slippage of mothers into filial roles and daughters into maternal roles indicates that these oppositions, virulent though their performance may be, are constantly being undone. Mother and daughter may never agree, but they are nevertheless so alike that they can be transformed into each other. Thus the familial relation of peasant mother and daughter symbolizes a more fundamental kinship based on their sexual nature as women.

The sexualized continuity of peasant mother and daughter is class-based. Neidhart's poems comically transpose their notions of women's sexuality into a fictive peasant realm, rendering these notions attributes of peasant women rather than attributes of all women as a group. In these poems it is safe for aristocratic audiences both to mock and to desire an imagined world in which illegitimate births are merely a nuisance, in which women overcome resistance to actively pursue the lovers they want, and in which erotic desires are fulfilled for young women and old women alike.

The Mother-Daughter Motif in Some Inauthentic Neidhart Poems

The manuscript Berlin mgf 779,[9] which was compiled in Nuremberg in the 1460s, assembles a huge collection of Neidhart poems. According to the description in Wießner's standard edition, it contains 395 authentic stanzas and 703 inauthentic ones. Among the inauthentic poems are a number of lengthy, comic mother-daughter exchanges that appear only in it and in the sixteenth-century printed books called *Neidhart Fuchs*. The

---

9. Berlin mgf 779, has been edited and published by Bennewitz-Behr (1981). I have also consulted Beyschlag (1989, 299–305). Berlin mgf 779 is in the Staatsbibliothek zu Berlin Preußischer Kulturbesitz. On Berlin mgf 779, see also Becker 1978 and Fritz 1969.

10. The peasant daughter establishes her sexual maturity by displaying her pubic hair to her mother. Woodcut from *Neidhart Fuchs*. Sixteenth century. Nuremberg, Germanisches Nationalmuseum, Bibl. Inc. 100996. 4v. Courtesy of the Germanisches Nationalmuseum.

mother-daughter poems of Berlin mgf 779 exaggerate certain possibilities inherent in the Neidhartian mother-daughter formula in order to heighten their drastic comic effect. First, certain mother-daughter poems of Berlin mgf 779 expand upon the potential for burlesque, most notably in the figure of the mother. Second, the mother-daughter poems of Berlin mgf 779 transform the opposition between mother and daughter, which is a virtually unchanging feature of the authentic Neidhart poems. In one case, the opposition remains, but the daughter bases her argument for sexual rebellion on her similarity to her mother. She thus articulates the sexual continuity underlying the opposing roles of mother and daughter. In a second case, the unresolved yet comic antagonism between mother and daughter is both strengthened and diminished, so that the inauthentic mother-daughter exchanges depict mother and daughter as rivals and as co-conspirators. As we shall see, these two motifs are in fact not mutually exclusive: in the course of the conversation between mother and daughter, rivalry can be transformed into solidarity.[10]

Before beginning my discussion, I wish to alert readers to the fact that the following pages contain long quotations, in English translation. These lengthy quotations are included because the texts, not well known in scholarly circles, are difficult to obtain since they are not included in Wießner's standard edition and Bennewitz's excellent transcription is not widely available in this country. They also give readers the means to evaluate my interpretations and to experience for themselves the drastic comic effects intended in these poems. The German originals are included in the appendix.

"A Dialogue": The Lusty Widow and Her Irate Daughter

The first poem of Berlin mgf 779 to be discussed here, no. 30, is titled simply "A Dialogue" [Ein wechsell]. The poem opens stereotypically, with the daughter giving a description of verdant spring (Natureingang). This is immediately echoed in the second stanza by the mother, who proclaims that her sense of youthfulness has also been renewed. This information alerts the reader to the expected formula: this is a reversed-roles poem, in which the daughter is the guardian and the mother is sexually active. The poem's thirteen stanzas do not undo the opposition between sexually wanton mother and socially conformist daughter. Rather, they

10. My discussion by no means exhausts the range of meanings in the inauthentic mother-daughter poems. Bennewitz points out that the poems stressing mother-daughter rivalry often show the daughter taking up a position that allies her with the father (1994, 187–88). She also discusses other inauthentic poems that produce yet different variations on the mother-daughter scheme (1994, 188–90).

heighten the mother-daughter conflict by adding narrative detail to the characterization of the wanton mother. She is a widow, fashioned according to the stereotype of the sexually insatiable widow who is a stock figure of late medieval fiction.[11] She is also financially well-situated, and the lover she is pursuing is a young man. The daughter is characterized chiefly by the way in which she mixes sound, if conventional, advice with indignant rebukes. As the argument progresses, both women use vulgar language and ribald metaphors that mark out with great emotional clarity the contours of their opposing positions: the mother is set on scandalizing her daughter with her wild behavior and increasingly smutty language, and the daughter becomes increasingly yet helplessly disgusted by her mother's intransigence.

> The daughter said: "How many speeches must I hear.
> Mother, you are making a fool of yourself
> by ignoring my advice.
> Don't you know that it is unseemly for old women
> to take up such lustiness?
> You should reconsider this sensibly."

> "I have reconsidered for the last time.
> Bring me my dress and my little wimple.
> I am going to wear them to spite everyone
> who begrudges me my joy as the days grow long.
> Daughter, I don't need your advice,
> and you are holding me back."

> "Listen, my advice is totally lost on you.
> Even though every word was well meant,
> Mother, you willfully take it all wrong.
> Having a good crutch at hand would suit you better
> and you should use it to go to church,
> instead of summer revels."

> "I'll do just fine without crutches.
> Right now I can, on one leg,
> leap as fleetly as a young deer.
> I am going to be happy for years because of a young man,
> all of twenty-four years old.
> I am going to do his will."

---

11. See, for example, Gautier le Leu, "The Widow," (1992) as well as the fifteenth-century German Shrovetide play "Der wittwen und tochter vasnacht" [The Widow and her Daughter] (Keller 1853–1856, 28: 97).

The daughter said: "Lady mother, you are unwise,
getting all dressed up for a young man.
He is only taking you for your money,
not your looks. Now pay attention to my words.
When the money is gone
he will beat you."

The mother said: "That's nonsense.
Even if I'm old I've got lots of money,
and if a young man comes forward
who can shake me at night like a warped door
so that my teeth rattle in my mouth,
he won't stay poor."

The daughter said: "As God is my witness,
it's going to be like skinning a smelly donkey
to sleep with you at night.
There will be no respite for him from your coughing and
    wheezing.
For God's sake, pull yourself together
And knock your head against the wall!"

The old one said: "Lady daughter, now be quiet.
Truly, you know that an expert can strum good notes
on an old fiddle.
I intend to lend my fiddle to a young man
who can dance and prance.
Let him give it a good shake for me.

When the bathhouse is poorly heated,
you must be beaten with a branch before you can feel
the heat that the heart desires."
"No matter how good the wood is, if the oven is bad
there's no enjoying the heat.
Mother, stop this bragging!

You promised my father, you should remember,
that you wouldn't take another man. Now you've changed your
    mind."
"I would have kept my promise
if he had recovered, so that he would think well of me.
Now he's dead. He can't order me around any more.
I want to enjoy myself."

The daughter said: "May the devil take you.
You are screwing around and you don't even have any teeth.
Your cheeks are full of wrinkles.

I was right to say every word I've said."
She hit the old one until she limped on one leg,
and went to the dance herself. (c 30, st. 3–13)

The sexual vitality that renders the young woman attractive is viewed as grotesque in the old woman, and the unseemliness of her desire is underscored by the many narrative details calling attention to her aged body: her wheezing and coughing, her "old fiddle" and "oven" (common euphemisms for female genitalia), her toothless mouth and wrinkled face. Interestingly enough, the text pays no attention to the daughter's body at all; the poem is entirely given over to the comic imagining of the mismatch between the mother's physical infirmities and her lust. The poem leaves no doubt that the mother is actively pursuing sexual pleasure. Yet when she first mentions her twenty-four-year-old boyfriend, she asserts that she is "going to do his will," as though he were the active and she the passive party. In late medieval and early modern German, "to do his will" is a stock euphemism for having sex. It is used by and about women at trials and hearings to mean having sex with a man; men never "do a woman's will" but rather "have their way" with women (Roper 1989b). The mother's use of this phrase is highly ironic, since "his will" is clearly her will, too. Every stanza of the poem undercuts the submissiveness and sexual passivity such a phrase imputes to women by confirming the mother's agency, volition, and active sexual desire.

The daughter's indignation is due primarily to what she perceives as the gross social inappropriateness of her mother's behavior, though we may speculate that seeing her inheritance thrown away by her mother on youthful playboys does not improve her temper. She suggests that the mother's young lover is responding to greed, not desire, in sleeping with her. In order to deter her mother, she expresses the practical concern that when the mother's money is gone, her boyfriend will beat her. The mother's response is twofold. She rejects the notion that she will run out of money, and she then takes up the image of battering and reinterprets it as a metaphor for vigorous sexual intercourse. The mother's speeches are marked by zestful metaphors for sex: rattled doors, strummed fiddles, heated bathhouses. This licentious language is also distastful to the daughter, and she characterizes it as boasting (*geuden*). Such vulgar speech is another example of the mother's unchastity. But even an appeal to the mother's deathbed promise to her husband not to take another man does not daunt the obstinate mother, and in the end, mother and daughter come to blows. Thus youth does indeed triumph, and the daughter, reclaiming the right of youth from her mother, goes to the dance herself.

Poem 30 keeps to the general formula of Neidhart's mother-daughter poems. The modifications it makes—increased narrative detail, concrete reminders of the physicality of the aged yet sexually desirous female body, smutty language—move the poem's intertextual referentiality away from the mother-daughter motif in thirteenth-century epic texts. Instead, this mother-daughter poem is closer to the late medieval genres of the fabliaux (*mære*) and the Shrovetide play, which share its love of raucous humor and drastic comic effect.

"The Sated Crow or the Hungry Crow": Imitation and Sexual Continuity Between Mother and Daughter

Poem 64 in Berlin mgf 776 has a more specific title than the one for no. 30. Following a proverb quoted in the poem, it is called "The Sated Crow or the Hungry Crow." This poem uses the stereotypes of the guardian mother and the rebellious daughter. In contrast to poem 30 and to the authentic Neidhart poems, there is little narrative or symbolic detail in this poem: no clothing, bodies, or babies; no narratives of trysts or fights. "The Sated Crow or the Hungry Crow" opens with a two-stanza *Natureingang*, but then it becomes a debate poem, in which the mother sets out in rather colorless and almost pedantic fashion the central concerns of guardianship, only to be vigorously refuted by her daughter. The mother scarcely exists as a character; she represents more a kind of disembodied, authoritative role. The role of the daughter, however, is elaborated and strengthened to such a degree that her arguments reveal the mother's authority to be weak and her teachings to be largely clichés. In the process of refuting her mother, the daughter articulates the sexual continuity between mother and daughter as an inborn trait: "Mother, I inherited it from you" (st. 3, 1.6). This statement expresses what I have argued is a fundamental premise of the Neidhartian mother-daughter texts, but its articulation by one of the women characters in the poems is unique.

> "Daughter, who told you
> about men?
> I don't care for this talk.
> It comes from the power of desire."
> "Mother, that I feel desire is not something I have acquired.
> I inherited it from you.
> The one I have chosen as my lover,
> even if it means angering the whole world,
> I will desire him always."
>
> "Daughter, wait one year
> so that I can advise you better."
> "Little Mother, you speak the truth,

but it's probably too late.
If I held a lover in my arms as you do, I would be full of joy.
Mother, you've got a man
who can love you well.
The sated crow and the hungry one
live very different lives."

"Daughter, obey me
if you wish to learn about honor."
"Mother, you've got a man
and I want one, too.
You deny me the right that you enjoy yourself.
Hell is full of people like that.
Mother, you do fine at night
with love, as you rightly deserve.
That's how you have been 'bedfellowed.' "

"Daughter, let your loving end
and follow my teaching."
"Alas, dear little mother,
you are committing a terrible sin.
I am wholeheartedly devoted to him, and I mean to let him know
    it.
Take your advice yourself.
You talk like someone who is done baking.
I long for the love of my friend.
I'm going to run away with him." (c 64, st. 3–6)

   With her forceful words and religious threats, the daughter brands her
mother a hypocrite. Her mother freely enjoys sexual pleasure; why
shouldn't the daughter do so as well? The daughter's descriptions of her
mother's frequent sexual relations are ambiguous. We cannot be sure
whether they refer to the mother's husband or to her lovers, though the
daughter's vehemence—"take your advice yourself"—leads us to believe
that it is the latter. If so, the daughter's words attack whatever notion of
honor the mother intended to advance—in fact, because of her daughter's
torrent of words, the mother never gets around to explaining what exactly
she means by honor. The daughter's statements may imply that whatever
the mother's concept of honor might be, it is merely a convenient mask
that conceals her own sexual escapades. The daughter's indignation is expressed in moralistic terms. In fact, the text makes it clear that both
mother and daughter are hypocrites. The daughter's attempt to justify her
own premarital fornication by calling the mother a sinful hypocrite is un-
reasonable, and the very irrationality of the argument indicates how completely the daughter is overcome by her own passion.

The most significant element of this poem is that the socialization ("teaching") intended by the mother comes too late. The daughter already knows what she needs to know about sex, and there is no need to teach her about it, because her knowledge of sexual desire is innate: "Mother, that I feel desire is not something I have acquired. I inherited it from you" (st. 3, ll. 5–6). What the mother might have taught the daughter in the year she proposes that the daughter wait (an echo of *Kudrun*) is left unsaid; presumably it would have been something along the lines of the mother's advice in *Die Winsbeckin,* a set of precepts for sexual self-control and socialization into cultural notions of womanly honor. But the daughter's instinctual capacity for feeling and expressing sexual desire has already asserted itself with such force that any concern for social norms has been swept aside.

The daughter knows the source of this desire; she has inherited it from her mother. The daughter asserts the fundamental, natural similarity between herself and her mother as a justification for her own wanton behavior. Her reprimands of her mother emphasize this fact, for they demand that the mother accept the daughter's choices on the grounds that she is merely following her mother's example and the inclinations inherited from her mother. The daughter is thus demanding that the mother recognize and accept their fundamental sexual kinship. In an angry and contradictory way, the daughter is in fact making her argument and her appeal on the grounds of solidarity between mother and daughter.

In "The Sated Crow or the Hungry Crow" a clear demarcation of opposing positions for guardian mother and wanton daughter is being eroded away. The authentic Neidhart poems represented the sexual kinship of mother and daughter through the interchangeability of their roles in the genre as whole. Here the daughter's arguments bring the sexualized, genealogical link between mother and daughter into the poem itself. The daughter establishes continuity between herself and her mother on the basis of their sexual nature. This argument changes the quality of the daughter's rejection of her mother, for she repudiates her mother's teachings in order to insist on the essential resemblance of mother and daughter. For her, the mother-daughter connection is based on a family likeness that expresses itself in their sexual nature.

"The Pan, A Dialogue": Rivalry and Solidarity Between Mother and Daughter

The final poem to be discussed in this chapter is no. 36 in Berlin mgf 779, entitled "The Pan, a Dialogue" (Die pfann ein wechsell), a title taken from an unusual image used in the poem. This poem briefly introduces the types of the guardian mother and the innocent daughter, only to abandon them entirely. Instead, the initial argument between mother and

daughter turns first into a disclosure of their rivalry and then into a dec-
laration of mutual aid and solidarity in the deceits necessary for carrying
on their love affairs. As in the previous poem, the stated premise of this
alliance is the sexual kinship between mother and daughter.

> "I want to go dancing this year
> on the wide green meadow, now that it is Maytime,"
> said a maid. "I am enjoying this.
> It has been said to me
> that love is sweet torment;
> now I am ready for love.
>
> I am ready for a man,
> just like my sister Irmelein who loved carrying on with men.
> Now where have they disappeared to, all those cowardly
>   fellows?
> Why, not a one of them has invited me yet,
> and I wouldn't put up a fuss
> or demand any binding promises.
>
> I am ready for love this year!
> If it is nice as people say, I'll do it even more.
> If it hurts, I'll put it off 'till next year.
> Now where is the blessed man
> who will start this thing with me?
> Let him see how I behave!"
>
> Her mother heard this.
> "Little daughter, stop this talk, for afterwards you will be
>   hurt.
> Wanting to make love when you are so young—
> Why, you aren't even sixteen years old!"
> "Little mother, I am sixteen-plus,
> and that's the best time.
>
> I've been benippled for a few years now,
> little mother. I tell you, I have grown everything a woman
>   needs.
> I've been waiting far too long.
> You told me yourself
> that you were only a virgin for twelve years
> and you survived it."
>
> "Daughter, if you want to make love,
> then find yourself a man whom you can win over.
> Choose a man for yourself whom you really like,

but let me have him first."
"Little Mother, I'd be happy to do that,
but that way you get them all!

What good is food from outside the home
if I can't eat it myself? Lady mother, you are unwise.
I know very well that you always take the best ones for yourself.
My father may be your husband,
but he can no longer master you.
You carry the longer knife.

I know very well that my father
has been your husband for along time; he asked you to him.
Look at you, still eating with the children out of one pan,
and taking twice as much for yourself!
Pfui! May the devil take you!
What do you want with strange men?"

"Daughter, be quiet.
Love a lot or a little, it's all right by me.
Even if I see it with both eyes,
I will keep quiet about it, little daughter.
Child, now you do the same for me,
and we will both love secretly.

If you should get a cradle from this,
little daughter, then our bickering won't help us a bit."
"Little mother, if I can get over that,
then the damage will only be half as bad.
No matter how I turn out,
pass that on to my children."(c 36, 2–11)

The poem begins by invoking the stereotypes of the innocent, dance-happy daughter and the guardian mother but immediately undercuts both. The daughter is a virgin, but she is no innocent. Rather, she expresses her sexual appetites frankly and unabashedly. As for the guardian mother, her assertion of authority in the opening lines of stanza 3 is surprisingly tentative and indecisive. The daughter sweeps aside this maternal claim to authority and exploits the intimacy of the mother-daughter relationship to claim for herself an authoritative voice by simply overtalking her mother and dominating the conversation. This gesture convinces the mother, for instead of restraining her daughter, she begins giving her advice on choosing lovers. At the same time that the mother acknowledges the daughter as her sexual equal, however, she also makes the daughter her rival, demanding that the daughter share her boyfriends.

But the daughter knows how to counter this challenge to her newly won authority. The family life that she and her mother share means that the daughter knows her mother's secrets. She scolds her mother roundly for her voracious appetites—for both food and men. Up until this point, the mother has been the master in the household, but with these arguments the daughter has mastered her mother, who now proposes a pact. Mother and daughter each promise to keep quiet about the other's love affairs, and in return they will cooperate in dealing with the daughter's offspring, who, the daughter assumes, will turn out like herself.

Mother and daughter have become versions of each other—in part, because the daughter wishes it to be so. They are so similar that they no longer oppose each other as proponents of honor or license, respectively, but have become instead potential rivals for the attention of lovers. It is the mother who, at the end of the poem, turns the equality of rivalry into the equality of solidarity. This mother-daughter relationship has failed as an apprenticeship in social conformity, but perhaps it can succeed, the mother proposes, as an apprenticeship in a kind of "secret society" of women, in which women help one another deceive husbands and fathers and share their secrets about finding and taking lovers. The mother offers to transform the mother-daughter relationship into a conspiracy bent on undermining the social order for the purpose of pursuing illicit bodily pleasure. The daughter wholeheartedly agrees. With this poem, we have moved close to the world of late medieval rhymed couplet texts such as the fabliaux and the *Minnerede*, in which women's innate lustfulness is represented as the foundation for their subversive solidarity against men. This theme is explored in more detail in the next chapter, whose primary text, *Stepmother and Daughter*, also shares the notion that the mother-daughter connection is a conspiracy intended to secure women's sexual pleasure while deceiving men.

7

"How a Mother Teaches Her Daughter Whoring"

The Rhymed Couplet Text Stepmother and Daughter

O Moder, ich well en Ding han!
Wat für'n Ding, min Herzenskind?
En Ding! En Ding!
Wellst du dann 'nen Mann han?
Jo, Moder, Jo!
Ihr sitt en gode Moder,
Ihr künnt dat Ding wal roden,
Wat dat Kind für'n Ding well han! ding derling ding ding!
—Anonymous Low German folksong (Kretzschmer 1840, 2:349)[1]

AN OLDER WOMAN teaches a young woman how to exploit her sexuality in order to cheat men, enrich herself, and become economically self-sufficient. The older woman socializes the younger one by first showing her how she is sexualized (i.e., reduced to a sexual function) and then showing her how to use this cultural assumption to her material advantage. The use of this literary convention spans many centuries and cultures of European literature.[2] Sometimes the older woman is servant or foster mother for the younger woman, but often the two women are kin:

1. Oh Mother, there's something I want! / What is it, my dearest child? / Something! Something! / Do you want a man? / Yes, Mother, Yes! / You are a good Mother, / You could guess the something / the something that the child wanted! ding derling ding ding!

2. These citations represent only a sample of relevant literature. See also the play *The Ghost (Mostellaria)* by Plautus (c. 254–184 B.C.), in which the relationship between a young courtesan and her aged female servant develops similar themes. For other examples from classical literature see Juvenal, "Against Women" (Humphries 1958, 71–72); Ovid, *Amores* 1. 8; and Lucian, "Mother Knows Best" (Turner 1990, 39–41). In early modern literature, see, for example, Pietro Aretino, *Ragionamenti della Nanna e della Antonia* (1534) as well as Fernando de Rojas, *Celestina* (1631).

mother and daughter. Female teacher and female student are then further characterized by means of family, kin, and descent. When a mother teaches her daughter whoring, the representation of kinship, the representation of cultural instruction, and the representation of the sexualization of women become inextricably linked. Mothers teach this sociosexual identity to their daughters, yet daughters may well inherit the disposition for it from their mothers. Such a configuration produces a discourse that suggests that the sexualization of women, past and present, is both learned by women and innate in women.

The imagery of nurture and nature thus combined produce one of the most frequent and ancient stereotypes of the mother-daughter relationship. The regularity with which it occurs permits one generalization: The reduction of the social and cultural identity of human beings born female to their sexual and reproductive functions is systemic and structural in Western European culture. It is a historical constant. Yet fixed images of women do not have fixed meanings. The appropriation and recirculation of stereotypes in different places and at different times produces new meanings. Texts containing such stereotypes negotiate, participate in, and help to shape their literary, social, and cultural worlds. In this chapter, the stereotypes of the whoring mother and her initiate daughter from the anonymous late medieval German text, *Stepmother and Daughter*, provide a case in point. *Stepmother and Daughter* represents the socialization and the sexualization of women in ways that both accord with and interrupt the norms and conventions for licit and illicit sexual relations between men and women in fifteenth-century urban Germany. In the varying redactions of *Stepmother and Daughter*, the images of female duplicity and disorderliness tell us much about the cultural contestations of urban, late medieval constructions of female honor and about the asymmetical power relations between men and women in late medieval urban Germany.

The tale scholars have dubbed *Stepmother and Daughter* (*Stiefmutter und Tochter*)[3] is a rhymed couplet text of about 230 lines belonging to the genre known as the *Minnerede* (discourse on love), which circulated widely in the late Middle Ages in Germany (Glier 1971). In his monumental compi-

---

3. That the earliest manuscript containing *Stepmother and Daughter*, the Sterzinger Miszellaneen-Handschrift (see table) has been dated to the first decade of the fifteenth century suggests that *Stepmother and Daughter* may have been written around the turn of the century, possibly in the late fourteenth century. The table also shows, however, that the work's popularity belongs decidedly to the fifteenth century. As a cultural and literary artifact, *Stepmother and Daughter* is a fifteenth-century text.

lation listing all known examples of *Minnereden* and their manuscripts, Tilo Brandis gives it the number 351 and assigns it to the group called "negative Minnelehre" [negative lessons about love] (1968, 132–33). Brandis lists eleven manuscripts containing *Stepmother and Daughter*, an unusually high number of manuscripts for any short rhymed couplet text. With one or possibly two exceptions, these manuscripts were compiled and used in southern German cities, where economic prosperity, cultural accomplishment, and civic pride flourished in the fifteenth century. All the manuscripts are compilation manuscripts—anthologies, as it were—containing vernacular literature of many kinds: rhymed couplet genres such as short narrative poems, fabliaux, and fables as well as love poetry, didactic and gnomic verse, and religious lyrics.[4] To these eleven manuscript witnesses can be added a further, related text bearing an authorial signature: Hans Düsch's printed lunation tract (a moon calendar) from late fifteenth-century Strasbourg.

The twelve texts we call *Stepmother and Daughter* (see table) share elements of the same basic story: out late one night, a male eavesdropper-poet overhears a mother initiating her still virginal daughter into a life built on exploiting sexuality by regaling the daughter with tales of her own erotic and criminal feats. The eavesdropper, the mother, and the daughter are all nameless. The version by Hans Düsch shows the greatest divergence from the eleven manuscript witnesses: Düsch recombines elements of the basic story with episodes of his own devising and changes the ending of the story. The eleven manuscripts containing *Stepmother and Daughter*, however, closely resemble one another, repeating whole sections of the text. Nevertheless, like most late medieval rhymed couplet texts, the manuscript versions of *Stepmother and Daughter* also show certain differences. These textual variations cover the whole range of variation common in pre-print culture, such as scribal error (misspellings, misunderstandings, transposed words, skipped lines) and scribal emendation (most commonly, spellings and word substitutions reflecting the speech habits in the region where the manuscript was being copied). The variations in the manuscripts of *Stepmother and Daughter* also include interventions that reshape the text, such as the deletion, addition, and rewriting of entire passages—transformations that approximate our notion of authorial adaption.

The most significant authorial modifications in the unsigned manuscript versions of *Stepmother and Daughter* are rewritings of the text's ending. They can be grouped into three redactions. The first I call the

4. On fifteenth-century compilation manuscripts, see Westphal 1993.

Table 1
Chronological List of Textual Witnesses Containing
Stepmother and Daughter (Brandis no. 351)

Library and call number	Date	Place of Origin
Sterzinger Miszellaneen-Hs	1400–1410	southern Tyrol (perhaps Neustift/Brixen)
Bamberg HV Msc. 569 (no. 1789) (previously known as Kuppitsch-Hs. C)	1453	perhaps Bavarian
Munich cgm 379	1454	Augsburg
Dresden M 50	1460–1462	Nuremberg
Munich cgm 270	1464	Augsburg
Leipzig 1590	1460–1465	Nuremberg
Weimar Q 564	1460–1475	Nuremberg
Prague X A 12 (= *Liederbuch der Klara Hätzlerin*)	1470–1471	Augsburg
London Ms. Add. 24946	1479–1480	Nuremberg (?)
Weimar O 145	1480–1490	Augsburg area
Basel, Öffentliche Bibliothek der Universität, Einblattdrucke saec. XV, no. 25, Hans Düsch, "Das Clärlein"	1482	Strasbourg
Munich cgm 5919	1501–1510	Regensburg

"framed narration" because the text is both opened and closed by the eavesdropping male narrator, whose words frame the lengthy speech by the mother that makes up the greater part of the text. In each of the manuscripts of version 1, the text concludes with a final speech by the narrator, although his actual words vary considerably from manuscript to manuscript.[5] Five manuscripts are examples of the "framed narra-

5. In all five manuscripts, the narrator concludes with a moralistic saying rhyming *êr* (honor) and *lêr* (teaching). In Weimar O 145 these are his final lines. Sterzing adds a curse and the word "amen." Prague X A 12 adds a pious saying. Munich cgm 270 and Munich cgm 5919 add two lines that call for drink (*Zutrunk*).

tion" version: the oldest one, the Sterzinger Miszellaneen handschrift, as well as Munich cgm 270, Prague X A 12, Weimar O 145, and Munich cgm 5919.[6]

The second redaction I call the "unframed" version. The narrator does not return to close the narrative frame. Instead, the text of version 2 concludes while the mother is still speaking. Version 2 is shorter than version 1, yet textually it follows version 1 very closely. Version 2 may well have derived from an imperfect copy of version 1 that was missing the ending, as from a scribal intervention to shorten the text. Three manuscripts are examples of version 2: Bamberg HV Msc. 569 (no. 1789), Munich cgm 379, and London Ms. Add. 24946. Version 2 will not be discussed in this book.[7]

The third version I call the "Nuremberg redaction" because my research has shown that it is likely to have been composed in Nuremberg. As in version 2, a male narrator opens the text but does not return to close it. The text concludes with the mother's voice. However, the Nuremberg redaction adds new material to the text, including a completely new ending. Three manuscripts are examples of version 3: Dresden M 50, Leipzig 1590, and Weimar Q 564.[8] As I shall demonstrate, the differences in the endings of version 1 (the framed narration) and version 3 (the Nuremberg redaction) provide significant evidence for showing how gender informs conflicting notions of women's honor.

6. The manuscripts of version 1 are described and/or edited in the following sources. On the Sterzinger Miszellaneen-Handschrift (Sterzinger Stadtarchiv, no signature), see the edition and commentary by Zimmermann (1980). On Munich cgm 270, see the description in the magnificant manuscript catalogue from the Bayerische Staatsbibliothek (Schneider 1973a, 189–208). Leiderer has edited twelve discourses of love from Munich cgm 270 and provides a valuable discussion of its sources (1972). On Prague X A 12 (Knihovna Národního musea), see n. 9, below. For a description of Weimar O 145, (Herzogin Anna Amalia Bibliothek) see Hanns Fischer's edition of Hans Folz (1961, XLVI-LVIII). For a lengthy description of Munich cgm 5919, see Meyer 1989, 1: 31–133 (for *Stepmother and Daughter* 102–103).

7. For a description of Munich cgm 379, see the manuscript catalogue of the Bayerische Staatsbibliothek (Schneider 1973b, 96–115). Munich cgm 379 is also discussed by Wachinger (1982) and Mück (1980, 281–89). For descriptions of London Ms. Add. 24946 (British Museum), see Mück (1980, 271–80) and Reichel (1985, 233). For a discussion of Bamberg HV Msc. 569 (no. 1789) (Staatsbibliothek Bamberg), see Schulz-Grobert (1989, 236–41).

8. Neither Dresden M 50 (Sächsiche Landesbibliothek) nor Leipzig 1590 (Bibliothek der Universität Leipzig) has been edited. See Reichel 1985 for a description of Dresden M 50 (226–27) and of Leipzig 1590 (232–33), as well as for a discussion of the interrelationship of these two manuscripts (44–58). Morgenstern-Werner (1990) has published a transcription of Weimar Q 564 (Herzogin Anna Amalia Bibliothek).

The Framed Narration

The 228-line version of *Stepmother and Daughter* from the compilation manuscript Prague X A 12, often called after the female scribe who compiled it in 1470 or 1471 "The Songbook of Klara Hätzlerin" (Liederbuch der Klara Hätzlerin), is the longest version of the "framed narration" redaction.[9] In Prague X A 12, *Stepmother and Daughter* has a unique and particularly apt descriptive title: "How A Mother Teaches Her Daughter Whoring" (wie ain můter ir dochter lernet půlen). It shares its opening, however, with all eleven manuscript witnesses: an eavesdropping male narrator begins recounting the circumstances that lead to the story.

> I left the house late one night
> and arrived at the chamber of love
> where I heard two people talking.
> I noted it well in my mind,
> a mother and her little daughter,
> saying what I expected to hear.

> Ich gieng ains nachtes von huse spat
> Und kam für liebes kemenat,
> Da hort ich reden zway darynn.
> Das merck ich wol in meinem synn,
> Ain můter und ir döchterlein.
> Die redten nach dem willen mein. (*ST*, ll. 1–6)

The narrator establishes himself as a framing and recording voice ("merck ich wol in meinem synn"). The daughter's voice follows in a short speech, complaining that she is tormented in body and spirit by longing. After these twelve introductory lines, the mother speaks. Diagnosing her daughter's problem as virginity, she launches into the text's main text: a two-hundred-line monologue of anecdotes and instructions about seducing, deceiving, and cheating men. Promising wealth and honor if her daughter follows her teachings, the mother boasts of the enterprising spirit she showed in her youth.

---

9. The text is cited according to Haltaus, ed., *Liederbuch der Clara Hätzlerin* (1966), abbreviated here as *ST*. All translations are my own. Haltaus's line numbering contains errors. I have chosen, however, to retain the edition's faulty line numbering so that the cited lines can be easily located. For this reason the number of actual lines cited does not always correspond to the stated line numbering.

On this manuscript see also Geuther 1899 and Schlosser 1965. For an excellent analysis of the social function of this genre of *Minnereden* in the late medieval urban milieu, see Wachinger 1982.

> When I was in your place
> I truly was a fine maid,
> and I could do more defrauding
> than one hundred others in the city.
> Whoever asked me for my affections,
> if I knew that he had much money,
> then I didn't say no, I gave him a date
> and I also took his goods for it.
> . . . .
> Like water running through a mill,
> so my wheels were turning.
> The first man I let in at the front,
> the second I sent out at the back,
> the third I kept in the house.
>
> Da ich was in deiner acht,
> Da was ich gar ain stoltze dieren,
> Und kund auch mer troffieren,
> Dann ander hundert in ainer Statt.
> Wer mich umb mein pûlschafft bat,
> West ich, das er hett pfenning vil,
> So liesz ich nit, ich gab Im zil,
> Ich nam auch sein gut daran.
> . . . .
> Wie rynnet wasser durch ain mül,
> Also giengen die reder mein.
> Den ainen liesz ich vornen ein,
> Den andern schickt ich hinden usz,
> Den dritten hielt ich in dem hus. (*ST*, ll. 20–27, 42–46)

The mother's strategies for duping men while enriching and enjoying herself, all while eluding male control, are legion: she begs off assignations with poor men by pretending fear of an unwanted pregnancy; she picks the pockets of her lovers; she sends two suitors ahead at haying (mowing) time, "so that, in case I were to lose one, I'd still have the other" [ob es wär, das ich ainen verlür / Das der ander by mir belib] (*ST*, ll. 62–63); she has sex with the master (*herr*) in the barn. She enjoys exploiting—repeatedly—the pretense of virginity, and she finds it funny that she can go off to "pick flowers" and "make garlands" and, in the process of making love in the fields, flatten the crops. The mother is also proud of her success at extorting money from wealthy lovers after the births of illegitimate children.

> Unmarried I bore seven children;
> not a one did I give to its true father.
> Rather, the one with the most wealth,

I would cast the child at his door in the morning
when people were going to and fro.
Then he was mocked by the whole world
and begged me by the love of God
to take the child back again.
He would pay out to me, with great shame,
more than ten pounds,
if only I would restore his honor.
He would have sworn that it was his
and he believed my talk,
but I only did it for profit,
naming him as the father.

Ich trůg auch ledig siben chind;
Chains ich dem rechten vater gab;
Nur welher hett die maisten hab,
Dem warf ichs morgens für die tür,
Da die lüt giengen hin und für.
Der ward dann vor der welt zu spott
Und bat mich dann fast durch gott,
Das ich das chind wider nem.
Er zalt mir uf mit grosser schäm
Mer dann zehen pfunt,
So ich Im nur der eren gunt.
Er hett gesworen, es wär sein
Und gelaubet der rede mein;
So tet ichs nur durch genyesz,
Das ich In den vater hiesz. (*ST*, ll. 86–100)

The mother goes on to recount an elaborate ruse (recounted in other
fabliaux as well) she has employed to obtain money from two gravely ill
suitors who have been injured, she says, in fighting over her. She ties a
wet sponge to her head, covers it with veil (the symbol of wifely honor)
and hat, and visits in turn, each of her suitors on his sickbed. She tells her
daughter of her sighing and weeping (that is, squeezing the sponge so
that "tears" will flow):

I said: "My hope, my dearest treasure,
Open your eyes, don't you recognize me?
If need be, I would die for you!"
I made my sighs terribly long.

Ich sprach: mein trost, mein höchster hordt,
Tů uff deine augen, chennst du mich?
Solt es sein, ich stürb für dich!
Ich macht mein seüftzen also langk. (*ST*, ll. 118–21)

At least one of the suitors sees through this ploy; she reports that he said: "Cut it out, you're making me sick" [hör uff, du machst mich kranck] (*ST*, l. 122). This response does not, however, slow her down; her lament, she assures her daughter, was sincere enough, because she was lamenting her own misfortune that the fellow survived and thus could not leave her any money. The mother states her creed plainly:

> Now, dear daughter, take this to heart:
> lie and cheat everybody.

> Nun, liebe dochter, nym dich an
> Lewig und betring yederman! (*ST*, ll. 139–40)

But the daughter still requires training in how to use her sexual charms to cheat men, so the mother now tutors her in the arts of flattery, entice-ment, seduction, and bargaining—all of which utilize tempting displays of the female body. To paraphrase the mother's instructions: keep a look-out from your window, and when a likely young fellow (*gesell*) comes by, ask someone else loudly who he is. When he comes back, stand in the doorway, and ask "Where are you going? Come in, I am sure I know you from somewhere." Rub your feet together, spin and dance in front of him, sit down, send for wine, put your head on his shoulder, wrap yourself around him like a fur coat, hold his hand and tell him that a man with such warm hands inflames you (*ST*, ll. 141–69).

> If he then becomes so bold
> that he grabs your bosom,
> say "Cut it out, hands off!"
> Tickle him under his arms
> and leave your bodice open
> on both sides.
> Then he will hardly be able to wait.
> He will peer in at your little breasts,
> and his desire will stand proud.

> Ist er dann so gar verwegen
> Und greifft dir zu dem pûsem ein,
> So sprich: hört uff, tût hin!
> Under den armen In kützel
> Und lasz offen deinen schützel
> Baidenthalb by der seitten.
> So mag er kaum erpeitten,
> Vil plick er zu den prüstlen tût,
> Damit so stoltzet Im der mût. (*ST*, ll. 170–78)

If an inexperienced fellow ("milichfriedel," *ST*, l. 185) should ask for your favors, demand an exorbitant amount of money and then bargain like a fishwife. In any case, helping poor fellows out in this way damages young women "as much as taking a sip of water hurts the Danube river" [als der Tonau ain trunck] (*ST*, l. 197), in other words, not at all. And by all means hang on to such a fellow, who can become your best beau ("lieber man," *ST*, l. 204); he will do everything you wish.

The narrative frame now begins to close. The daughter replies that she is expecting just such a fellow this evening, one who is coming with a heavy purse that she can now, by following her mother's teachings, lighten. The narrator—who with the daughter's words has been pulled into the framed story, because he may be the suitor in question—now closes the frame. He has learned his lesson, which he sums up with the proverb: "the apple never falls far from the tree" [Der Apfel will nach dem stamm / geratten! dacht ich mir] (*ST*, ll. 214–15). Enlightened and considerably sobered, the narrator runs away from the house, denouncing the women to passersby, and ending with a pious warning.

> Away from the house I quickly rushed.
> Many a one got fixed up there,
> and I denounced the falsity of the young woman
> as a crowd of fools appeared.
> First and foremost I reacted to the old woman.
> May the devil break her bones,
> for then many a good apprentice would have peace,
> and many a daughter would be virtuous
> who now relies on fickleness
> and does not preserve her honor.
> Those who follow such advice
> often come to harm.
> May God have mercy on the righteous!

> Vom dem hus da eylt ich schier.
> Da ward manigem gerüft,
> Der Jungen valschait ich da brüft,
> Es kamen tûmeling ain schar,
> Aller erst nam ich der alten war.
> Der tewffel zerpräch ire glid,
> So hätt manig gût gesell frid,
> Und wär auch maniger dochter gût,
> Die sich verlat uf wanckel mût,
> Und bewart auch nit ir Er!
> Die volgen ainer sölichen ler,
> Den chomt es oft ze schaden!
> Gott wöll die frumen begnaden! (*ST*, ll. 216–28)

Conflicting Views of Women's Honor and Sexual Behavior

The distinction between female honor and female dishonor is contested on the basis of gender in the framed version of *Stepmother and Daughter* in Prague X A 12. At the outset, the mother states categorically that her teachings are compatible with maintaining womanly honor; she promises her daughter that if she follows her advice, "Then wealth and honor will become yours" [So widerfert dir gut und Er] (*ST*, l. 18).[10] Through her example, the mother teaches her daughter to act out the chastity, passivity, fidelity, and obedience that define socially sanctioned female honor even as she transgresses against them: she feigns virginity even though she is sexually active; she pretends to fear pregnancy before marriage; she takes on respectable work such as field labor and uses it as an opportunity to find sexual partners; she dons the veil signifying wifely honor in order to exploit financially the convention of the loving, grieving wife. The mother's transgression is most obvious in her reproductive role, when she exploits the social conventions for establishing paternity in order to support herself and her numerous illegitimate children. For the mother, as we shall see, female honor does not reside in a woman's body. For her, female honor is, to quote Lyndal Roper, "not so much a thing as a self-description to which women might lay claim by devising their own stories." (1989b, 57).

The narrator, on the other hand, wishes the reader to believe that he has narrowly escaped being ensnared by two dishonorable women, of whom the older one is the more reprehensible because she purposefully leads her youthful daughter away from maintaining womanly honor. The narrator lays claim to a construction of female honor that is strictly and narrowly defined by women's sexual activity: virtuous women are either unmarried virgins or faithful, obedient, and chaste wives; disreputable women are sexually promiscuous. For the narrator, women's honor resides in women's bodies, and sexually active behavior by women "is perceived as dishonorable and as a potential challenge to the sexual prowess and honor of men" (Roper 1994, 72).

The narrator and the mother represent conflicting perspectives on the questions of women's honor and women's sexual behavior. The historical context suggests that women's honor and their sexual activity were perceived as interdependent categories in late medieval German society.[11] In

10. The mother in pseudo-Neidhart poem number 32 from manuscript Berlin mgf 779 says virtually the same thing: "Little daughter, if you follow my advice, then both respect and honor will become yours" [tohterlein, / volgestu meiner lere, / so widerfert dir paide wird und ere] (song no. 32, st. 5) (Bennewitz-Behr 1981, 88–89).

11. On the issue of women's honor in late medieval and early modern Germany, see Roper 1989b and 1994, as well as Burghartz 1990, 1991, and 1992.

L'Enseigne à Bière. Holzschnitt. Paris. Bibliothèque Nationale. Lucas de Leyde. tom. II.
(Aus der Sammlung des Abbé de Marolles.)

11. In the interior of a tavern, a man and a young woman are seated at a table. They fondle each other; the man appears to draw the woman toward himself, while the woman touches the man's face with her right hand and picks his pocket from behind his back with her left hand. They share the table with an elderly woman who drinks from a goblet. Two male figures spy on the scene. From the doorway, a young boy peers in; from the window, an elderly male figure dressed as a fool points to the young couple and speaks the words on the scroll: "acht, hoet. varen. sal" [Pay attention to the way the wind blows]. Lucas van Leyden, *A Tavern Scene* (also known as the *Prodigal Son*). Woodcut, 1518–1520. Paris, Bibliothèque Nationale.

medieval German cities, a woman's legal situation was ambiguous. The historian Merry Wiesner points out that women were "simultaneously independent legal persons (they owned property, inherited wealth, received wages, paid taxes) and dependent parts of a legal entity, the family, whose financial decisions they did not officially control" (1986, 31). As daughters, wives, and to a lesser extent, widows, women were supposed to belong to a household in which they were subject to paternal rule, represented primarily by fathers and husbands. Women's social honor was determined largely by their sexual comportment as chaste daughters or faithful wives; indeed, a woman's reputation for chastity was a *Rechtsgut*, a legal, material entity for which a woman could juridically demand compensation. Women's honor was seen to be a key issue influencing individual morality, economic well-being, and the stability of the social order. Unmarried women who lived on their own, unsupervised by a male head of the household, were always regarded with suspicion by city councils.

Yet late medieval German cities abounded with single women (whether or not yet married) who lived independently and whose occupations gave them access to unsupervised and unsupervisable spaces: wage laborers, bathhouse workers, washerwomen, farm laborers, domestic servants (Wiesner 1986, 32–34). Such working women were viewed with suspicion but tolerated out of necessity. The fictional mother and daughter in *Stepmother and Daughter* belong to this category of socially and economically marginal women: they are unmarried; they live alone; the mother has worked as a farm laborer (driving cattle and mowing), and at one point she calls herself a maidservant (*dieren, ST*, l. 21). The suspicion society cast upon such lower-class women is reflected in the conflicting accounts the mother and the narrator offer of women's honor. While the narrator wishes to expose mother and daughter as dishonorable, the mother insists that her honor is intact and that her daughter, too, can preserve her good name.

The issue around which these conflicting accounts of honor coalesce is sex. In order to see the significance of this conflict, we must examine more closely the social and economic parameters of the sex work the mother undertakes. From around 1350 until the advent of the Reformation, medieval German cities took an active role in regulating and organizing the business of sex work, i.e., prostitution.[12] In the fifteenth century civic brothels flourished, organized and run by town authorities. The munici-

---

12. Studies of medieval prostitution have multiplied in recent years. On medieval France see Otis 1985. On medieval England see Karras 1989 and 1996. On fifteenth- and sixteenth-century Germany, see Roper 1989a, P. Schuster 1992 and Beate Schuster 1991 and 1995.

pal brothel was "designated for one particular group of men—journeymen and apprentices not yet married" (Roper 1989a, 92). Brothels were highly regulated. The occupation of brothel keeper was dishonorable but highly lucrative. In the Augsburg of this period, all brothel keepers were apparently men (Roper 1989a, 97). Prostitution, too, was dishonorable; whether it was a lucrative venture for the individual women seems dubious.[13] The Nuremberg brothel ordinances from the fifteenth century legislate against a number of practices that may well have been commonplace: buying and selling women; keeping women against their will and compelling them to work when ill or pregnant; brothel keepers charging exorbitant fees for rent and food; allowing women to refuse customers in order to accommodate their "best beau" (*lieber man*; the phrase used in the brothel ordinance is also used by the mother in *Stepmother and Daughter*) (Baader 1861, 117–21). Such practices certainly suggest that brothel life "was the antithesis of the ideal of the free citizen controlling his own labour" (Roper 1989a, 97).

Institutionalizing prostitution was justified in part because it was understood to provide an outlet for the sexual energies of the numerous unmarried men, apprentices and journeymen, who also populated these cities. Civic brothels "legitimated the social construction of male desire as a force which must have an outlet or cause chaos" (Roper 1989a, 100). The institutionalization of prostitution was viewed as protection of the virtue of honorable wives and daughters, who would otherwise have been endangered by the unfulfilled sexual urges of these unmarried men. In turn, brothels also functioned to clearly separate honorable women from dishonorable ones. The history of the era suggests that secular authorities attempted to strictly patrol the boundary between honorable and dishonorable women. Prostitutes and brothels were segregated and restricted to certain parts of the city—usually on the margins, beside a minor city gate, or just outside the city walls. The sumptuary laws of the period, which insisted on visual demarcations of estate and rank for virtually all city inhabitants, legislated special clothing and colors for whores (P. Schuster 1992, 145–53).

Mother and daughter in *Stepmother and Daughter* exchange sex for money and have multiple sex partners, yet there is no sign in the text that they are brothel prostitutes. On the contrary—the monetary success of much of the sex work the mother does depends on successfully maintain-

---

13. Christine de Pisan's description of a prostitute's life in her *Treasure of the City of Ladies* is illuminating: "How can she tolerate indecency and living, drinking and eating entirely among men more vile than swine—men who strike her, drag her about and threaten her, and by whom she is always in danger of being killed?" (1985, 172). See also B. Schuster 1991.

ing a reputation of womanly honor, and on avoiding being perceived as a prostitute. Instead, the sex work in which mother and daughter engage exploits the access to unsupervised space that is a condition of their legitimate, low-class employment as laborers, servants, and serving women. In this regard, their sex work most closely parallels the free-lance prostitution that existed alongside brothel prostitution in medieval German cities. Nonliterary evidence of free-lance prostitution suggests that free-lance prostitutes plied their trade through streetwalking and with the help of go-betweens, procurers, and procuresses (figures also familiar from contemporary fiction). Wiesner suggests that even during the era of civic brothels the majority of women who made all or part of their living by prostitution did so illicitly (1986, 106–109). Such illicit prostitution was often part-time work, combined with some of the professions already mentioned, such as washing, farm work, and day labor. In "Die meisterliche Predigt" (The masterly sermon), the fifteenth-century Nuremberg poet Hans Rosenplüt, for example, complains about adultery between married men and housemaids. The men, he claims, linger on the street at night and proposition maidservants on their way to fetch wine. The maids willingly agree to engage then and there in a hasty sexual union in exchange for money (1990, ll. 67–87).

German cities attempted repeatedly—but unsuccessfully—to eliminate such free-lance prostitution, in part to protect the monopolies of the civic brothels and in part to control women's sexual behavior and to segregate dishonorable from honorable women. The competition between these two forms of prostitution figures in another poem by Hans Rosenplüt, *Die fünfzehn Klagen A* (The Fifteen Laments, Version A):

> The common women [i.e., brothel prostitutes] also lament their
>   estate,
> Their meadow has become too sparse:
> The "corner women" [i.e., free-lance prostitutes] and the
>   housemaids,
> they overgraze daily their meadow.
>
> Die gemeinen weib clagen auch iren orden,
> Ir weide sei vil zu mager worden:
> Die winkelweiber und die hawßmeide,
> Die fretzen teglich ab ir weide. (1990, ll. 31–34)

In Rosenplüt's text women pursuing other occupations (housemaids, even nuns) "poach" on the brothel prostitute's rightful territory. His text thus supports the nonliterary evidence in suggesting that brothel prostitution, though a dishonorable profession, was seen as a licit activity, while free-lance prostitution was an illicit activity that muddled the boundary between honorable and dishonorable behavior.

In *Stepmother and Daughter*, besides engaging in sex for pleasure and in the outright exchange of sex for money or favors, the mother, by extorting payments from her suitors and from the fathers of her illegitimate offspring, also exploits established social conventions for resolving illicit sexual liaisons between masters and servants or clerics and their concubines. In households, illicit sexual liaisons between masters and their servants, for example, were not necessarily considered adultery or fornication in the full, serious, public sense, as long as they did not become a public affront to domestic and work relations (Roper 1989a, 198), and as long as the obligations entailed by the relationship could be contractually discharged (Roper 1989a, 196). Ecclesiastical courts and local tradition often dealt with cases involving loss of virginity or the birth of a child outside of wedlock, both of them cases in which a woman had lost her honor. In such instances, the seduced virgin or abandoned mother could be compensated. The woman was asked to calculate an appropriate figure as her compensation claim, "insisting on her worth in a direct calculus of honor and money" (Roper 1989b, 57); reluctant men were forced to meet their financial obligations. Roper documents sixteenth-century cases in which women resorted to tactics of shame and public ridicule in order to enforce their claims—a seduced maid servant, for example, jumped up on her seducer's marriage cart and refused to get off until she had received payment (Roper 1989a, 198).

Such practices and customs are exploited by the mother in *Stepmother and Daughter* seven times with seven illegitimate children (*ST*, ll. 86–100, quoted earlier). In the context of womanly honor, the sevenfold repetition of this action hints that after each illegitimate—and hence dishonorable— birth, the mother was able to reclaim enough honor to be able to reassert its loss. Like Roper's maidservant, the mother does not count on any sort of legal authority to assert her claim to monetary compensation but instead depends on public ridicule to tarnish the father's respectability. The mother thus bypasses questions of her own honor by defaming that of men. The mother also exploits other kinds of customary compensation for illicit sexual liaisons, as she shows in tales of escapades in which she claimed and benefited from female honor. With the sponge ruse, for example, she posed as a grief-stricken lover or concubine in order to seek a share of a dying man's estate. Moreover, the mother's final instruction that the daughter attach herself to a best beau (*lieber man*) hints that sexual promiscuity is no barrier to a long-term, financially secure relationship such as concubinage, perhaps even marriage.

In *Stepmother and Daughter*, the mother exploits socially sanctioned registers of femininity for her own purposes, seeking both to evade patriarchal control and to pass on to her daughter the knowledge of how to do so. Through her example, she shows her daughter how to support herself both with respectable work and by exploiting male lust when and how she chooses. The mother teaches her daughter to turn to her own benefit virtually every honorable female role while transgressing against the main precept of female honor: that honorable women remain chaste. The mother negotiates the contradictory social customs regarding female promiscuity according to the principle that a woman can remain honorable and benefit from notions of female honor so long as she controls how the story of her honor is told.

From the narrator's point of view, the figure of the mother illustrates what Roper calls "the long association of women, lust, and luxury" (1989a, 176). For the narrator, the mother is fraudulent on every level: sexual, social, moral, and economic. Yet the contradictory interpretations of female honor claimed by the mother and by the narrator in *Stepmother and Daughter* reveal another level of meaning: that of social satire. The mother is, after all, a successful businesswoman; for her, sex is a commodity. She rejects poor customers and services the rich, she turns potential disasters to her financial advantage, and she is a shrewd bargainer. Her complete disdain for men after they have satisfied her economic needs parodies both the expected male attitude towards a prostitute, who is expendable once she has satisfied the customer's sexual needs, as well as an unscrupulous merchant's attitude toward his customers:

> After their pockets were empty
> I was completely indifferent to them.
>
> Wann In was der pewtel lär
> So waren sy mir gantz unmär. (*ST*, ll. 75–76)

The mother's success parodies the mercantile spirit of the late medieval German city. It inverts the commercial values that were a source of local wealth and pride, values represented by the mother through her entrepreneurial drive, her shrewd business sense, her delight in driving a good bargain, her pleasure in getting something for nothing. Through the figure of the mother, *Stepmother and Daughter* represents commerce as an appetite for fraud.

The Socialization and Sexualization of Women

The mother in *Stepmother and Daughter* passes her knowledge on to her daughter. The daughter in turn is a willing pupil, ready to accept and practice what the mother teaches. For these two women, the mother-daughter relationship represents connection in the form of economic and social solidarity and mutual aid. The disagreement, anger, and separation that figured so prominently in the early Neidhart poems are conspicuously lacking here. For the narrator of *Stepmother and Daughter*, the connection between mother and daughter has a further ramification: it means that the daughter duplicates her mother. This idea is expressed clearly in the the narrator's closing proverb, "the apple never falls far from the tree" [Der Apfel will nach dem stamm / geratten! dacht ich mir] (*ST*, ll. 214–15). For the narrator, the predictability of the proverb creates its explanatory force. The apple tree always produces apples; this daughter will not only imitate her mother, she will become exactly like her. With these words the narrator establishes the mother-daughter connection in a biological metaphor suggesting the enduring, innate identities of the natural world. In this way the narrator suggests that the continuity of such practices among lower-class women is not due to the material and social conditions of their existence. Rather, it suggests that such practices persist because lower-class daughters inherit from their mothers a nature given to fraud and promiscuity, making them susceptible to their mothers' teachings.

The socialization of the daughter acted out in *Stepmother and Daughter* raises interesting questions about the sexualization of women. Early in the poem the daughter states outright that she feels sexual desire:

> The daughter spoke the first word:
> "Such a terrible longing has seized
> my proud body, my fresh spirit!
> It must be time, and I feel it's right,
> that I should seek and find a man
> who could cure my longing."
>
> Die dochter sprach am ersten wort:
> Sich sënt usz der massen hart
> Mein stoltzer leib, mein frischer mût!
> Es wär wol zeit und deucht mich gût,
> Das ich sûchet und ainen fünd,
> Der mir mein senen püszen künd! (*ST*, ll. 7–12)

The mother concurs with this opinion: her daughter's virginity is the cause of her suffering ("Der magtumb dir gar nachent leit," *ST*, l. 15). At the same time, the mother shows the daughter that the sexualization of women—their reduction to a sexual and reproductive role—is not innate to or natural to women. Rather, it is a social construction, one that must be learned and that can be exploited by women for their own economic gain. The mother shows the daughter how she has been sexualized, then socializes her by teaching her how to make use of that condition.

The male narrator plays a different role in the text's sexualization of women. First, we should recall that he eavesdrops on the women and secretly overhears their talk. The mother's story and the daughter's reactions, as we hear them, are recorded by means of this rhetorical device of the eavesdropping male narrator,[14] which creates a discourse of women's secrets: knowledge that women share with other women and conceal from men. This narrative framing characterizes the socialization of the daughter by the mother as such a narrative of women's secrets; the daughter confesses her sexual desire to her mother and the mother reveals her methods to her daughter only because they believe that they are alone. The frame of the eavesdropper thus seems to reveal as an objective truth that women consciously, intentionally, and calculatingly exploit their power to arouse men, an appearance of truth that derives from the fact that this message issues in an unguarded moment from the mouths of the women themselves. The socialization of women that mother and daughter act out is thus revealed as a female conspiracy that is profoundly, and secretly, contemptuous of men.

The recording frame of the eavesdropping male narrator invites us to interpret *Stepmother and Daughter* as expressing a deep anxiety that no woman is fundamentally honorable—that *all* women, not just those who occasionally exchange sex for money, participate either openly or secretly in the duplicity enacted by mother and daughter in this text. The rhetorical construction of the narrative in *Stepmother and Daughter* legitimates (to paraphrase Roper) a social construction of female desire as a natural urge to defraud that must be regulated, controlled, and constrained or cause chaos.[15]

Like so many medieval fabliaux, *Stepmother and Daughter* is a story about conflicts of economic, social, and moral power between men and women. Yet it reminds us that the asymmetrical power relations between the sexes in late medieval Europe were socially constructed and socially contested. *Stepmother and Daughter* is also a tale of resistance and women's economic self-sufficiency. The mother exploits even her fertility to gain

14. On the use of the motif of the eavesdropping male narrator in medieval literature, see Joldersma (1984) and Spearing (1993).

15. Roper (1988) demonstrates how in the 1540s the Augsburg city council took a view of the mother-daughter relationship similar to the one expressed by the unnamed narrator of Prague X A 12. Believing that the mother-daughter relationship was primarily a sexual alliance and that some lower-class mothers deliberately exploited and abused their parental role in order to encourage their daughters to engage in premarital sex with upper-class men, the city council sought to criminalize such parental behavior and prosecuted some mothers as procuresses.

power that is derived from men but not accountable to them. Though intended perhaps as a story of disorder, it is also the story of defiance, insubordination, and subversion. The mother's resourcefulness, her derring-do, and her good humor, fascinate and impress; she is, above all, a survivor. For her, woman's honor is a self-description, a story that a woman tells about herself. As the story closes, the narrator strives to establish a didactic and moralizing tone that will counteract the mother's advice and example. Yet the narrator, who scurries away with a pious warning on his lips, seems anxious and timid in comparison to the enterprising mother. In the final lines the narrator strives to recuperate the conventional assumption that there is a fixed difference between honorable and dishonorable women, but since that assumption rests on the understanding that woman's honor is a possession which once lost can never be restored, it is disrupted by the mother's stories.

The Nuremberg Redaction

The three compilation manuscripts Dresden M 50, Leipzig 1590, and Weimar Q 564 contain a distinct version of *Stepmother and Daughter* that makes substantial additions to the text and gives it a unique ending.[16] The changes begin with the title: the Dresden and Leipzig manuscripts call the text *Stepmother and Daughter,* a title unique to the Nuremberg redaction (Dresden M 50: "Die stiefmuter und di tochter"; Leipzig 1590: "Von der stiefmuter und dochter"; Weimar Q 564: "Die stieffmuter"). Changes continue in the narrator's initial lines, which are the first five lines of the poem. While retaining the framework and repeating the lines and rhymes of the base text (for comparison, see ll. 1–5 of Prague X A 12, quoted on p. 194, above), the text makes two changes that begin the process of subtly altering the text's message: the adjective *liebes*, charac-

---

16. Dresden M 50 and Leipzig 1590 are line by line the same text, with only minor spelling and transcription deviations and obvious scribal errors, such as when Dresden skips line. Weimar also follows Dresden and Leipzig line for line, but it abbreviates the poem by deleting the middle section. In other words, Weimar shares the first thirty-six lines with Dresden and Leipzig, then deletes the next eighty-some lines, and then picks up the last fifty-six lines. Perhaps an entire folio was passed over or missing. Deliberate abbreviation seems unlikely. Additionally, all three manuscripts transmit *Stepmother and Daughter* as a part of collections of poetry by Hans Rosenplüt (Reichel 1985). Dresden and Leipzig have the same cluster of Rosenplüt texts appearing with *Stepmother and Daughter;* in Weimar Q 564, *Stepmother and Daughter* is the last of collection of Rosenplüt and Pseudo-Rosenplüt Shrovetide plays and poems that close the manuscript (Morgenstern-Werner 1990).

terizing the chamber where the conversation takes place as a "chamber of love" (*liebes kemenat*), is removed, and the mother (*mûter*) becomes stepmother (*stieffmuter*).

> I left the house late one night
> and passed by a chamber
> where I heard two people talking.
> I noted it well in my mind,
> a stepmother and her little daughter. (ll. 1–5)

> Ich ginge eins nachcz von hause spat
> Da kam ich fur ein kemnat
> Da horet ich zwey reden ynn
> Das merkt ich eben in meinem synn
> Ein stieffmuter und ir tochterlein. (Dresden M 50)

> Ich ging eins nachtz von hause spat
> Do kam ich für ein kemnat
> Do hört zweÿ reden In
> Das merckt ich eben in meinen synn
> Ein Stieffmuter und ein töchterlein. (Weimar Q 564)

> Ich ging eins nachtes spat
> Do kam ich fur ein kemnat
> Do hort ich zway reden ynn
> Das merckt ich eben yn mein sin
> Ein stiefmuter und yr tochterlein. (Leipzig 1590)[17]

Following the basic story, the daughter speaks, and then the mother's voice takes over the text. Unlike the characters in Prague X A 12, neither daughter nor narrator speaks again; the mother's voice continues through to the end, closing the text.

Version 3, the Nuremberg redaction, retains the incidents recounted in version 1, exemplified by Prague X A 12: the extortion of money through childbirth, the false laments at the lover's sickbed, the specific advice for the daughter. Its general tendencies, however, are to shorten the text, to add more manifestly obscene passages, and, moreover, to make the mother explicitly a prostitute, as can be seen in the following passage:

---

17. Because the three manuscripts differ so little, in the following I supply text only from Dresden M 50.

And when I was in your situation
I was truly a free-living maid
and I could always do more flirtatious courting
than thirty others in one city.

Und da ich was in deiner acht
Da was ich gar ein freÿe diren
Und konde auch allwegen mer hoffiren
Dann annder dreyszig in ein stat. (Dresden M 50, ll. 18–21)

For the sake of comparison, the corresponding passage from Prague X A 12:

And when I was in your situation
I was truly a proud maid
And I could do more cheating
than one hundred others in one city.

Da ich was in deiner acht,
Da was ich gar ain stoltze dieren,
Und kund auch mer troffieren,
Dann ander hundert in ainer Statt. (Prague X A 12, ll. 20–23)

In the first twenty-five lines of the text, the mother has already become a "free-living maid," not a "proud" one, and her behavior is no longer cheating (*troffieren*) but acting in the manner of courtesan (*hoffieren*).[18]

Although the Nuremberg version is shorter than the long, framed version represented here by Prague X A 12, it contains original interpolations. These include three lines containing an obvious reference to a man's erection,

I told him about the school of pleasure,
so that before my eyes he became a stool,
that is, his third leg grew.

Ich sagt im von der frewden schul
Das er vor mir warde zu einem stul
Das im ward wachszen das dritte peÿn. (Dresden M 50, ll. 37–39)

as well as a new example of how the mother exploits the virginity ruse:

18. The change from *troffieren* to *hoffieren* makes sense semantically, but it could have originated in a scribal misreading, since the graphemes for *tr* and *h* in fifteenth-century hands can resemble each other closely.

I looked around for a rich man next,
and I led him away into my bed.
Then and there he was my best beau,
and with me he was so happy
for he believed he was mowing the first grass.
But the stubble he found wasn't green
and he was fishing in an empty pond.

Nach dem reichsten ich umb ganimpt
Den furt ich in mein pett hindan
Der was dann da mein liebster man
Mit mir er dann so frolich was
So meynt er dann er meet das erste grasz
So vand er kainem der grunner stupffel
Und vyschet da in leren tumpffel. (Dresden M 50, ll. 44–50)

A salient difference between the Nuremberg redaction and the other versions of the *Stepmother and Daughter* is the allusion to male and female sexual organs: the erect penis (the third leg of the stool) and the woman's pubic hair and vagina (stubble and pond) from the above examples, as well as a later reference to the female sexual organs as a "fiddle": "he will grab you on your fiddle" [Das er dir wird greiffen zu der fideln] (Dresden M 50, l. 172). Such references focus attention on the bodily mechanics of sexual intercourse, explicitly eroticizing the narrative. Because this sexual language has the effect of shifting the first version's uneasy balance between sex and honor towards an emphasis on sex, the Nuremberg version further undermines the mother's claims that she has maintained her womanly honor.

The sexualization of the mother's story continues in the new ending, which fundamentally recasts the issue of the mother's honor. After recommending that the daughter bargain with any inexperienced fellow (*milichfriedel*) who might come her way, the mother continues:

Therefore follow me, dear child,
for there certainly is much trickery
by which many a daughter supports herself.
For if it is bestowed upon you
to enter the order
in which I have become lazy and fat,
then you have heard the proper rule.
You can't thresh with a flail
nor can you fell trees with an axe.
So live off people
And don't wait any longer than this year.
Let this advice be your dowry.

Darumb so volg mir liebes kint
Wann noch wol sovil ludel sind
Davon sich manige tochter nert
Und ist es dir dann auch beschertt
Das du dann solt kumen in den orden
Darinnen ich faul und veist bin worden
So hast du gehortt die rechten regel
Du kanst nicht dreschen mit dem flegel [Leipzig: *schlegel*]
Und auch nicht mit der hawen rewten
Darumb so ner dich unter den lewten
Und beytt nicht lennger dann noch hewer
Die lere die hab dir zu einer haüszstewer. (Dresden M 50, ll. 184–95)

Conduct, Dowry, Estate

In this new ending, the mother casts her teachings in three contexts: the literary context of the conduct book (teaching, *lere*), the legal context of marriage (dowry, *haüszstewer*), and the sociological context of the estate (estate, order, *orden*). Conduct books and similar texts consisting of precepts from the old for the young are legion in medieval literature (see chap. 5). In the manuscript versions of *Stepmother and Daughter*, the mother announces at the outset that she is presenting a *ler*, advice and instruction. This reference places *Stepmother and Daughter* in a parodic relation to the genre of conduct literature, since the mother's instructions invert the notion of moral and ethical teaching informing the "bestsellers" of the genre such as *Cato*.[19] In Prague X A 12 it is the narrator who at the end returns us to the moral sphere by reminding us that the mother's teachings (*lere*) are harmful (ll. 226–27). The last line of the Nuremberg redaction, too, contains a specific reference to *lere*, but here again the word is spoken by the mother, who reinvokes the tradition of conduct literature to emphasize that everything she has said is an example of it. Since no moral is supplied, readers remain within the framework of the mother's story and are left to supply for themselves the parodic intent behind these words.

The advice the mother has given her daughter is to be the daughter's dowry. The mention of a dowry, a parental bequest to a daughter on her marriage, is another new feature of the Nuremberg redaction. Intended to provide a measure of financial security when a daughter marries, the dowry is, of course, supposed to be composed of material goods: money,

---

19. For an edition of *Cato*, see Zarncke 1852. The work is discussed by Sarah Westphal (1993, 44–46).

household furnishings, furniture, land. Its transfer from the bride's family to the bride and groom is one of the signs that a full, legal marriage has taken place. The satiric intent of the text's last word, dowry, is self-evident. The mother's dowry is but words. Her teachings are a mock dowry that at best may allow the daughter to accrue some material manifestations of economic well-being on her own. Further, the rules for conduct being passed on make it implausible that the daughter will ever be able to enter into the honorable state of marriage.

In Prague X A 12 the distinction between honorable and dishonorable women is a point of contention. The narrator seeks to draw a clear line between the categories and place mother and daughter on the side of dishonor. The mother, in contrast, seeks to create a mode of living for herself and her daughter that continually rewrites the boundary between honor and dishonor. The mother's words in the closing lines of the Nuremberg redaction resolve the problem by simply doing away with the clash between honor and dishonor. Instead, the mother places herself in the category of dishonor by invoking a series of distinctions from the medieval social hierarchy of estates.

This set of distinctions begins on line 188, when the mother refers to her profession as an order (*orden*). *Orden* has a double meaning. First, it is used to mean "clerical or monastic order." The mother's notion that the daughter is entering the "order" to which the mother already belongs certainly summons up the image of lascivious nuns common in late medieval literature. The further reference to "proper rule" (*rechte regel*, l. 190) confirms this reading, for *rule* is the technical term for the code of conduct that governed monastic houses.

Orden also has a second common meaning: "estate." In its usage in medieval Europe, *estate* is a political, sociological, and legal term that amalgamates class, caste, and profession. The tripartite division of noblemen, churchmen, and peasants represents the classic medieval model of estates. In the later Middle Ages, as new professions and classes—patricians, merchants, craftsmen—arose and proliferated, the term *estate* became increasingly elastic and was also used to define social groups by means of their work or profession. The mother refers indirectly to two such categories in lines 191–92: those of peasant ("you can't thresh with a flail") and woodsman or day laborer ("nor can you fell trees with an axe"). Such an estate, too, might have a rule (*regel*), a code of conduct considered binding for its members. Thus, when the mother describes herself as belonging to an *orden*, she uses the term in the same manner that it is used by the poet Rosenplüt in "The Fifteen Laments" mentioned earlier: "The common women [i.e., prostitutes] also lament their estate" [Die gemeinen weib clagen auch iren orden] (l. 31), a text contemporaneous with *Stepmother and Daughter*. The mother may well be implying that she belongs to the estate of prostitution, for in late medieval Germany, prostitution was considered an estate, albeit one on the very lowest rung of society's ladder.[20]

The dishonorable life of trickery and deceit (*ludel*, l. 185) which the mother recommends to her daughter is not only an estate, it is also gender specific. The daughter can join neither the estate of the laborer nor that of the peasant; lacking flail or axe, she is not "equipped" to do so. The sexualization of the narrative is thus carried into the estates register as well, for while the daughter lacks a phallus, the text has made clear to us that she possesses the necessary sexual "equipment" to be a prostitute. In this sense, the daughter's dowry from her mother is no more and no less than her sex.

Prague X A 12 both constructs the mother as the site of social disorder and seeks to contain the threat of chaos she embodies by means of the rhetorical device of the eavesdropping male narrator. In allowing his voice to close the frame around mother and daughter, Prague X A 12 seeks to establish a moralizing, didactic tone that can counteract the mother's self-descriptions, which establish a different understanding of female honor. In contrast, the Nuremberg redaction of *Stepmother and Daughter* dispenses with the moralizing narrator but has the mother express a self-understanding that clearly places her in the category—the *estate*—of dishonorable women. The problem of female disorderliness as a violation of male dominance is thus resolved in a twofold manner. First, the disorderly mother knows her place. She does not seek to rewrite the difference between female honor and female dishonor but rather accepts the dominant moral standards. Second, she does so by invoking the estates register. This register restores order to the text by asserting that there is a specific cultural and social space reserved for disorderly, dishonorable women, a space at the bottom of the social hierarchy.

The Strasbourg Lunation Tract "Das Clärlein"

The early Strasbourg printer Hans Düsch adapted a version of the *Minnerede Stepmother and Daughter* for a printed broadside intended for distribution in 1482. The work's time-limited purpose as a lunation tract (a calendar giving the dates and times of the new moon in 1482) virtually guaranteed their disposal. However, because three copies of the broad-

---

20. Westphal provides an illuminating and original discussion of the use, both serious and parodic, of the register of instruction to the estates in fifteenth-century Nuremberg manuscripts (1993, 150–63).

side were reused as endpapers by a Basel bookbinder (probably in the 1480s), they accidently survived into our time.[21] On the basis of philological evidence, Eckehard Simon suggests that the 1482 broadside might in fact be a reprint of a lunation tract from an earlier year (1988, 54–55). Such ghostly evidence of a lost source further indicates the wide popularity that *Stepmother and Daughter* must have enjoyed.

Düsch's version borrows short passages from *Stepmother and Daughter* and adapts new material in the same vein around them. New are, of course, the calendrical calculations, which are inserted with little regard for the sense of the mother-daughter narrative. More significant for an interpretation of the mother-daughter motif, however, is that Düsch eliminates the eavesdropping narrator altogether and instead expands the characterization of mother and daughter. The daughter receives a name: Clärlein. In Düsch's text alone the daughter's maturing, young body is specifically contrasted to the mother's aged one, and only in Düsch's text does the mother declare herself beyond sexual pleasure. These adaptations intensify the work's voyeuristic quality, encouraging its readers to view the women as purely sexual beings reduced to their sexual functions.

> I ask you, tell me, dear Clärlein,
> Haven't you found any short hairs,
> rubbing you under your chemise?
> That is odd, almost impossible.
> It seems to me from your breasts
> that I should fashion some clothing for you
> so that old men and young boys
> can ogle you mightily.
> . . . .
> I myself can no longer enjoy sex,
> For I am too old,
> wrinkled, dried up, and misshapen.

> Ich bitte dich, sag mir, liebes clerlin,
> Befindestu noch nyrgent herlin,
> Das dir berure din under hemde?
> Das ist seltczam und fast fremde.
> Mich beduncket an dynen brusten,
> Ich solte dir cleydung zu rusten,
> Das alte man und junge knaben

---

21. Kully provides an edition of the poem (1978), which is further discussed by Simon in his work on German lunation tracts (1988).

> Groß uff sehen uff dich haben.
> . . . .
> Ich mag myn selber nit genyessen,
> Dan ich bin hin fur me zu alt,
> Gerumpffen durre und ungestalt. (ll. 19–26, 32–34)

The mother is very much the same as in the basic story. While virtually all of the dramatic episodes have been removed (the children at the doorstep, the mowing scenes, the ill rivals, the sponge ruse, the sickbed conversations), much of her advice is exactly the same—the extortion of money for illegitimate children, the petty thievery, the instructions on how to pick up a man—and the new elements only amplify her duplicity. She expands on her instructions in thievery, adds clergy to her list of potential clients, and includes the church and the market as places to meet men. She also specifically cautions against marriage:

> If you should enter into marriage,
> you will encounter the same as many others,
> who build on the state of marriage
> and regret it eternally thereafter.
>
> Soltestu kommen in die ee,
> So beschehe dir wie maniger me,
> Die uff elichen stat buwet
> Und die es dar nach ewig ruwet. (ll. 55–58)

This advice has been given because the daughter, after admitting that she has noticed changes in herself, asks her mother's help in making a marriage for herself. The daughter's remark signals the two further changes in the basic story: on the formal level, the text is more clearly a dialogue because the daughter speaks more often, and on the thematic level, the characterization of the daughter has been altered. Instead of promising to follow her mother's advice as the daughter in Prague X A 12 does, Clärlein describes herself as hardworking and pious (ll. 49–50) and as desiring a life of honor. The difference between honorable and dishonorable women is thus transposed into the mother-daughter relationship itself. Düsch's new ending capitalizes on the dissimilarity of mother and daughter. In it, the daughter violently rejects her mother:

> Mother, those who burden their children with vice
> should be drowned.
> I would rather die
> than earn my bread in this way.

> "Muter, man solt die erdrencken,
> Die kinder laster an hencken.
> Ich wolte vil lieber sterben,
> Dann myn narung so erwerben." (ll. 221–24)

Clärlein takes over the moralizing voice that was reserved for the male narrator of Prague X A 12. Clärlein's revulsion against her mother's advice is so great that she would prefer death to becoming like her mother. Of all the daughters in the various texts of *Stepmother and Daughter*, Clärlein alone stakes out a position opposing her mother. She achieves a voice very different from her mother's—perhaps this is why she also receives a name, while her mother, like all the mothers and daughters in the other manuscript witnesses, remains anonymous. Yet the position Clärlein stakes out conforms to patriarchal notions of woman's honor and marriage; hers is the story of complicity. Much like in the *Eneasroman*, the daughter attains a voice different from her mother's, but at the cost of repudiation, of reviling her mother, of wishing her mother dead. The price the daughter pays to attain her allegiance with the patriarchal social order is the loss of her alliance with her mother.

The socialization of women acted out in the three adaptations of *Stepmother and Daughter* produces three very different results. In Prague X A 12, narrator and mother present contradictory views of women's honor, and the text balances uneasily between them. Furthermore, because the daughter follows her mother's teachings, the mother-daughter relationship is viewed either as the site of solidarity and mutual aid towards economic self-sufficiency (the women's point of view) or as the site in which moral weaknesses and criminal tendencies inherent in lower-class women are reinforced by the intimacy of the mother-daughter relationship (the narrator's point of view). In the Nuremberg version, the cultural and gendered friction around the notion of female honor has been removed. Instead, the mother herself thinks in the dominant social categories. She knows her place and does not contest the view that labels her dishonorable. In this version, we do not learn what the daughter thinks, for her voice is particularly muted. Accordingly, the problem of continuity between mother and daughter is absent from the Nuremberg version altogether. "Das Clärlein," on the other hand, focuses its interpretive energies precisely on the issue of continuity in the mother-daughter relationship. The distinction between honorable and dishonorable is created within the mother-daughter relationship itself. The daughter is given the moralizing and conformist voice that is reserved for the narrator in Prague X A 12 and that is absent from the Nuremberg version altogether. By having the daughter reject her mother, Düsch ruptures the mother-daughter relationship.

These three adaptions of *Stepmother and Daughter* create different stories about female honor and female dishonor, about female orderliness and female disorderliness, and about the mother-daughter relationship. It is worth remembering that the manuscripts and the printed broadside containing these adaptations are virtually contemporaneous with one another: Dresden M 50 and Leipzig 1590 date from the early 1460s, Prague X A 12 dates from 1470, and the Strasbourg lunation tract dates from 1482. The different adaptations of *Stepmother and Daughter* discussed in this chapter do not show a progression or an evolution in their notions of honor or in their notions of what the mother-daughter relationship can or should be. Rather, they are simultaneous responses to a common set of issues about gender that differ for local reasons. Yet viewed as a whole, the adaptations of *Stepmother and Daughter* testify to the abiding struggle of late medieval urban German culture to demarcate and regulate the boundaries of acceptable female behavior.

Looking Beyond the Middle Ages

In the middle of the sixteenth century, the prolific poet of reformed Nuremberg, Hans Sachs, wrote a short dialogue between a mother and daughter. Sachs fashions a text that seeks to recuperate the socialization of women to the new, reformed model for living that viewed the God-fearing, patriarchal, Protestant household as the center of morality in civic and religious life. In "A Mother's Conversation with Her Daughter about Her Son-in-Law" [Gesprech der mutter mit irer tochter von irem ayden],[22] Sachs turns the disreputable urban women of *Stepmother and Daughter* into honorable, upright matrons. He also locates the mother-daughter dialogue in an estate we have not yet encountered: the household of a craftsman. Further, he transforms the mother into a stern representative of the new Protestant norms, gives the daughter equal time for her complaints, and replaces all talk about sex or romantic love with talk about food and money.

Like his anonymous predecessors, Sachs employs the motif of the eavesdropping male narrator in an opening that is powerfully reminiscent of *Stepmother and Daughter*. Sachs is careful, however, to identify his speakers as honorable, respectable women (*erebare frauen*), a designation that has class as well as moral valence.

---

22. In Keller (1870, 356–63); cited hereinafter by page number.

> It hasn't been long since it happened
> that I secretly sneaked by a room
>
> . . . .
> where there were two honorable women.
> I listened secretly to them.
>
> Es ist nicht lang, das es geschach,
> Ich haymlich schlich für ein gemach.
>
> . . . .
> Da warens erbarer frawen zwu.
> Den thet ich haymlich losen zu. (356, ll. 1–2, 9–10)

What the narrator overhears would warm the heart of any member of the Nuremberg city council, which as in other Reformed cities had taken over the policing of domestic affairs that previous to the Reformation had been carried out by ecclesiastical authorities. The newly married daughter has come home to complain about her husband, in whose eyes she cannot do anything right. He scolds and nags and complains, and the daughter is sick and tired of living with him. However, she receives no sympathy from her mother, whose answers repeatedly and exclusively emphasize the obligations of marriage and the subservience of wives to their husbands:

> The mother said: "That's no good.
> You must strive to do his will.
>
> . . . .
> You must give in,
> For now it cannot be otherwise."
>
> Die muter sprach: "Es taug mit nichten.
> Du must seins willens dich befleysen.
>
> . . . .
> Du must nach-geben,
> Wann es kan nun nit anderst sein." (357, ll. 19–20, 29–30)

The daughter's litany of complaints continues. She reveals that her husband mistreats the servants, to which the mother replies that the daughter should then treat them well. The daughter laments that her husband is jealous and won't allow her to talk to the servants, to which the mother replies that it is up to the daughter to always comport herself humbly and modestly at home and in public. The daughter confesses her husband withholds money for food, to which the mother replies that young people ought to be frugal. Only the daughter's complaint that her husband follows her around in the kitchen demanding that she account for every penny arouses the mother's ire on her daughter's behalf. The mother suggests that the daughter banish her husband from the domestic realm with the following words:

> "Husband, you are in charge of the workshop;
> Now leave me alone in the kitchen!
> I will manage your kitchen well;
> I have been raised to manage a household.
> Otherwise everyone will mock you."

> "Mein mann, du warrt der werckstatt dein
> Und laß mich inn der kuchen sein!
> Ich will dein kuchen recht verwalten.
> Ich bin erzogen beym haußhalten.
> Sunst wurd dein spotten yederman." (359, ll. 26–30)

But the daughter's grievances are still not complete. She confides that her husband speaks ill of others, defrauds and cheats others, and comes home drunk. The mother's advice on dealing with each of these moral failings remains the same: the daughter is to gently remind her husband of the consequences of his actions. The mother closes the conversation with a short speech on a wife's duty to transform and educate her husband with tenderness and gentle words. She then sends her daughter back to her new home:

> "Return home to your house!
> Obey my proper teachings!
> You mustn't complain to me anymore."

> "Ker widerumb heym in dein hauß!
> Halt dich meiner getrewen leer!
> So darffst du mir nit klagen meer." (363, ll. 23–25)

The last words of the poem belong to the narrator, who praises virtuous wives and wishes for peace and friendship in marriage.

The mother in *Stepmother and Daughter* exploited the social order and embodied excess; the mother in this text lives according to Protestant values, advocating frugality and female subservience and domesticity. She has been transformed into the strict custodian of a morality that enforces separate codes of conduct and work for men and for women. The son-in-law has serious moral failings both as head of the household and as a citizen, yet his drunkenness, jealousy, harassment of the servants, miserliness, and dishonesty are never condemned by the mother. Instead, she apparently views such actions as normal behavior for a young man, which is now to be lovingly corrected by a patient and forgiving wife. The only shortcoming the mother openly criticizes, the son-in-law's interference in kitchen business, is his only action violating the clear separation of labor based on gender. Meddling in his wife's domestic sphere is unmanly, and it makes the young husband vulnerable to the mockery of all society.

The mother's words to her daughter also make it clear that the daughter must conduct herself according to very different standards than her husband. Indeed, it is the mother's belief that in time the daughter's exemplary behavior as a modest, frugal, virtuous, and obedient wife will correct the husband's excesses. By instructing her daughter vigorously about the virtues of female obedience and domesticity, the mother proves that her own home is a model of household righteousness, a domestic microcosm of the greater civic righteousness of the city. No wonder Sachs can close the text so optimistically, in spite of the son-in-law's flagrant moral transgressions. Sachs's eavesdropping confirms a vision—a fantasy, perhaps?—of the inner and outer harmony of the reformed, Lutheran city that has "enshrined marriage, the union between the sexes, as the foundation of social existence" (Roper 1989b, 259). In choosing the formal device of a mother-daughter dialogue to convey this message, Sachs confirms that the stability of the new, reformed moral order is founded upon women's knowledge of and acquiescence in their subservient status as wives and upon a strict separation of labor that restricts women's work to a private, domestic, nonremunerative sphere. Sachs's text anticipates the early modern proliferation of conduct manuals for young girls, which also stress wifely subservience and domesticity as female virtues (Barth 1994). Like these, it is one of many texts for and about mothers and daughters heralding the changes in gender ideologies that accompanied the economic, political, and social rise of the bourgeoisie in early modern Europe.

Looking Back at the Middle Ages

IN THIS STUDY I have taken my bearings from contemporary feminist theory to interpret the mother-daughter relationship in male-authored medieval German literature as an intergenerational quest for similarity and dissimilarity—connection that values difference—in social contexts that frequently place all women at a disadvantage. Using the issue of similarity and dissimilarity as a structural guide, I have shown how mother-daughter fictions rehearse conflicting assumptions about medieval cultural norms. Fictional mothers and daughters play out contradictions in medieval society at large: aristocratic concepts of lineage that relied on but tried to limit women's political role (*Eneasroman*); structures for allocating economic resources that fostered but also curtailed noblewomen's influence (*Nibelungenlied*); the conflict between dominant, patrilineal kinship structures and muted, bilineal ones (*Kudrun*); women's success or failure in transferring their knowledge to one another (*Tristan*); women's methods for achieving agency and solidarity in a social sphere increasingly restricted to marriage and sexuality (*Winsbeckin* and the Neidhart corpus); the construction of conflicting accounts of poor women's honor in late medieval urban Germany (*Stepmother and Daughter*).

What kinds of reading strategies has the mother-daughter relationship made meaningful for medieval German literature? First, an exploration of the mother-daughter relationship reasserts the importance of social history for interpreting medieval German literature. It has shown that larger cultural processes such as changes in aristocratic concepts of lineage and kinship and in the allocation of material and political resources within noble families leave a recoverable trace in medieval German fictions. It shows further that literary texts can contribute insights to the history of the family, especially in areas lacking profile in the kinds of documents that have survived (court records, property transactions, wills, geneaologies) and upon which historians tend to rely.

A second, related conclusion is that cross-genre analyses of the mother-daughter relationship make visible the issue of class in medieval German literature. My exploration of the mother-daughter relationship has shown that the literary conversation between mother and daughter about sex and love falls out along lines of genre and class. Aristocratic mothers try to channel their daughters' desire in class-specific ways to secure familial honor, status, and power; mothers and daughters of the lower classes, by contrast, illustrate the belief that any tenet for the social control of sexuality placed in the hands of women is bound to fail. Readings of literary texts thus explore how the gendering of women's bodies is a function of class. Indeed, the mother-daughter relationship shows the necessity of bringing issues of class to bear on issues of gender.

Third, the study of the mother-daughter relationship has shown that there is no single, unifying notion of femininity in the medieval patriarchal social order. Just as the medieval world knew different, sometimes contradictory, modes of sexualizing women, so it knew different, sometimes competing, modes of creating femininity. The exchange between mother and daughter creates a complicated field of polarities and oppositions that opens up a range of alternatives and resistances around notions of femininity and the areas of knowledge and life events commonly associated with it: sexual desire, motherhood, reproduction, marriage, gender, sexuality. When viewing the mother-daughter motif across genres, there is no correlation between generational role and the adoption of conformist or subversive notions of femininity: some mothers teach socially conformist notions of femininity, while others teach subversive ones; some daughters choose to follow the dominant social expectations for women, others to flaunt them. Mother-daughter stories are neither timeless fables about female maturation nor allegories about femininity as difference or impossibility, but rather socially, historically, and economically conditioned narratives telling how the cultural production of femininity differs according to genre, time, and place. Studying medieval mothers and daughters shows that feminist readings of the literature of the distant past can profitably seek not a grand synthesis on the issue of gender but rather the clusters of ideas about gender that arise and change over time.

My final conclusion addresses the relationship between historical reconstructions of medieval women's lives and their representations in fiction. This book has also been about finding sites in literary texts from which could emerge women's voices that the historical evidence would allow us to imagine as authentic. Such a statement requires several qualifications. I do not argue that literary characters are real people, nor do I wish to attribute to medieval women themselves the misogyny informing much medieval literature. Nor do I wish to project into texts of the past a modern concept of interiority and selfhood. In charting this course I have no desire to erase the loss of authentic medieval German women's voices. Like the loss of medieval voices from the lower classes, it is real and inescapable.

Yet I am convinced that medieval women would have told us different stories than medieval men; the material, economic, and cultural conditions of their lives were too different—solely because they were women—for this not to have been so. It also seems to me that just as medieval society did not produce a single set of meanings about mothers and daughters, so it was hardly possible for it to produce a single, monolithic, unified male perspective. Rather, the dominant medieval social order, which asserted in multiple ways the dominance of men and the subordination of women, was in fact a diffuse, contradictory, and flexible set of institutionalized power relations. What matters for my way of reading are the contradictions, the ways in which different medieval power relations and different medieval discourses amend and dispute one other. Historical research has shown conclusively that these contradictions derive from the real material and historical circumstances of medieval women's lives. By revealing to us the contradictions upon which medieval assumptions about women's power, women's sexuality, and women's relationships to one another rest, careful readings of medieval German literature can open up a space in which we can comprehend more fully the complexity of the dilemmas faced by medieval women and the range of choices open to them. Modern scholarship can never reconstruct an authentic woman's voice from the past, but it can frame in all its complexity the conflicting ideas, attitudes, and beliefs within and through which medieval female voices would have emerged.

Appendix

Works Cited

Index

The German Language Texts
of the Neidhart Poems

from Sommerlied 7

"Ez meiet hiuwer aber als ê.
von dem touwe",
sprach ein frouwe,
"springent bluomen unde klê.
nahtegal diu singet ûf der linden
ir süezen sanc.
Merze vor den reien spranc:
bî dem sult ir mich vinden."

"Tohter, wende dînen muot
von dem touwe!
ganc her, schouwe:
disiu mære sint niht guot.
warne dich engegen dem scherpfen winder!
(wilt aber hin,)
ahte niht ûf Merzen sin:
des rede drinc hin hinder!

Und reie alsô, swiez dir ergê,
ob er dich triege,
daz ein wiege
vor an dînem fuoze iht stê!
sich, sô wirt dîn fröude harte kleine
und mac geschehen,
sô dû bluomen wellest sehen,
daz nâch dir iht weine."

"Muoter, ir sorget umbe den wint.
mirst unmære

The "Sommerlieder" (summer songs) are quoted from Wießner (1984). The inauthentic poems from Belin mgf 779 follow Bennewitz-Behr (1981). Accent marks, as well as punctuation that interrupts the syntax, have been removed from the inauthentic poems.

solhiu swære:
wîp diu truogen ie diu kint.
ich wil mîner fröude niht enlâzen
durch iuwern rât.
reichet mir mîn liehte wât:
diu wiege var verwâzen!"

Nu hœret, wie ez ir ergie!
si biegen beide
dô mit leide.
diu muoter einen rechen vie:
den begreif diu tohter bî der grœze.
si nam zehant
in der alten ûz der hant.
dô gienc ez an die stœze. (st. 1–5)

Sie stiezen beide ein ander wol.
diu alte sprach:
"ditz ungemach
nam vernt ich von dir niht vür vol;
nu bin ich leider kranc an mînem lîbe
gæbest dû Merzen tusent marc,
er næm dîn niht ze wîbe." (st. 5a)

from Sommerlied 23

"Tohterlîn, lâ dich sîn niht gelangen!
wil dû die ritter an dem reien drangen,
die dir niht ze mâze ensulen sîn,
tohterlîn,
dû wirst an dem schaden wol ervunden.
    der junge meier muotet dîn." (st. 6)

"Sliezet mir den meier an die versen!
jâ trûwe ich stolzem ritter wol gehersen:
zwiu sol ein gebûwer mir ze man?
der enkan
mich nâch mînem willen niht getriuten:
    er, wæn, mîn eine muoz gestân." (st. 7)

Tohterlîn, dû wilt dîn lop verliesen,
wiltû her Kuonzen meiers sun verkiesen.
der hât doch beide rinder unde swîn,
korn unt wîn.
wiltû nû daz allez samt verliesen?
    des meiers sun begeret dîn. (st. 7a)

"Tohterlîn, lâ dir in niht versmâhen!
dû wilt ze tumbe ritters künde vâhen:
daz ist allen dînen vriunden leit.
manegen eit
swüere dû: des wis nu âne lougen,
    dîn muot dich allez von mir treit!" (st. 8)

"Muoter mîn, ir lâzet iuwer bâgen!
ich wil mîne vriunde durch in wâgen,
den ich mînen willen nie verhal.
über al
müezen sîn die liute werden inne:
    mîn muot der strebt gein Riuwental." (st. 9)

Diu muoter diu krift eine kunkel swære.
"nû var hin! dû bist mir gar unmære."
si gap ir einz, daz in dem hûse erschal;
über al
gap si ir vil starke slege schiere
    und schihte sî gein Riuwental. (st. 9a)

"Tohterlîn, nu waz geschach dir nehten?
ich hôrt dich in der louben lûte brehten
mit einem stolzen ritter: daz ist wâr.
bint ûf dîn hâr!
er hât sô vil getiselt und getaselt
    mit dir: daz ist wol offenbâr." (st. 9b)

"Muoterlîn, nu zürnet niht sô sêre!
ez wirbet einer mich (des habt ir êre:
dâ von lâzet trûren über al!)
gein Riuwental:
dar wil er mich wirdiclîchen setzen;
    dâ singet wol diu nahtigal." (st. 9c)

from Sommerlied 1

Ein altiu diu begunde springen
hôhe alsam ein kitze enbor: si wolde bluomen bringen.
"tohter, reich mir mîn gewant:
ich muoz an eines knappen hant,
der ist von Riuwental genant.
traranuretun traranuriruntundeie."

"Muoter, ir hüetet iuwer sinne!
erst ein knappe sô gemuot, er pfliget niht stæter mînne."

"tohter, lâ mich âne nôt!
ich weiz wol, waz er mir enbôt.
nâch sîner minne bin ich tôt.
traranuretun traranuriruntundeie." (st. 1–2)

from Sommerlied 17

"Dâ wil ich dîn hüeten", sprach des kindes eide.
"nu gê wir mit ein ander zuo der linden beide!
ich bin mîner jâre
gar ein kint,
wan daz mînem hâre
die locke sint
grîse:
di wil ich bewinden
   mit sîden.
    tohter, wâ ist mîn rîse?"

"Muoter, die rîsen die hân ich vor iu behalten;
diu zimet einer jungen baz dan einer alten
ze tragen umbe ir houbet
an der schar.
wer hât iuch beroubet
der sinne gar?
slâfet!
waz, ob iu nu ringer
   getroumet,
    daz ir iuch anders zâfet?" (st. 5–6)

from *Song No. 30* (old numbering Song No. 29) Ein wechsell [A Dialogue]

Die tochter sprach wie mang Rede Ich muß horen.
muterlein Ir wolt euch selber toren.
vber get Ir meinen Rate.
wisset das es alten weiben vbel an stat.
das sie solich vppigkait begynnen.
Ir sult euch pas versynnen.

Ich han mich wol versunnen an ein ende.
pring mir mein Rockel vnd mein klaynes gepende.
das wil ich den zu lait tragen.
die mir freuden wendent gein den liechten tagen.
tochter Ich bedarff nicht ewer lere
Ia sawmet Ir mich sere

Sich mein lere ist gancz an euch verprochen.
was ich euch zugute hab gesprochen.

muter das habt Ir nu fur ein haβ.
euch gezeme ein gute krucken pas.
In ewr hant wenn Ir zu kirchen gienget.
denn Ir den Summer empfienget.

Der krucken geczeich ich wol zu rate.
seit Ich an einem pain mag so drote.
gespringen als ein kiczelein.
Ich will Jarlach fro durch einen Iungen sein.
der Ist wol bey vier vndzwainczig Jaren.
des willenn will ich faren.

Die tochter sprach fraw muter Ir seit vnweis.
das Ir euch auff einen Iungen wolt preisen.
der nympt euch durch das gutlein.
vmb ewer schon nicht vernempt die rede mein.
wenn denn das gutel hat ein ende.
so pert er euch die lende.

Die muter sprach Ir redt von thumben dingen.
pin ich alt so han ich uil pfennigen.
vnd schuβ sich ein Iunger fur.
der mich des nachtes rutelt als ein Jrre thur.
das mir die zene erklafften in dem munde.
des armut gar verswunde.

Die tochter sprach des sey got mein vrkunde.
es thett Im recht als er ein fulen esell schunde.
der nachtes bej euch slaffenn musβ
dem wirt hustens keychens von euch nymer puβ.
Ir selt euch durch got haben sawr.
slacht ewer haupt vmb ein mawre.

Die alt die sprach fraw tochter des gesweiget.
Ja wisst ir das man gute noten geiget.
auff alten fideln der sie kan.
Ich will mein fidell leyhen einem Iungen man
der wol tanczen vnd Rayen kan.
der rutelt mirs vondan

Welich badstub wirt gehiczet also linde.
ein man geleckett uil ee er empfunde.
hicze der sein hercz begert.
wie gut die scheiter sind vnd ist pos der hert.
von hicz empfecht er doch uil selten freuden.
muter Ir last ewer gewden.

Ir gehiest meinem vater Ir solt gedencken.
das Ir nit mannes nempt nu wolt Ir wencken.
das thett alles vmb das.
ob er genes das er mich hielt des paß
Nun ist der todt. er kan mir nicht gepieten.
Ich wil mich freuden nyeten.

Die tochter sprach so euch der teufell schende.
nu mynnt Ir man vnd habt doch nyndert zene.
Die wengel sind euch runczel voll.
das red Ich als tewer ich soll.
Sie sluge die alten das sie hangk an einem payne.
die Iunge spranck an dem Rayne. (st. 3–13)

from Song no. 64 *Die statt kraw oder die wanndt kraw* [The sated crow or the hungry crow]

Ich frew mich sprach ein thumme maidt.
Ich hor die vogelein schallen.
die sind an freuden vnuerczaitt.
das muß mir wolgefallen.
Man sicht auff dem anger der plumen mangerlaj.
der will ich brechen ein krenczlein.
mir vnd dem gesellen mein.
so er ymer selige muß sein.
an seiner hand ich raye

Tochter wer hat dir gesagt
von der geselschafft.
die rede mir nicht wol behagt.
es kumpt von mynne krafft
Muter das ich mynn das ist mir nicht angepunden
Es ist mir von euch angeporn.
den ich mir han zu lieb erkorn.
vnd wer es aller werlt zorn.
den mynn ich zu allen stunden.

Tochter beitt noch ein Jar.
das ich dich bas berate.
muterlein ir sagt mir war.
es kumpt mir leicht zu spate.
hett ich lieb am arm als ir so wer Ich freuden reiche.
muter Ir habt einen man.
derr euch vil woll treuten kan.
der satten kraw vnd auch der wann
der leben ist vngeleich.

Tochter pis mir vnterthan.
vnd wiltu eren leren.
muter ir habt einen man.
also hett ich auch gern.
das ir mir das recht nicht gebt. das ir doch haben wollet.
dauon so ist die helle voll.
muter euch ist des nachtes wol.
mit mynnen als euch von recht soll.
also habt ir euch gesellet.

Tochter las dein mynnen sein.
vnd volg meiner lere.
O we liebes muterlein.
Ir versundet euch gar sere.
Ich bin Im gancz von herczen holdt. des bring ich In wol Innen.
dauon gebt euch selber rat.
Jr redt als/als der gepachen hatt.
mein mut nach freundes mynnen statt.
mitt dem wil ich von hynnen. (st. 2–6)

from Song no. 36 (old numbering no. 35)
Die pfann ein wechsell [The pan, a dialogue]

Ich will hewer rayen.
auf dem grunen anger weitt gein dem sussen myen.
sprach ein maidt. ich frew mich lieber mere.
mir ist von der mynn gesaitt
die sey ein susse arbaitt.
nu pin Ich mynnepare

Ich bin als mann zame.
als mein swester Jrrmelein. die man gern neme.
wo sind nu die laidigen mann verswunden.
Das mich Ir keiner nicht empitt.
vnd ichs doch so wol er lidt.
Ich leg Im vngepunden.

Zwar Ich will hewer mynnen.
thut es als woll als man da gicht. Ich will sein mer begynnen
tut es we Ich glob sein hincz pis Jare.
wo ist nu ein selig man.
der von ersten hebet an.
der schaw wie ich gepere.

Das erhort Ir aide.
tochterlein der red empir Es kompt dir nach zu laide.
willtu mynnen in so grosser Jugent.

du hast noch nicht sechczehen Jare.
muterlein ich han sie gar.
nu in der pesten tugendt

Vor mengem Jar mir brosset.
muterlein Ich sag euch/das mir ist gar geschossett.
Ich han zu lang vber recht gepiten.
Ja habt ir mir selber gesait.
Ir wert nur zwolff Iar ein maid.
vnd habt es doch erliten

Tochter wiltu mynnen.
so such dir einen man. den du magst gewynnen.
nym dir einen der dir wol gefalle.
den will ich vor dir gewern.
muterlein das tet ich gern.
also nempt Ir sie alle

Was hulff mich fremde speis.
der ich nicht genyessen kan. fraw muter Ir seit vnweis.
Ich wais woll ir nempt euch stett das pesser.
nein vater der ist ewer man.
der euch des nicht gemaistern kan.
ir tragt das lenger messer.

Ich wais wol das mein atte.
lang ist ewer man gewesen. der euch zu Im pete.
ir esset noch mit kinden auß der pfanne.
vnd peisset anderthalben ab.
pfuh das euch der teufel hab.
was wolt Ir fremder manne

Tochter zweig still.
mynn wenig oder uil. das ist mein guter will.
Sehe ich es an mit paidenn meinen augen.
Ich verswig es tochterlein.
also thu du kind das mein.
vnd mynn wir paide togen

Gewynnstu dann ein wiegen.
tochterlein so hilft vns nicht vnser paider kriegen.
Muterlein wenn ich das vberwinde.
so ist der schad wol halber hin.
wie ich denn geraten pin.
das erb auff meine kinde (st. 2–11)

Works Cited

Abbreviations

ATB   Altdeutsche Textbibliothek
Euph   Euphorion
DVjs   Deutsche Vierteljahresschrift für
Literaturwissenschaft und Geistesgeschichte
GAG   Göppinger Arbeiten zur Germanistik
GQ   German Quarterly
MLR   Modern Language Review
MTU   Münchener Texte und Untersuchungen
PBB   Beiträge zur Geschichte der deutschen Sprache und Literatur
(Tü)   (Tübingen)
ZfdPh   Zeitschrift für deutsche Philologie
ZfdA   Zeitschrift für deutsches Altertum

Anderson, Philip N. 1985. "Kriemhild's Quest." *Euph* 79: 3–12.
Andersson, Theodore M. 1987. *A Preface to the Nibelungenlied.* Stanford: Stanford Univ. Press.
Ashley, Kathleen, and Pamela Sheingorn, eds. 1990. *Interpreting Cultural Symbols: Saint Anne in Late Medieval Society.* Athens and London: Univ. of Georgia Press.
Atkinson, Clarissa W. 1991. *The Oldest Vocation: Christian Motherhood in the Middle Ages.* Ithaca: Cornell Univ. Press.
Baader, Joseph. 1861. "Ordnung der Gemeinen Weiber in den Frauenhäusern." In *Nürnberger Polizeiordnungen aus dem XII bis XV Jahrhundert,* 117–21. Bibliothek des Litterarischen Vereins, vol. 63. Stuttgart: Litterarischer Verein.
Barth, Susanne. 1994. *Jungfrauenzucht: Literaturwissenschaftliche und pädagogische Studien zur Mädchenerziehungsliteratur zwischen 1200 und 1600.* Ph.D. diss., University of Cologne, 1993. Stuttgart: M&P.
Bäuml, Franz. H., ed. 1969. *Kudrun: Die Handschrift.* Berlin: de Gruyter.
Becker, Hans. 1978. *Die Neidharte: Studien zur Überlieferung, Binnentypisierung und Geschichte der Neidharte der Berliner Handschrift germ. fol. 779 (c).* GAG, vol. 255. Göppingen: Kümmerle.
Behagel, Otto, ed. 1882. *Heinrichs von Veldeke Eneide.* Heilbronn: Henninger.
Behr, Hans-Joachim. 1985. " 'der werden lop' und 'gotes hulde': Überlegungen zur konzeptionellen Einheit des Winsbecke." *Leuvense Bijdragen* 74: 377–94.
Bekker, Hugo. 1987. *Gottfried von Strassburg's Tristan: A Journey Through the Realm of Eros.* Studies in German Literature, Linguistics, and Culture, vol. 29. Columbia, S.C.: Camden House.

235

Benecke, G. F., and K. Lachmann, eds. 1968. *Hartmann von Aue: Iwein*. Revised by Ludwig Wolff. 7th ed. Berlin: de Gruyter.

Benjamin, Jessica. 1988. *The Bonds of Love: Psychoanalysis, Feminism, and the Problem of Domination*. New York: Pantheon.

Bennett, Judith M. 1989. "Feminism and History." *Gender and History* 1(3): 251–72.

———. 1996. *Ale, Beer, and Brewsters in England: Women's Work in a Changing World, 1300–1600*. New York: Oxford Univ. Press.

Bennett, Ralph Francis. 1937. *The Early Dominicans: Studies in Thirteenth-Century Dominican History*. Cambridge: Cambridge Univ. Press.

Bennewitz, Ingrid. 1994. "'Wie ihre Mütter'?: Zur männlichen Inszenierung des weiblichen Streitgesprächs in Neidharts Sommerliedern." In *Sprachspiel und Lachkultur: Beiträge zur Literatur- und Sprachgeschichte. Rolf Bräuer zum 60. Geburtstag*. Edited by Angela Bader, Annemarie Eder, Irene Erfen, and Ulrich Müller, 178–93. Stuttgarten Arbeiten zur Germanistik, vol. 300. Stuttgart: Hans-Dieter Heinz.

Bennewitz-Behr, Ingrid. 1981. *Die Berliner Neidhart-Handschrift c (mgf 779): Transkription der Texte und Melodien*. In collaboration with Ulrich Müller. GAG, vol. 356. Göppingen: Kümmerle.

Beyschlag, Siegfried. 1975. *Die Lieder Neidharts: Der Textbestand der Pergament-Handschriften und die Melodien. Text und Übertragung. Einführung und Worterklärung. Konkordanz*. Melodies edited by Horst Brunner. Darmstadt: Wissenschaftliche Buchgesellschaft.

Beyschlag, Siegfried, and Horst Brunner, eds. 1989. *Herr Neidhart diesen Reihen sang: Die Texte und Melodien der Neidhartlieder mit Übersetzungen und Kommentaren*. GAG, vol. 468. Göppingen: Kümmerle.

Bloch, R. Howard. 1991. *Medieval Misogyny and the Invention of Western Romantic Love*. Chicago: Univ. of Chicago Press.

Bobertag, Felix, ed. 1885. "Neidhart Fuchs." In *Deutsche National-Litteratur*, vol. 11, *Narrenbuch*, 141–292. Berlin: Spemann.

Bodel, Jehan. 1989. *La Chanson de Saisnes*. Edited by Annette Brasseur. 2 vols. Geneva: Droz.

Brandis, Tilo. 1968. *Minnereden: Verzeichnis der Handschriften und Drucke*. MTU, vol. 25. Munich: Beck.

Brundage, James A. 1989. "Prostitution in the Medieval Canon Law." Reprinted in *Sisters and Workers in the Middle Ages*, edited by Judith M. Bennett, Elizabeth A. Clark, Jean F. O'Barr, B. Anne Vilan, and Sarah Westphal-Wihl, 79–99. Chicago: Univ. of Chicago Press.

Bumke, Joachim. 1979. *Mäzene im Mittelalter: Die Gönner und Auftraggeber der höfischen Literatur in Deutschland 1150–1300*. Munich: Beck.

———. 1986. *Höfische Kultur. Literatur und Gesellschaft im hohen Mittelalter*. 2 vols. Munich: Deutscher Taschenbuch Verlag. Translated as *Courtly Culture: Literature and Society in the High Middle Ages*. Berkeley: Univ. of California Press, 1991.

———. 1990. *Geschichte der deutschen Literatur im hohen Mittelalter*. Vol. 2 of *Deutsche Literatur in Mittelalter*, 3 vols., edited by Joachim Bumke, Thomas Cramer and Dieter Kartschoke. Munich: Deutscher Taschenbuch Verlag.

Bumke, Joachim, Thomas Cramer, and Dieter Kartschoke. 1990. *Deutsche Literatur in Mittelalter*. 3 vols. Munich: Deutscher Taschenbuch Verlag.

Burghartz, Susanna. 1990. *Leib, Ehre und Gut: Delinquenz in Zürich Ende des 14. Jahrhunderts.* Zurich: Chronos.

———. 1991. "Kein Ort für Frauen? Städtische Gerichte im Spätmittelalter." In *Auf der Suche nach der Frau im Mittelalter: Fragen, Quellen, Antworten,* edited by Bea Lundt, 49–64. Munich: Fink.

———. 1992. "Rechte Jungfrauen oder unverschämte Töchter? Zur weiblichen Ehre im 16. Jahrhundert." In *Frauengeschichte—Geschlechtergeschichte,* edited by Karin Hausen and Heide Wunder, 173–83. Frankfurt am Main: Campus Verlag.

Burns, E. Jane. 1985. "The Man behind the Lady in Troubadour Lyric." *Romance Notes* 25(3): 254–70.

Buschinger, Danielle. 1976. *Eilhart von Oberg: Tristrant. Édition diplomatique et traduction en français moderne.* GAG, vol. 202. Göppingen: Kümmerle.

Buschinger, Danielle, and Wolfgang Spiewok, eds. 1991. *Tristan und Isolde in europäischen Mittelalter: Ausgewählte Texte in Übersetzung und Nacherzählung.* Stuttgart: Reclam.

Campbell, Ian R. 1978. *Kudrun: A Critical Appreciation.* Anglica Germanica, ser. 2. Cambridge: Cambridge Univ. Press.

Carter, Susanne, comp. 1993. *Mothers and Daughters in American Short Fiction: An Annotated Bibliography of Twentieth-Century Women's Literature.* Bibliographies and Indexes in Women's Studies, no. 19. Westport, Conn.: Greenwood.

Cazelles, Brigitte. 1991. *The Lady as Saint: A Collection of French Hagiographic Romances of the Thirteenth Century.* Philadelphia: Univ. of Pennsylvania Press.

Chodorow, Nancy. 1978. *The Reproduction of Mothering: Psychoanalysis and the Sociology of Gender.* Berkeley: Univ. of California Press.

———. 1985. "Gender, Relation, and Difference in Psychoanalytic Perspective." In *The Future of Difference,* edited by Hester Eistenstein and Alice Jardine, 3–19. New Brunswick, N.J.: Rutgers Univ. Press.

Christine de Pisan. 1985. *The Treasure of the City of Ladies or The Book of the Three Virtues.* Translated by Sarah Lawson. London: Penguin.

Classen, Albrecht. 1989. "Matriarchy versus Patriarchy: The Role of the Irish Queen Isolde in Gottfried von Strassburg's *Tristan.*" *Neophilologus* 73(1): 77–89.

Deist, Rosemarie. 1986. *Die Nebenfiguren in den Tristanromanen Gottfrieds von Straßburg und Thomas' de Bretagne und im "Cligès" Chrétiens de Troyes.* GAG, vol. 435. Göppingen: Kümmerle.

Dietz, Reiner. 1974. *Der Tristan Gottfrieds von Strassburg: Probleme der Forschung (1902–1970).* Göppingen: Kümmerle.

Dittrich, Marie-Luise. 1966. *Die "Eneide" Heinrichs von Veldeke.* Part 1 of *Quellenkritischer Vergleich mit dem Roman d'Eneas und Vergils Aeneis.* Wiesbaden: Franz Steiner.

Donovan, Josephine. 1989. *After the Fall: The Demeter-Persephone Myth in Wharton, Cather, and Glasgow.* University Park: Pennsylvania State Univ. Press.

Duby, Georges. 1980. *The Chivalrous Society.* Translated by Cynthia Posten. Berkeley: Univ. of California Press.

Duvernoy, Jean, trans. and ed. 1978. *Le Registre d'inquisition de Jacques Fournier,* 3 vols. Civilisations et Sociétés, vol. 43. Paris: Mouton.

Ehlert, Trude. 1986. "Die Frau als Arznei: Zum Bild der Frau in hochmittelalter-licher deutscher Lehrdichtung." *ZfdPh* 105: 42–62.

Ehrismann, Otfrid. 1987. *Nibelungenlied: Epoche, Werk, Wirkung.* Munich: Beck.

Erb, Elke. 1985. "Das Thema startet." In *Luchterhand Jahrbuch der Lyrik 1985,* edited by Christoph Buchwald and Ursula Krechel, 66–67. Darmstadt: Luchterhand.

Erler, Mary. 1992. Review of Louise Mirrer, ed., *Upon My Husband's Death: Widows in Literature and Histories of Medieval Europe.* In *Medieval Feminist Newsletter* 14(fall): 30–31.

Facinger, Marion F. 1968. "A Study of Medieval Queenship: Capetian France 987–1237." *Studies in Medieval and Renaissance History* 5: 3–47.

Farrell, Michèlle Longino. 1991. *Performing Motherhood: The Sévigné Correspondence.* Hanover, N.H., and London: Univ. Press of New England.

Ferrante, Joan M. 1975. *Woman as Image in Medieval Literature, from the Twelfth Century to Dante.* New York: Columbia Univ. Press.

Fischer, Hanns, ed. 1961. *Hans Folz: Die Reimpaarsprüche.* MTU, vol. 1. Munich: Beck.

———. 1983. *Studien zur deutschen Märendichtung.* Edited by Johannes Janota. 2d ed. Tübingen: Niemeyer.

Fisher, Sheila, and Janet E. Halley. 1989. "The Lady Vanishes: The Problem of Women's Absence in Late Medieval and Renaissance Texts." In *Seeking the Woman in Late Medieval and Renaissance Writings: Essays in Feminist Contextual Criticism,* edited by Sheila Fisher and Janet E. Halley, 1–17. Knoxville: Univ. of Tennessee.

Flax, Jane. 1978. "The Conflict between Nurturance and Autonomy in Mother-Daughter Relationships and Within Feminism." *Feminist Studies* 4(1): 171–89.

———. 1985. "Mother-Daughter Relationships: Psychodynamics, Politics, and Philosophy." In *The Future of Difference,* edited by Hester Eisenstein and Alice Jardine, 20–40. New Brunswick, N.J.: Rutgers Univ. Press.

Forsyth, Louise. 1981. "The Radical Transformation of the Mother-Daughter Relationship in Some Women Writers of Quebec." *Frontiers* 6(1): 44–49.

Frakes, Jerold C. 1984. "Kriemhild's Three Dreams: A Structural Interpretation." *ZfdA* 113: 173–87.

Freed, John B. 1977. *The Friars and German Society in the Thirteenth Century.* Cambridge, Mass.: Medieval Academy of America.

———. 1990. "German Source Collections: The Archdiocese of Salzburg as a Case Study." In *Medieval Women and the Sources of Medieval History,* edited by Joel T. Rosenthal, 80–121. Athens: Univ. of Georgia Press.

———. 1995. *Noble Bondsmen: Ministerial Marriages in the Archdiocese of Salzburg, 1100–1343.* Ithaca: Cornell Univ. Press.

Freeman, Michelle. 1988. "The Power of Sisterhood: Marie de France's 'Le Fresne.'" In *Women and Power in the Middle Ages,* edited by Mary Erler and Maryanne Kowaleski, 250–64. Athens: Univ. of Georgia Press.

Freud, Sigmund. [1925] 1982. "Einige psychische Folgen des anatomischen Geschlechtsunterschieds." In *Sexualleben,* Studienausgabe, vol. 5, 253–66. Frankfurt am Main: Fischer.

———. [1931] 1982. "Über die weibliche Sexualität." In *Sexualleben,* Studienausgabe, vol. 5, 273–94. Frankfurt am Main: Fischer.

————. [1933] 1982. "Die Weiblichkeit." In *Vorlesungen zur Einführung in die Psychoanalyse*, Studienausgabe, vol. 1, 554–65. Frankfurt am Main: Fischer.

Fritz, Gerd. 1969. *Sprache und Überlieferung der Neidhart-Lieder in der Berliner Handschrift germ. fol. 776 [c]*. GAG, vol. 12. Göppingen: Kümmerle.

Gaunt, Simon. 1992. "From Epic to Romance: Gender and Sexuality in the *Roman d'Eneas*." *Romanic Review* 83(1): 1–27.

Gautier le Leu. 1992. "The Widow." In *Woman Defamed and Woman Defended: An Anthology of Medieval Texts*, edited by Alcuin Blamires, assisted by Karen Pratt and C. W. Marx, 135–44. Oxford: Oxford Univ. Press.

Geary, Patrick J. 1992. *Readings in Medieval History*. Vol. 2. Lewiston, N.Y.: Broadview.

Geuther, Karl. 1899. *Studien zum Liederbuch der Klara Hätzlerin*. Halle: Niemeyer.

Gibbs, Marion E., and Sidney M. Johnson, trans. 1992. *Kudrun*. Garland Library of Medieval Literature, series B, vol. 79. New York: Garland.

Glier, Ingeborg. 1971. *Artes amandi: Untersuchungen zu Geschichte, Überlieferung und Typologie der deutschen Minnereden*. MTU, vol. 34. Munich: Beck.

Gold, Penny Schine. 1985. *The Lady and the Virgin: Image, Attitude, and Experience in Twelfth-Century France*. Chicago: Univ. of Chicago Press.

Goody, Jack. 1983. *The Development of the Family and Marriage in Europe*. London: Past and Present Publications.

Gottfried von Strassburg. 1984. *Tristan und Isolde*. Edited by Rüdiger Krohn. 3 vols. [Middle High German with modern German on facing pages]. Stuttgart: Reclam.

Gravdal, Kathryn. 1989. *Vilain and Courtois: Transgressive Parody in French Literature of the Twelfth and Thirteenth Centuries*. Lincoln: Univ. of Nebraska Press.

————. 1991. *Ravishing Maidens: Writing Rape in Medieval French Literature and Law*. Philadelphia: Univ. of Pennsylvania Press.

————. 1992. "Chrétien de Troyes, Gratian, and the Medieval Romance of Sexual Violence." *Signs* 17(3): 558–84.

Grave, Jacques Salverda de, ed. 1925–1929. *Eneas: Roman de XIIe siècle*. Les classiques française du moyen âge. Paris: Champion.

Green, Monica H. 1990. "Female Sexuality in the Medieval West." *Trends in History* 4(4): 127–58.

————. 1993. "Recent Work on Women's Medicine in Medieval Europe." *Society for Ancient Medicine Review* 21 (Dec.): 132–41.

Groos, Arthur. 1976. " 'Amor and his Brother Cupid': The 'two loves' in Heinrich von Veldeke's *Eneit*." *Traditio* 32: 239–55.

Grundmann, Herbert. [1935] 1966. *Religiöse Bewegungen im Mittelalter: Untersuchungen über die geschichtlichen Zusammenhänge zwischen der Ketzerei, den Bettelorden und der religiösen Frauenbewegungen im 12. und 13. Jahrhundert und über die geschichtlichen Grundlagen der deutschen Mystik*. Reprint, Darmstadt: Wissenschaftliche Buchgesellschaft.

Gudde, Erwin Gustav. 1934. *Social Conflicts in Medieval German Literature*. University of California Publications in Modern Philology, vol. 18. Berkeley: Univ. of California Press.

Haigh, Samantha. 1994. "Between Irigaray and Cardinal: Reinventing Maternal Genealogies." *MLR* 89(1): 61–71.

Haltaus, Carl, ed. [1840] 1966. *Liederbuch der Clara Hätzlerin.* With an afterword by Hanns Fischer. Deutsche Neudrucke, Texte des Mittelalters, no. 85. Berlin: de Gruyter.

Hatto, A. T., trans. 1960. *Gottfried von Strassburg's Tristan.* London: Penguin.

———, trans. 1965. *The Nibelungenlied.* London: Penguin.

Haymes, Edward R. 1979. "Hagen the Hero." *Southern Folklore Quarterly* 43(1–2): 149–55.

———. 1986. *The Nibelungenlied: History and Interpretation.* Urbana: Univ. of Illinois Press.

Heinrich von Veldeke. 1986. *Eneasroman.* Edited by Dieter Kartschoke, after the text by Ludwig Ettmüller. [Middle High German with modern German on facing pages]. Stuttgart: Reclam.

Henkel, Nikolaus. 1988. *Deutsche Übersetzungen lateinischer Schultexte: Ihre Verbreitung und Funktion im Mittelalter und in der frühen Neuzeit.* Zurich: Artemis.

Herlihy, David. 1985. *Medieval Households.* Cambridge: Harvard Univ. Press.

Herrmann, Petra. 1984. *Karnevaleske Strukturen in der Neidhart-Tradition.* GAG, vol. 406. Göppingen: Kümmerle.

Hinnebusch, William A. 1966. *The History of the Dominican Order.* Vol. 1, *Origins and Growth to 1500.* Staten Island, N.Y.: Alba House.

Hirsch, Marianne. 1981. "Mothers and Daughters: A Review Essay." *Signs* 7(1): 200–22.

———. 1989. *The Mother/Daughter Plot: Narrative, Psychoanalysis, Feminism.* Bloomington: Indiana Univ. Press.

Hoffmann, Werner. 1967. *Kudrun: Ein Beitrag zur Deutung der nachnibelungischen Heldendichtung.* Germanistische Abhandlungen, vol. 17. Stuttgart: Metzler.

———. 1976. "Die Kudrun: Eine Antwort auf das Nibelungenlied (1970)." In *Nibelungenlied und Kudrun,* Wege der Forschung, vol. 54, edited by Heinz Rupp, 599–620. Darmstadt: Wissenschaftliche Buchgesellschaft.

Homans, Margaret. 1986. *Bearing the Word: Language and Female Experience in Nineteenth-Century Women's Writing.* Chicago and London: Univ. of Chicago Press.

Humphries, Rolfe, trans. 1958. *The Satires of Juvenal.* Bloomington: Indiana Univ. Press.

Irigaray, Luce. 1981. *Le corps-à-corps avec la mère.* Montreal: Les Éditions de la pleine lune.

Jaeger, C. Stephen. 1985. *The Origins of Courtliness: Civilizing Trends and the Formation of Courtly Ideals, 939–1210.* Philadelphia: Univ. of Pennsylvania Press.

Janssen, Hildegard. 1980. *Das sogenannte "genre objectif": Zum Problem mittelalterlicher literarischer Gattungen dargestellt an den Sommerliedern Niedharts.* GAG, vol. 281. Göppingen: Kümmerle.

Joldersma, Hermina. 1984. "The Eavesdropping Male: 'Gespielinnengesprächslieder' from Neidhart to the Present." *Euph* 78: 199–218.

Jones, William Jervis. 1990. *German Kinship Terms (750–1500): Documentation and Analysis.* Studia Linguistica Germanica, vol. 27. Berlin: de Gruyter.

Jöst, Erhard, ed. 1980. *Die Historien des Neithart Fuchs: Nach dem Frankfurter Druck von 1566.* Litterae, vol. 49. Göppingen: Kümmerle.

Karras, Ruth Mazo. 1989. "The Regulation of Brothels in Later Medieval England." *Signs* 14(2): 399–433. Reprinted in *Sisters and Workers in the Middle Ages*, edited by Judith M. Bennett, Elizabeth A. Clark, Jean F. O'Barr, B. Anne Vilan, and Sarah Westphal-Wihl, 100–134. Chicago: Univ. of Chicago Press.

———. 1996. *Common Women: Prostitution and Sexuality in Medieval England*. New York: Oxford Univ. Press.

Kartschoke, Dieter. 1983. "Didos Minne—Didos Schuld." In *Liebe als Literatur: Aufsätze zur erotischen Dichtung in Deutschland*, edited by Rüdiger Krohn, 99–116. Munich: Beck.

Kasten, Ingrid. 1988. "Herrschaft und Liebe: Zur Rolle und Darstellung des 'Helden' im Roman d'Eneas und Veldekes Eneasroman." *DVjs* 62(2): 227-45.

Keller, Adelbert von, ed. 1853–1856. *Fastnachtspiele aus dem 15. Jahrhundert,* Bibliothek des litterarischen Vereins in Stuttgart, vol. 28–30, 46. Tübingen: Laupp.

———. 1870. *Hans Sachs: Werke. Bd. 4.* Bibliothek des litterarischen Vereins in Stuttgart, vol. 105. Tübinger: Laupp.

Kellermann-Haaf, Petra. 1986. *Frau und Politik im Mittelalter: Untersuchungen zur politischen Rolle der Frau in den höfischen Romanen des 12., 13. und 14. Jahrhunderts.* GAG, vol. 456. Göppingen: Kümmerle.

Kieckhefer, Richard. 1990. *Magic in the Middle Ages.* Cambridge: Cambridge Univ. Press.

———. 1991. "Erotic Magic in Medieval Europe." In *Sex in the Middle Ages: A Book of Essays*, edited by Joyce E. Salisbury, 30–55. Vol. 3 of Garland Medieval Casebooks. New York: Garland.

Kienast, Walther. 1975. "Von Ausbruch des deutschen Thronstreites bis zur Schlacht von Bouvines (1198–1214)." In *Deutschland und Frankreich in der Kaiserzeit (900–1270): Weltkaiser und Einzelkönige.* 2d ed. Monographien zur Geschichte des Mittelalters, vol. 9, part 3. Stuttgart: Anton Hiersemann.

Kloepfer, Deborah Kelly. 1989. *The Unspeakable Mother: Forbidden Discourse in Jean Rhys and H.D.* Ithaca: Cornell Univ. Press.

Kraft, Helga, and Barbara Kosta. 1983. "Mother-Daughter Relationships: Problems of Self-determination in Novak, Heinrich and Wohmann." *GQ* 56: 74–88.

Kraft, Helga, and Elke Liebs, eds. 1993. *Mütter—Töchter—Frauen: Weiblichkeitsbilder in der Literatur.* Stuttgart: Metzler.

Kraus, Carl von, ed. 1978. *Deutsche Liederdichter des 13. Jahrhunderts.* 2d ed. Tübingen: Niemeyer.

Krechel, Ursula. 1977. "Meine Mutter." *In Nach Mainzl! Gedichte.* Darmstadt: Luchterhand.

Kretzschmer, August, ed. 1840. *Deutsche Volkslieder mit ihren Original-Weisen.* 2 vols. Berlin: Vereins-Buchhandlung. Reprint, Hildesheim: Olms, 1969.

Kristeva, Julia. 1985. "Stabat mater." In *The Female Body in Western Culture: Contemporary Perspectives*, edited by Susan Rubin Suleiman, 99–118. Cambridge: Harvard Univ. Press.

Kudrun. 1965. Edited by Karl Bartsch. 5th ed., revised by Karl Stackmann. Deutsche Klassiker des Mittelalters. Wiesbaden: Brockhaus.

Kuhn, Hugo. 1953a. "Winsbecke." In *Die Deutsche Literatur des Mittelalters: Verfasserlexikon,* vol. 4, edited by Karl Langosch, 1013. Berlin: de Gruyter.

————. 1953b. "Winsbeckin." In *Die Deutsche Literatur des Mittelalters: Verfasser-lexikon*, vol. 4, edited by Karl Langosch, 1016. Berlin: de Gruyter.

————. 1976a. "Gottfried von Straßburg." In *Die deutsche Literatur des Mittelalters: Verfasserlexikon*, edited by Kurt Ruh, vol. 3, 153–68. 2d ed. Berlin: de Gruyter.

————. 1976b. "Kudrun." In *Nibelungenlied und Kudrun*, Wege der Forschung, vol. 54, edited by Heinz Rupp, 502–14. Darmstadt: Wissenschaftliche Buch-gesellschaft.

Kully, Rolf Max. 1978. "Das Clärlein: Ein erotisches Kalendergedicht auf das Jahr 1482 von Johannes Erhard Düsch." *ZfdA* 107: 138–50.

Knust, Jaap, ed. 1939. *Het levende lied in Nederland uit den volksmond opgeteekend en bewerkt voor zang (blokfluit) en piano*. Amsterdam: H. J. Paris.

Langgässer, Elisabeth. 1981. *Gedichte*. Frankfurt am Main: Ullstein.

Lasker-Schüler, Else. 1986. *Gedichte, 1902–1943*. Munich: Deutscher Taschenbuch Verlag.

Lauretis, Teresa de. 1987. "The Violence of Rhetoric: Considerations on Represen-tation and Gender." In *Technologies of Gender: Essays on Theory, Film, and Fiction*, 31–50. Bloomington: Indiana Univ. Press.

Lawson, Richard H. 1989. "The Changing Maternal Perspective in Brother Her-mann's *Leben der Gräfin Iolande von Vianden*." In *Medieval German Literature: Pro-ceedings from the 23rd International Congress on Medieval Studies*, GAG, vol. 507, edited by Albrecht Classen, 117-27. Göppingen: Kümmerle.

————. 1991. "Countess Yolanda of Vianden: A Reconsideration." In *Women as Protagonists and Poets in the German Middle Ages: An Anthology of Feminist Ap-proaches to the Study of Middle High German Literature*, GAG, vol. 528, edited by Albrecht Classen, 105–15. Göppingen: Kümmerle.

————, trans. 1995. *Brother Hermann's Life of the Countess Yolande of Vianden*. Co-lumbia, S.C.: Camden House.

Leiderer, Rosmarie. 1972. *Zwölf Minnereden des Cgm 270*. Texte des späten Mit-telalters und der frühen Neuzeit. Berlin: Erich Schmidt.

Leitzmann, Albert, ed. 1962. *Winsbeckische Gedichte nebst Tirol und Fridebrant*. 3d ed., revised by Ingo Reiffenstein. ATB, vol. 9. Tübingen: Niemeyer.

Lemmer, Manfred. 1981. *"der Dürnge bluome schînet dur den snê": Thüringen und die deutsche Literatur des hohen Mittelalters*. Eisenach: Wartburg-Stiftung.

Leyser, Karl. 1968. "The German Aristocracy from the Ninth to the Early Twelfth Century: A Historical and Cultural Sketch." *Past and Present* 41: 25–53.

————. 1970. "Maternal Kin in Early Medieval Germany: A Reply." *Past and Pre-sent* 49: 126–34.

Loerzer, Eckart. 1971. *Eheschließung und Werbung in der "Kudrun."* MTU, vol. 37. Munich: Beck.

McConnell, Winder. 1988. *The Epic of* Kudrun: *A Critical Commentary*. GAG, vol. 463. Göppingen: Kümmerle.

Mälzer, Marion. 1991. *Die Isolde-Gestalten in den mittelalterlichen deutschen Tristan-Dichtungen: Ein Beitrag zum diachronischen Wandel*. Heidelberg: Carl Winter Uni-versitätsverlag.

Meier, John, ed. 1889. *Bruder Hermann: Leben der Gräfin Iolande von Vianden*. Ger-manistische Abhandlungen, vol. 7. Breslau: Wilhelm Koebner; reprint, Hildesheim: Olms, 1977.

Meister, Peter. 1990. *The Healing Female in the German Courtly Romance*. GAG, vol. 523. Göppingen: Kümmerle.

Mens-Verhulst, Janneke, Karlein Schreurs, and Liesbeth Woertman, eds. 1993. *Daughtering and Mothering: Female Subjectivity Reanalysed*. London: Routledge.

Meyer, Dieter H. 1989. *Literarische Hausbücher des 16. Jahrhunderts: Die Sammlungen des Ulrich Mostl, des Valentin Holl und des Simprecht Kröll*. 2 vols. Würzburg: Königshausen + Neumann.

Meyer, Ruth. 1995. *Das St. Katharinentaler Schwesternbuch: Untersuchungen—Edition—Kommentar*. MTU, vol. 104. Tübingen: Niemeyer.

Miklautsch, Lydia. 1991. *Studien zur Mutterrolle in den mittelhochdeutschen Großepen des zwölften und dreizehnten Jahrhunderts*. Ph.D. diss., University of Vienna, 1990. Erlanger Studien, vol. 88. Erlangen: Palm und Enke.

Minis, Cola. 1959. *Textkritische Studien über den Roman d'Eneas und die Eneide von Henric van Veldeke*. Studia Litteraria Rheno-Traiectina, vol. 5. Groningen: J. B. Walters.

Morgenstern-Werner, Elisabeth. 1990. *Die Weimarer Liederhandschrift Q 564 (Lyrik Handschrift F)*. GAG, vol. 534. Göppingen: Kümmerle.

Morrison, Susan Signe. 1994. "Women Writers and Women Rulers: Rhetorical and Political Empowerment in the Fifteenth Century." *Women in German Yearbook* 9: 25–48.

Mück, Hans-Dieter. 1980. *Untersuchungen zur Überlieferung und Rezeption spätmittelalterlicher Lieder und Spruchgedichte im 15. und 16. Jahrhundert: Die "Streuüberlieferung" von Liedern und Reimpaarreden Oswalds von Wolkenstein*. vol. 1, *Untersuchungen*. GAG, vol. 263. Göppingen: Kümmerle.

Müller, Heidy Margrit. 1991. *Töchter und Mütter in deutschsprachiger Erzählprosa von 1885 bis 1935*. Munich: Iudicium Verlag.

Mustard, Helen M., and Charles E. Passage, trans. 1961. *Wolfram von Eschenbach: Parzival*. New York: Vintage.

Das Nibelungenlied. 1979. Edited by Karl Bartsch and Helmut de Boor. 21st ed., revised and edited by Roswitha Wisniewski. Deutsche Klassiker des Mittelalters. Wiesbaden: Brockhaus.

Nolte, Theodor. 1985. *Das Kudrunepos—ein Frauenroman?* Untersuchungen zur deutschen Literaturgeschichte, vol. 38. Tübingen: Niemeyer.

O'Barr, Jean, Deborah Pope, and Mary Wyer, eds. 1990. *Ties that Bind: Essays on Motherhood and Patriarchy*. Chicago: Univ. of Chicago Press.

Opitz, Claudia. 1987. *Frauenalltag im Mittelalter: Biographien des 13. und 14. Jahrhunderts*. Ergebnisse der Frauenforschung, vol. 5. Weinheim: Beltz.

———. 1988. "Von Familienzwist zum sozialen Konflikt: Über adlige Eheschließungspraktiken im Hoch- und Spätmittelalter." In *Weiblickheit in geschichtlicher Perspektive: Fallstudien und Reflexionen zu Grundproblemen der Frauenforschung*, edited by Ursula A. J. Becher and Jörn Rüsen, 116–49. Frankfurt am Main: Suhrkamp.

———. 1990. "Allein gegen alle? Weibliche Identitäten, Familieninteressen und Eheschließungskonflikte in mittelalterlichen Frauenbiographien." In *Evatöchter und Bräute Christi: Weiblicher Zusammenhang und Frauenkultur im Mittelalter*, edited by Claudia Opitz, 15–29. Weinheim: Deutscher Studienverlag.

———. 1991. "Emanzipiert oder marginalisiert? Witwen in der Gesellschaft des späteren Mittelalters." In *Auf der Suche nach der Frau im Mittelalter: Fragen, Quellen, Antworten*, edited by Bea Lundt, 25–48. Munich: Fink.

———. 1992. "Mutterschaft und Vaterschaft im 14. und 15. Jahrhundert." In *Frauengeschichte—Geschlechtergeschichte*, edited by Karin Hausen and Heide Wunder, 137–53. Frankfurt am Main: Campus Verlag.

Otis, Leah Lydia. 1985. *Prostitution in Medieval Society: The History of an Urban Institution in Languedoc*. Chicago: Univ. of Chicago Press.

Parsons, John Carmi. 1993. "Mothers, Daughters, Marriage, Power: Some Plantagenet Evidence, 1150–1500." In *Medieval Queenship*, edited by John Carmi Parsons, 63–78. New York: St. Martin's Press.

Patterson, Lee. 1987. *Negotiating the Past: The Historical Understanding of Medieval Literature*. Madison: Univ. of Wisconsin Press.

Patze, Hans. 1974. "Politische Geschichte im hohen und späten Mittelalter." In *Geschichte Thüringens*, edited by Hans Patze and Walter Schlesinger, vol. 2, *Hohes und spätes Mittelalter*, 1–214. Mitteldeutsche Forschungen, vol. 48/II, part 1. Cologne and Vienna: Böhlau.

Payen, J. C. 1989. *Tristan et Iseut. Les Tristan en vers. Édition nouvelle. Texte, traduction, notes critiques, bibliographie et notes*. Paris: Garnier.

Payne, Karen, ed. 1983. *Between Ourselves: Letters Between Mothers and Daughters 1750–1982*. Boston: Houghton Mifflin.

Pearlman, Mickey, ed. 1989. *Mother Puzzles: Daughters and Mothers in Contemporary American Literature*. Contributions in Women's Studies, no. 110. New York: Greenwood.

Pearson, Mark. 1992. "Sigeband's Courtship of Ute in the *Kudrun*." *Colloquia Germanica* 25.2: 101–11.

Peters, Ursula. 1981. *Fürstenhof und höfische Dichtung: Der Hof Hermanns von Thüringen als literarisches Zentrum*. Konstanzer Universitätsreden 113. Konstanz: Universitätsverlag Konstanz.

Rasmussen, Ann Marie. 1993. "Bist du begehrt, so bist du wert: Magische und höfische Mitgift für die Töchter." In *Mütter—Töchter—Frauen: Weiblichkeitsbilder in der Literatur*, edited by Helga Kraft and Elke Liebs, 7–35. Stuttgart: Metzler.

———. 1996a. " 'Ez ist ir g'artet von mir': Queen Isolde and Princess Isolde in Gottfried von Strassburg's *Tristan und Isolde*." In *Arthurian Women: A Casebook*, edited with an introduction by Thelma S. Fenster, 41–58. New York: Garland.

———. 1996b. "Zur wissenschaftlichen Analyse von Müttern und Töchtern im Mittelalter." *Das Mittelalter. Perspektiven mediävistischer Forschung* 1(2): 27–37.

Rassow, Peter. 1950. *Der Prinzgemahl: Ein pactum matrimoniale aus dem Jahre 1188*. Quellen und Studien zur Verfassungsgeschichte des Deutschen Reiches im Mittelalter und Neuzeit, vol. 8, part 1. Weimar: H. Böhlaus Nachfolger.

Reichel, Jörn. 1985. *Der Spruchdichter Hans Rosenplüt: Literatur und Leben im spätmittelalterlichen Nürnberg*. Stuttgart: Franz Steiner.

Rich, Adrienne. 1983. "Compulsory Heterosexuality and Lesbian Existance." Reprinted in *The Signs Reader: Women, Gender, and Scholarship*, edited by Elizabeth Abel and Emily K. Abel, 139–68. Chicago: Univ. of Chicago Press.

————. 1986. *Of Woman Born: Motherhood as Experience and Institution.* New York: Norton.

Ringler, Siegfried. 1980. *Viten- und Offenbarungsliteratur in Frauenklöstern des Mittelalters: Quellen und Studien.* MTU, vol. 72. Munich: Artemis.

Rojas, Fernando de. [1631] 1987. *Celestina.* Translated by James Mabbe. Reprint, edited by Dorothy Sherman Severin, Warminster: Aris.

Roper, Lyndal. 1988. "Mothers of Debauchery: Procuresses in Reformation Augsburg." *German History* 6(1): 1–19.

————. 1989a. *The Holy Household: Women and Morals in Reformation Augsburg.* Oxford: Clarendon Press.

————. 1989b. "Will and Honor: Sex, Words, and Power in Augsburg Criminal Trials." *Radical History Review* 43: 45–71. Reprinted in Roper 1994, 53–78.

————. 1994. *Oedipus and the Devil: Witchcraft, Sexuality and Religion in Early Modern Europe.* New York: Routledge.

Rosenplüt, Hans. 1990. *Reimpaarsprüche und Lieder.* Edited by Jörn Reichel. ATB, vol. 105. Tübingen: Niemeyer.

Rosenthal, Joel T., ed. 1990. *Medieval Women and the Sources of Medieval History.* Athens: Univ. of Georgia Press.

Rothstein, Robert A. 1989. "The Mother-Daughter Dialogue in the Yiddish Folk Song: Wandering Motifs in Time and Space." *New York Folklore* 15(1–2): 51–65.

Ruh, Kurt. 1977. *Höfische Epik des deutschen Mittelalters. Vol. 1, Von den Anfängen bis zu Hartmann von Aue.* 2d ed. Grundlagen der Germanistik, vol. 7. Berlin: Erich Schmidt.

————. ed. 1976–. *Die deutsche Literatur des Mittelalters: Verfasserlexikon.* 9 vols. to date. 2d ed. Berlin: de Gruyter.

Rushing, James A., Jr. 1995. *Images of Adventure: Ywain in the Visual Arts.* Philadelphia: Univ. of Pennsylvania Press.

Rusinek, Bernd A. 1986. "Veldekes *Eneide*: Die Einschreibung der Herrschaft in das Liebesbegehren als Unterscheidungsmerkmal der beiden Minnehandlungen." *Monatshefte* 78(1): 11–25.

Sawyer, Birgit, and Peter Sawyer. 1993. *Medieval Scandinavia: From Conversion to Reformation, circa 800–1500.* Nordic Series, vol. 17. Minneapolis: Univ. of Minnesota Press.

Schieb, Gabriele, and Theodor Frings, eds. 1964–70. *Henric van Veldeken. Eneide.* 3 vols. Berlin: Akademie Verlag.

Schlosser, Horst Dieter. 1965. "Untersuchungen zum sogenannten lyrischen Teil des Liederbuches der Klara Hätzlerin." Ph.D. diss., University of Hamburg.

Schneider, Karin. 1973a. *Catalogus codicum manu scriptorum Bibliothecae Monacensis.* Vol. 5, part 2. *Die deutschen Handschriften der Bayerischen Staatsbibliothek München: cgm 201–350.* Wiesbaden: Harrassowitz.

————. 1973b. *Catalogus codicum manu scriptorum Bibliothecae Monacensis.* Vol. 5, part 3. *Die deutschen Handschriften der Bayerischen Staatsbibliothek München: cgm 351–500.* Wiesbaden: Harrassowitz.

Schöning, Brigitte. 1989. "Name ohne Person: Auf den Spuren der Isolde Weißhand." In *der frauwen buoch: Versuch einer feministischen Mediävistik,* edited by Ingrid Bennewitz. GAG, vol. 517. Göppingen: Kümmerle.

Schulz-Grobert, Jürgen. 1989. "Kuppitschs Handschrift C: Zu ihrem Verbleib." *ZfdA* 118: 236–41.

Schulze, Ursula. 1983. "Amîs unde man: Die zentrale Problematik in Hartmanns Erec." *PBB (Tü)* 105(1): 14–47.

Schuster, Beate. 1991. "Frauenhandel und Frauenhäuser im 15. und 16. Jahrhundert." *Vierteljahresschrift für Sozial- und Wirtschaftsgeschichte* 78: 172–89.

———. 1995. *Die freien Frauen: Dirnen und Frauenhäuser im 15. und 16. Jahrhundert.* Frankfurt am Main: Campus Verlag.

Schuster, Peter. 1992. *Das Frauenhaus: Städtische Bordelle in Deutschland (1350–1600).* Paderborn: Schöningh.

Schweikle, Günther. 1986. "Pseudo-Neidharte?" In *Neidhart,* edited by Horst Brunner, 334–54. Wege der Forschung, vol. 556. Darmstadt: Wissenschaftliche Buchgesellschaft.

———. 1990. *Neidhart.* Stuttgart: Metzler.

Schwietering, Julius. 1961. "Natur und *art.*" *ZfdA* 91: 108–37.

Schwob, Ute-Monica. 1982. " 'Herrinen' in Troiler Quellen: Zur rechtlichen und sozialen Stellung der adeligen Frau im Mittelalter." In *Die Iwein-Fresken von Rodenegg und andere Zeugnisse der Wechselwirkung von Literatur and bildender Kunst: Literatur und bildende Kunst im Tiroler Mittelalter,* Innsbrucker Beiträge zur Kulturwissenschaft, Germanistische Reihe, vol. 15, edited by Egon Kuhebacher, 157–82. Innsbruck: Institut für Germanistik der Universität Innsbruck.

Shadis, Miriam Teresa. 1994. "Motherhood, Lineage, and Royal Power in Medieval Castile and France: Berenguela de León and Blanche de Castile." Ph.D. diss., Duke University.

———. 1996. "Piety, Politics, and Power: The Patronage of Leonor of England and her Daughters Berenguela of León and Blanche of Castile." In *The Cultural Patronage of Medieval Women,* edited by June Hall McCash, 202–27. Athens: Univ. of Georgia Press.

Shafi, Monika. 1991. "Die überforderte Generation: Mutterfiguren in den Romanen von Ingeborg Drewitz." In *Women in German Yearbook,* edited by Jeanette Clausen and Sara Friedrichsmeyer, 23–42. Lincoln: Univ. of Nebraska Press.

Sheingorn, Pamela. 1993. " 'The Wise Mother': The Image of St. Anne Teaching the Virgin Mary." *Gesta* 32(1): 69–80.

Simon, Eckehard. 1986. "Neidhart und Neidhartianer: Zur Geschichte eines Liedkorpus." In *Neidhart,* Wege der Forschung, vol. 556, edited by Horst Brunner, 196–250. Darmstadt: Wisenschaftliche Buchgesellschaft.

———. 1988. *The Türkenkalender (1454) attributed to Gutenberg and the Strasbourg Lunation Tracts.* Speculum Anniversary Monographs, vol. 14. Cambridge, Mass.: Medieval Academy of America.

Solterer, Helen. 1991. "Figures for Female Militancy in Medieval France." *Signs* 16(3): 522–49.

———. 1995. *The Master and Minerva: Disputing Women in French Medieval Culture.* Berkeley: Univ. of California Press.

Spearing, A. C. 1993. *The Medieval Poet as Voyeur: Looking and Listening in Medieval Love-Narratives.* Cambridge: Cambridge Univ. Press.

Spitz, Ellen Handler. 1990. "Mothers and Daughters: Ancient and Modern Myths." *Journal of Aesthetics and Art Criticism* 48(4): 411–21.

Stein, Peter K. 1984. "Tristan." In *Epische Stoffe des Mittelalters,* edited by Volker Mertens and Ulrich Müller, 365–94. Stuttgart: Kröner.

Stiller, Nikki. 1980a. "Eve's Orphans: Mothers and Daughters in Medieval English Literature." In *The Lost Tradition: Mothers and Daughters in Literature,* edited by Cathy N. Davidson and E. M. Broner, 22–32. New York: Ungar.

———. 1980b. *Eve's Orphans: Mothers and Daughters in Medieval English Literature.* Contributions in Women's Studies, vol. 16. Westport, Conn.: Greenwood.

Stuard, Susan Mosher. 1987. "The Dominion of Gender: Women's Fortunes in the High Middle Ages." Chap. 6 in *Becoming Visible: Women in European History,* edited by Renate Bridenthal, Claudia Koonz, and Susan Stuard, 2d ed., 153–74. Boston: Houghton Mifflin.

Suleiman, Susan Rubin, ed. 1985. *The Female Body in Western Culture: Contemporary Perspectives.* Cambridge: Harvard Univ. Press.

Sullivan, Joseph Martin. 1994. "Das Leben der Gräfin Iolande von Vianden: The Ideal Religious Woman and Medieval Hagiography." M.A. thesis, University of Texas at Austin.

Thomas, J. W., trans. 1978. *Eilhart von Oberg's Tristrant.* Lincoln: Univ. of Nebraska Press.

———. 1984. *Heinrich von Veldeke, Eneit.* Garland Library of Medieval Literature, vol. 49B. New York: Garland.

Turner, Paul, trans. 1990. *Lucian: Satirical Sketches.* Bloomington: Indiana Univ. Press.

Valtink, Eveline, ed. 1987. *Mütter und Töchter: Über die Schwerigkeit einer Beziehung und die Bildung weiblicher Identität.* Hofgeismarer Protokolle: Tagungsbeiträge aus der Arbeit der Evangelischen Akademie Hofgeismar, vol. 241. Hofgeismar: Evangelische Akademie Hofgeismar.

Wachinger, Burghart. 1973. *Sängerkrieg: Untersuchungen zur Spruchdichtung des 13. Jahrhunderts.* MTU, vol. 42. Munich: Beck.

———. 1982. "Liebe und Literatur im spätmittelalterlichen Schwaben und Franken: Zur Augsburger Sammelhandschrift der Clara Hätzlerin." *DVjs* 56: 386–406.

Wack, Mary F. 1990. *Lovesickness in the Middle Ages: The Viaticum and Its Commentaries.* Philadelphia: Univ. of Pennsylvania Press.

Wailes, Stephen L. 1983. "The Romance of *Kudrun.*" *Speculum* 58(2): 347–67.

Walters, Suzanna Danuta. 1992. *Lives Together/Worlds Apart: Mothers and Daughters in Popular Culture.* Berkeley: Univ. of California Press.

Walther, Ingo F., ed. 1988. *Codex Manesse: Die Miniaturen der Großen Heidelberger Liederhandschrift.* In collaboration with Gisela Siebert. Frankfurt am Main: Insel.

Walther von der Vogelweide. 1965. *Gedichte. Studienausgabe.* Edited by Karl Lachmann. 13th ed., revised and edited by Hugo Kuhn. Berlin: de Gruyter.

Weeks, Laura D. 1990. "'I Have Named Her Ariadna . . .': The Demeter-Persephone Myth in Tsvetaeva's Poems for Her Daughter." *Slavic Review* 49(4): 568–85.

Weigel, Sigrid. 1983. "Die geopferte Heldin und das Opfer als Heldin: Zum Entwurf weiblicher Helden in der Literatur von Männern und Frauen." In *Die verborgene Frau: Sechs Beiträge zu einer feministischen Literaturwissenschaft,* Argument-Sonderband, vol. 96, 138–52. Berlin: Argument-Verlag.

Westphal, Sarah. 1993. *Textual Poetics of German Manuscripts 1300–1500.* Columbia, S.C.: Camden House.

———. 1996. "Camilla: The Amazon Body in Medieval German Literature." *Exemplaria* 8(1): 231–58.

Westphal-Wihl, Sarah. 1989. *"The Ladies' Tournament:* Marriage, Sex, and Honor in Thirteenth-Century Germany." *Signs* 14(2): 371–98. Reprinted in *Sisters and Workers in the Middle Ages,* edited by Judith M. Bennett, Elizabeth A. Clark, Jean F. O'Barr, B. Anne Vilan, and Sarah Westphal-Wihl, 162–89. Chicago: Univ. of Chicago Press.

Wiesner, Merry E. 1986. *Working Women in Renaissance Germany.* New Brunswick, N.J.: Rutgers Univ. Press.

———. 1994. *Women and Gender in Early Modern Europe.* Cambridge: Cambridge Univ. Press.

Wießner, Edmund, ed., with Hanns Fischer. 1984. *Die Lieder Neidharts.* 4th ed., revised by Paul Sappler. ATB, vol. 44. Tübingen: Niemeyer.

Wild, Inga. 1979. *Zur Überlieferung und Rezeption des 'Kudrun'–Epos: Eine Untersuchung von drei europäischen Liedbereichen des "Typs Südeli".* GAG, vol. 265. Göppingen: Kümmerle.

Wilms, P. Hieronymus. 1928. *Das älteste Verzeichnis der deutschen Dominikanerinnenklöster.* Quellen und Forschungen zur Geschichte des Dominikanerordens in Deutschland, vol. 24. Leipzig: Harrassowitz.

Wiltenburg, Joy A. 1992. *Disorderly Women and Female Power in the Street Literature of Early Modern England and Germany.* Charlottesville: Univ. Press of Virginia.

Wolff, Robert Lee. 1952. "Baldwin of Flanders and Hainaut, First Latin Emperor of Constantinople: His Life, Death, and Resurrection, 1172–1225." *Speculum* 27: 281–322.

Wolfram von Eschenbach. 1965. *Parzival. Studienausgabe.* Edited by Karl Lachmann. 6th ed. Berlin: de Gruyter.

Yunck, John A., trans. 1974. *Eneas: A Twelfth-Century French Romance.* Records of Civilization: Sources and Studies, vol. 93. New York and London: Columbia Univ. Press.

Zarncke, Friedrich. 1852. *Der deutsche Cato: Geschichte der deutschen Übersetzung der im Mittelalter durch dem Namen Cato bekannten Distichen bis zur Verdrängung derselben durch die Übersetzung Seb. Brants am Ende des 15. Jahrhunderts.* Leipzig: Georg Wigands.

Zimmermann, Manfred, ed. 1980. *Die Sterzinger Miszellaneen-Handschrift: Kommentierte Edition der deutschen Dichtungen.* Innsbrucker Beiträge zur Kulturwissenschaft, Germanistische Reihe, vol. 8. Innsbruck: Institut für Germanistik.

Zink, Michel. 1995. *Medieval French Literature: An Introduction.* Translated by Jeff Rider. Medieval and Renaissance Texts and Studies, vol. 110, no. 19. Binghamton, N.Y.: Medieval and Renaissance Texts and Studies.

Index

Page numbers in *italics* denote illustrations.